THE CHARTING OF THE OCEANS

Circulus articus:
Oceanus occidentalis
Terra del Rey de portuguall
Has antilhas del Rey de castella:
Este he o marco dantre castella e portuguall
Toda esta terra he descoberta p mandado del Rey de castella
Linha equinocialis:
Mare oceanus:
Tropicus capricorni:
Pollus antarticus:

THE CHARTING OF THE OCEANS

TEN CENTURIES OF MARITIME MAPS

PETER WHITFIELD

POMEGRANATE ARTBOOKS

Title page: Detail from the Cantino chart of the world, 1502. See page 27.
Half-title: Detail from Christopher Saxton's wall map of England and Wales, 1583 (issued *c.*1640). The British Library Maps C.7.d.7.
Facing Contents page: Title-page of Mortier's *Neptune François*, 1693.

First published 1996 by The British Library
Published in North and South America by
Pomegranate Artbooks, PO Box 6099, Rohnert Park, California 94927

ISBN 0-7649-0009-9

Designed by John Mitchell
Typeset by Bexhill Phototypesetters, Bexhill-on-Sea, East Sussex
Printed in Italy by Grafiche Milani

CONTENTS

LE
NEPTUNE
FRANÇOIS
Jan van Vianen fecit

To the memory of
Francis Edward Whitfield
1901–1996

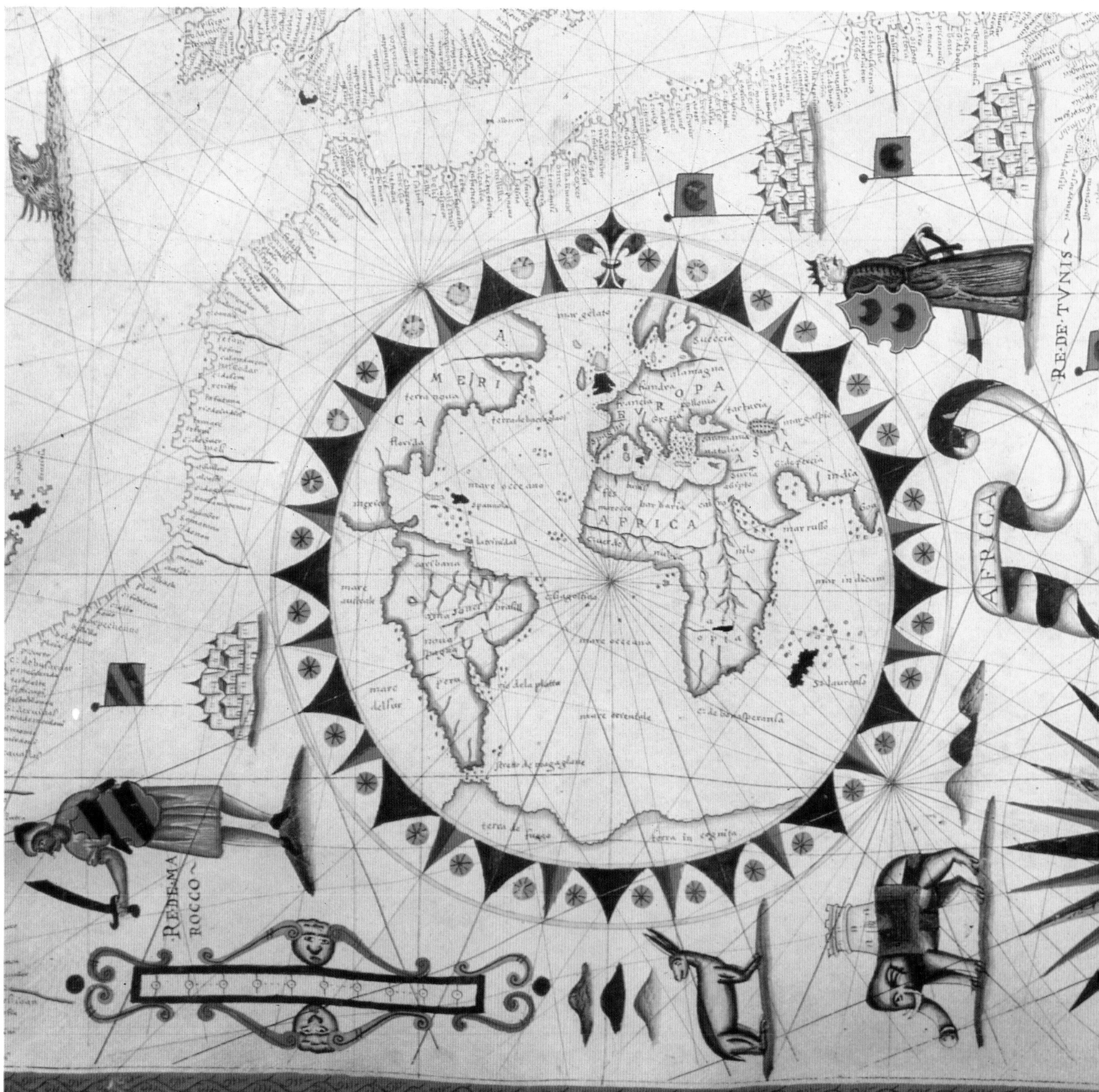
RE·DE·TVNIS
AFRICA
RE DE MA
ROCCO
AMERICA
EVROPA
ASIA
AFRICA

Introduction

IN September 1522 a small ship, the *Victoria*, anchored off the coast of Spain near Seville with eighteen men on board. The ship was laden with spices and exotic cargo, but the men were in the last stages of exhaustion and malnutrition. They were the survivors of a fleet of five ships and 270 men who had left Seville exactly three years before under the command of Ferdinand Magellan on the greatest adventure in maritime history, the first circumnavigation of the earth. With their return, man's knowledge of the sphericity of the earth was brought down from the theoretical level into the realm of human experience. When Magellan set sail, seafaring traders had been sailing the coasts and islands of the world for centuries, but it was the European explorers in the age of the Renaissance who set out into the unknown on deliberate ocean-crossing voyages. The decades 1490–1520 formed a pivotal moment in world history, when Europeans broke out from their own region and unwittingly began the process of creating the one world in which we now live: Magellan's first encirclement of the earth is a clear symbol of that unique dynamic.

In this historic movement, mastery of the sea was the vital catalyst. A number of technical changes came together to make ocean voyages possible: the compass, celestial navigation, improved shipbuilding, and guns to meet whatever challenge might appear. The political geography of the fifteenth century, with Moslem occupation of the Middle East, forced European explorers onto the oceans of the south and west. The new discoveries overseas created a distinct sense of European destiny and domination, that the world was there to be explored and plundered. In this culture, greed was dignified by religious motives; as one Spanish historian wrote, what they sought in the new world was 'To serve God and His Majesty, to give light to those who sat in darkness, and to grow rich, as all men desire to do.' The Treaty of Tordesillas in 1494, in which the Pope's authority divided the newly-discovered territories between Spain and Portugal, was an act of overwhelming global arrogance. This spirit is perfectly captured by Marlowe's Tamburlaine as he broods over the world map, surveying Asia, Africa and Europe, lamenting 'And shall I die and this unconquered?'.

The history of the sea-chart brings into focus Europe's changing knowledge of the world from the fifteenth to the nineteenth century. The world on these charts expands from the Mediterranean to embrace and map the Atlantic and Indian Oceans in the sixteenth century, the Pacific Ocean in the eighteenth century, and the Polar Regions in the nineteenth century. These charts express both the geography and the politics of their time. The making of sea charts by European nations clearly depended on their ability to gather maritime information, and on their commercial need for them. Thus between the years 1400 and 1900, Italian chartmakers were succeeded by the Portuguese, the Spanish, the Dutch, the French and the British, as each of these nations grew in maritime power. It is impossible to understand the progress of charting without being constantly aware of this political background. The sea chart is also part of the history of navigation, and the means the seafarer used to locate himself upon the earth's surface, astronomical or otherwise, is inseparable from the history of the charts themselves.

DETAIL FROM World Chart by Joan Oliva, 1599. See page 52.

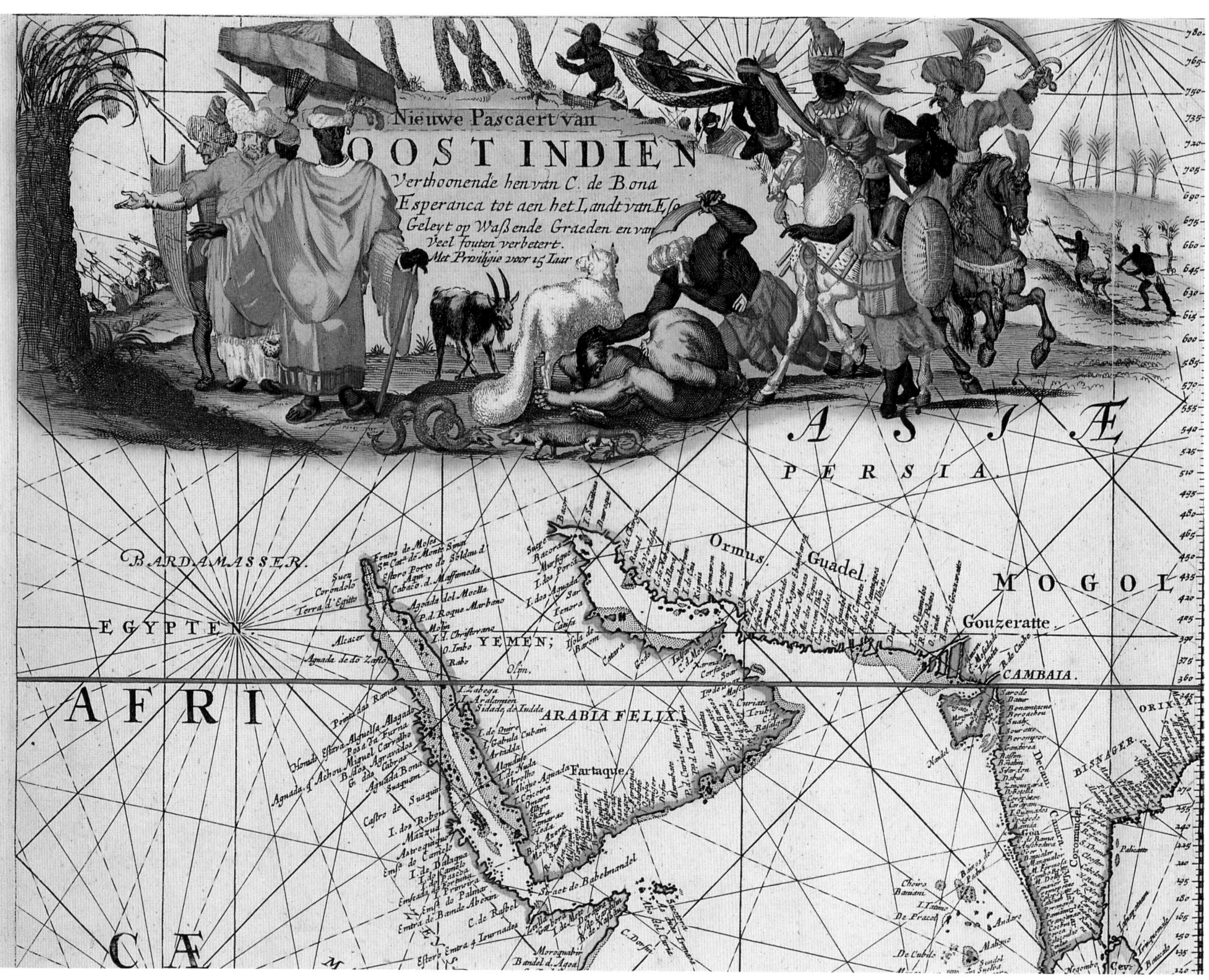
Nieuwe Pascaert van
OOST INDIEN
Verthoonende hen van C. de Bona
Esperanca tot aen het Landt van Eso
Geleyt op Waßende Graeden en van
Veel fouten verbetert.
Met Privilegie voor 15 Iaar
ASIÆ
PERSIA
BARDAMASSER
Ormus
Guadel
MOGOL
EGYPTEN
YEMEN
Gouzeratte
CAMBAIA
AFRI
ARABIA FELIX
Fartaque
Straet de Babelmandel
BISNAGER
ORIX
CÆ

This book is an entirely Euro-centred study, because the charting of the world's oceans was a European enterprise. Even among the Chinese there appears to have been no tradition of nautical mapping, and the Japanese sea-charts which exist from the seventeenth century onwards were based entirely on the European model. If seafarers from Asia or America had discovered and colonized medieval Europe, world history would have been re-written. The courage and achievements of the early mariners and explorers command our admiration, but this is not to underestimate the often catastrophic impact which European expansion had on Africa, America or Asia. These meetings of cultures were portrayed in many contemporary publications, and we now turn away in disgust from the endless scenes of brutality in books such as de Bry's *Voyages*. The callousness of the early explorers and adventurers was no doubt another expression of the iron endurance which they demanded of themselves. Europe's long maritime age from 1500–1900 witnessed a deliberate European assault on the world. This was a historical tide which has now ebbed in the direct political sense, although its legacy will probably be permanent.

Sea-charts had for many centuries a fluid relationship to topographical maps. For the modern chart, the depiction of geographical features – coasts, islands, estuaries – is not an end in itself, but is used as a framework for further navigational information. The contemporary chart embodies this data in a language of its own which must be mastered if the chart is to be of use. This was not always so, and many charts from the fifteenth to the nineteenth century were really dual-purpose maps, showing land features too. The historical reason for this is clear: sea charts were often the only maps available for many parts of the world, especially islands, and the chartmaker was fulfilling a dual role by mapping the interiors. The modern nautical chart carries so much coded data that it is perhaps closer to a technical diagram than a topographical map, and it is increasingly one part of a technical system of navigation. The charts of the past were closer to the general map: they were more readily understood, and they served as direct geographical pictures of the coasts and islands of the world.

* * * * * *

I am grateful to a number of scholars and librarians who have helped in the research for this book: Ken Atherton and Helen Breeze of the U.K. Hydrographic Office; Derek Howse, formerly of the National Maritime Museum; Francis Herbert of the Royal Geographical Society; Tony Campbell and the staff of The British Library; Kathy Houghton secured the pictures. The study of the charting of the world's oceans draws together some intriguing strands of western history: the interrelation between the technical and the political, and the fusing of greed, cruelty and courage. While mainly hugging the shore of this vast subject, I have been occasionally drawn into open sea, into a wider narrative of man's enduring relationship to the oceans that surround him.

DETAIL FROM a map of the Indian Ocean by van Keulen, see page 84.

Navigation before Charts

THE idea that seas and rivers are great dividers of peoples is a myth. Deserts and mountains have separated civilizations, while throughout history rivers and seas have been the means of communication, travel and trade. In the history of Europe from ancient times, the Mediterranean was a superhighway through which ran all the shaping forces of civilization. For the peoples of the Middle East, the waters of the Persian Gulf and the Arabian Sea offered possible routes to trade, wealth, adventure or conquest. The literature of the west and the east, from the *Odyssey* to the tale of Sinbad the Sailor, bears witness to the hold which the sea exercised over the imagination of these cultures. Emperors and pirates, poets and saints, merchants and warriors all felt the lure and the challenge of the sea.

Our knowledge of seafaring in the Mediterranen region reaches back some 5,000 years, to the most important innovation in maritime history – the sail, which replaced human power with wind power, and which made possible the movement of large quantities of goods and people. By 2500 BC Egyptian ships were leaving the mouth of the Nile to trade in Canaan, while Sumerian craft from the rivers Tigris and Euphrates were venturing out from the Persian Gulf to trade with the Indus Valley peoples. At the same time in the north, Bronze Age peoples were migrating and trading between mainland Europe and Britain and Scandinavia. Around 1500 BC the Greeks of Mycenae were able to launch a seaborne invasion of Crete. By 800 BC the Phoenicians had established colonies in Spain and North Africa, and were trading as far afield as Britain. How was all this achieved? How did these seafarers navigate? No sea-chart of any kind has survived from this era, nor is there any evidence that they existed. The belief that all these voyages were accomplished by 'hugging the coastline' cannot be sustained. Even within the Mediterranean, the routes to islands like Cyprus, Crete, Malta or Sardinia necessitated crossing miles of open sea out of sight of land. And even if the intention had been to follow the shoreline, darkness, fog and adverse weather might easily cut a vessel off from the coast, and it passes belief that these mariners were all hopelessly lost once out of sight of land. Yet there was no compass, no chart, and no accurate means of measuring direction or distance. From marine archaeology we know a good deal about ancient shipbuilding and warfare, but about the navigation of this era we know almost nothing. Without doubt there must have been a body of knowledge transmitted by oral teaching, which underlay these voyages of migration, trade or conquest. Scattered literary references – for example in Homer, Herodotus or Aristotle – give certain clues, as does the shared experience of seamen the world over.

The most basic form of navigation is dead reckoning, which means observing one's speed and direction over a given length of time, and estimating one's position in relation to the point of departure and the destination. The weakness of dead reckoning is that there is no objective control, and errors will accumulate. With frequent checks by the sighting of familiar landmarks the system works well enough, indeed the landmarks provide a chain of navigation points, but once out of sight of land, some other way – however elementary – of gauging direction is required.

ODYSSEUS'S SHIP. From an Athenian vase, late 6th century BC. The famous story from the *Odyssey* in which Odysseus is lashed to the mast in order to resist the sirens' song. The ship is a sailing galley, the classic Mediterranean vessel for thousands of years, having one large central sail and any number of oars, from a dozen to several hundred.
British Museum, Dept. of Greek and Roman Antiquities.

EGYPTIAN SHIPS *c.*1500 BC, redrawn from stone reliefs on the tomb of Hatshepsut at Deir-el-Bahri. These pictures illustrate an Egyptian trading voyage to the land of 'Punt' – perhaps Ethiopia. The ships are clearly seagoing vessels, larger than the Nile felucca. On the left, sails are shown furled at the harbourside, while on the right the huge sails are being used as well as the oars. The hieroglyphic text describes the cargo: ebony, ivory, gold and a live panther.

British Museum.

The cardinal points of direction were given by the sun: east and west correspond to sunrise and sunset, south and north to the direction of light and of shadow. At night too the stars appear to rise in the east, and their rotation about a fixed northern star was noticed. Although the path of the sun was perfectly familiar, it was difficult to observe directly, whereas the night sky, with its pivotal point, could serve as a more accessible map to the experienced eye. The Greek writer on astronomy, Aratus, described the constellation of Ursa Minor, and adds that 'by her guidance the men of Sidon (*i.e.* the Phoenicans) steer the straightest course'. Ursa Minor contains the present Pole Star Polaris and its ancient counterpart Kochab. Homer testifies to the importance of the circumpolar stars, which are ever-visible:

> . . . the Great Bear which wheeling round
> Looks ever towards Orion and
> Dips not into the waters of the deep.

Describing the shipwreck of St Paul, the writer of the book of Acts expresses the danger in which the seafarer found himself when 'neither sun nor stars in many days appeared' (*Acts* 27:20). In addition to these fundamental rules of astro-navigation, it seems that meteorology offered the earliest systematic form of direction-finding in the form of the winds. The skilled Mediterranean seafarer could readily distinguish the cold north wind from the warm south wind, the blustery west from the cool, moist easterly. Eight wind directions were identified by name, and they may have been used on shipboard in the form of an inscribed eight-pointed star, the wind-rose, which thus functioned as a type of compass, based not on magnetic direction-finding but on the mariner's reading of the wind. Aristotle endorses this scheme in his *Meteorologia*, and adds two more winds at North-North-East and North-North-West to make ten. Aristotle's model is effectively a diagram of the circular horizon, for he adds the solstitial points of sunrise and sunset. A century after Aristotle, Timosthenes of Rhodes designed a twelve-point wind-rose in which the winds are named after the countries from which they blow. This scheme of the twelve winds survived into the post-classical and medieval era – they are shown on medieval *mappae mundi* – and Renaissance mapmakers depicted them as human faces around the edges of their maps. The Tower of the Winds in Athens, its eight sides facing the original eight wind directions, was built around the year 100 BC as a kind of public compass.

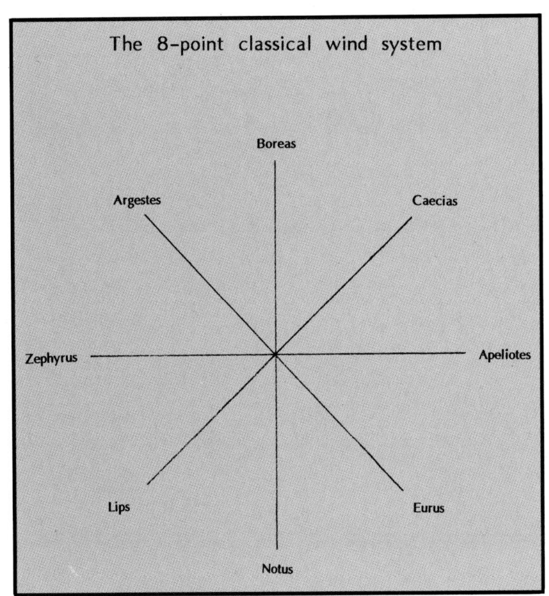

THE EIGHT CLASSICAL WINDS. The earliest 'compass' used by Mediterranean seafarers was based not on magnetic direction, but on the mariners' ability to recognise the character and direction of the wind. This system was endorsed by scientific writers such as Aristotle, and an alternative twelve-wind system was also developed. These eight or twelve winds were personified as faces around the edges of medieval and Renaissance maps.

After *The History of Cartography* Vol. 1, p.145.

By that date Greek science had made such advances in spherical geometry that theories of latitude and longitude were now current. Hipparchus drew up a star catalogue in the second century BC giving star positions on the celestial sphere in a form of celestial latitude and longitude. The method of determining a latitude on earth from the altitude of the Pole Star followed naturally from this. The extent to which a theoretical basis for cartography and navigation had been established is shown in the work of Eratosthenes who accurately calculated the circumference of the earth by measuring an arc of 7 degrees on its surface. No doubt this was specialized knowledge, and was out of reach of the seafarer. Nevertheless several clues suggest an empirical grasp of the form of the earth. Herodotus gives an account which he heard of a Phoenician expedition around the coast of Africa around 600 BC, from the Red Sea around the entire continent and back to the Mediterranean. It sounds improbable but for a phrase Herodotus uses when the Phoenicians were sailing west towards the Cape that 'they had the sun upon their right hand'. Could such a detail have been based on anything other than an authentic eyewitness account? Similarly, around the year 330 BC, the Greek mariner Pytheas reportedly sailed from Marseilles out into the Atlantic and northwards around the coast of Britain, beyond Orkney to the legendary land of Thule – the end of the world. At more than 60 degrees north, Pytheas claimed that the summer sun never sets at night: could such a description arise from purely theoretical knowledge? For centuries the Pillars of Hercules would mark the limit of the known world, and the open sea to the west would be populated with legendary islands such as Atlantis, the Hesperides, Avalon and Lyonesse.

In the familiar waters of the Mediterranean by the third century BC the wind-rose was used to underlay the earliest known writen aids to navigation – the pilot book or *periplus*. This listed ports in various regions with the courses to be steered between them, expressed in terms of wind direction and days' sailing. Additional information on landmarks and anchorages might also be given. A small number of these texts survive and cover ports from the Iberian Peninsula to the Indus, but there is no evidence that graphic charts of any kind were produced to accompany these *periploi*. One of the oldest known is the *periplus* of Scylax, dating from *c.*500 BC, covering virtually the entire Mediterranean but at a very elementary descriptive level:

> Coasting from the Pillars of Hercules to Cape Hermaea is two days; from Cape Hermaea to Cape Soloeis coasting is three days, and from Cape Soloeis to Cape Cerne seven days coasting. This whole coasting from the Pillars to Cerne Island takes twelve days. The parts beyond the Isle of Cerne are no longer navigable because of shoals, mud and seaweed. The traders here are Phoenicians.

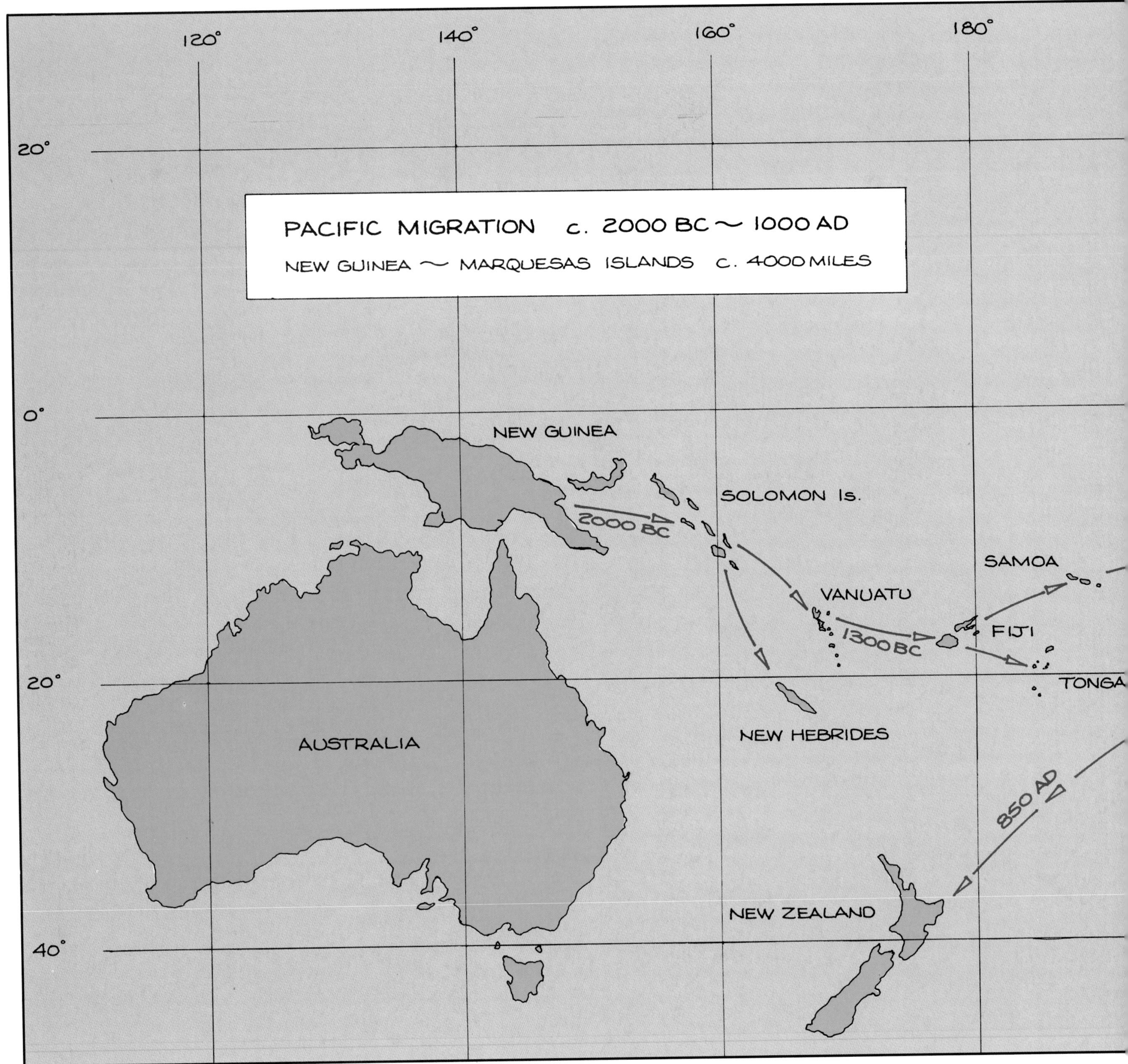

PACIFIC MIGRATION. Archaeological evidence has permitted the dating of the spread of Polynesian culture across vast distances in the Pacific. How these voyages were planned and navigated remains a mystery.

Drawing by Peter Sullivan.

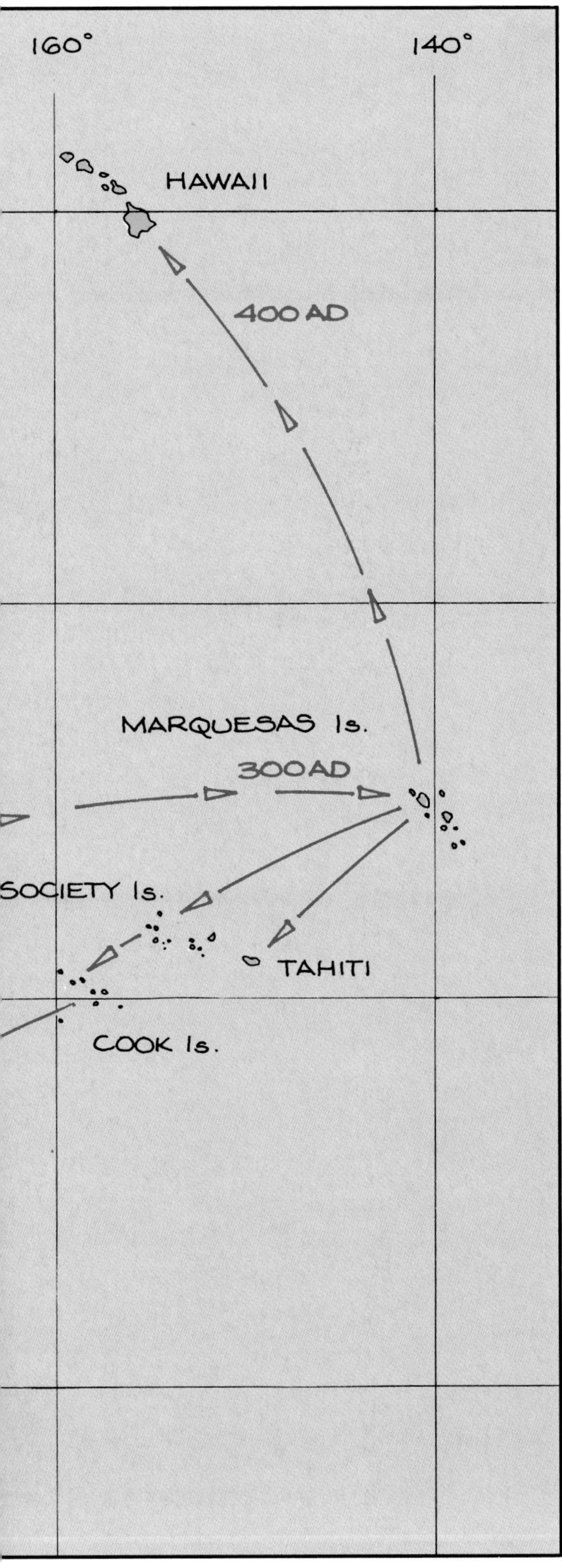

The underlying system of navigation here is a primitive form of dead reckoning: there is no mention of astro-navigation, or of any form of position-finding other than gauging the sailing time. The mariners who compiled them had no means of determining latitude and longitude, and no means of carrying out compass surveys of coastlines. Hence they could not lay a graphic framework within which to plot the positions of these ports. There was no cartographic method for constructing land surveys which might have served as a model for such charts. There was, in short, no cartographic awareness among mariners at this time, although a theoretical basis for scientific mapping was established among Hellenic scientists.

However conjectural our knowledge of early navigation, there is no such uncertainty about the importance of seafaring in the history of the Mediterranean. The spread of Hellenic culture was largely sea-based, and the great cities of Byzantium, Syracuse, Naples and Marseilles originated as Greek colonies. Simultaneously the Phoenician colony of Carthage would grow into a maritime power capable of threatening Rome. The twin motives for the exploitation of sea power were what they have always been: trade and warfare. The ship of this time was the sailing galley, in which oar and sail were combined.

THE MARSHALL ISLANDS from a native map of the early 19th century, constructed from sticks and shells (*right*) with the equivalent area from a modern map. The two main chains of the islands are over 100 miles apart and stretch for over 500 miles north-south: the geographical accuracy of the native map is generally excellent, but we have no real knowledge of how it was arrived at.

By courtesy of the International Cartographic Association.

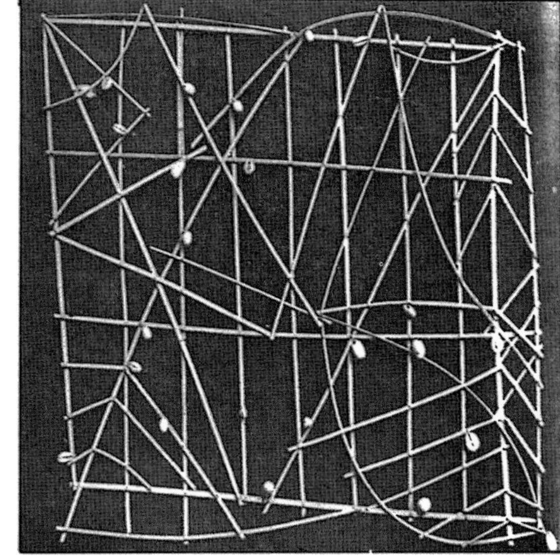

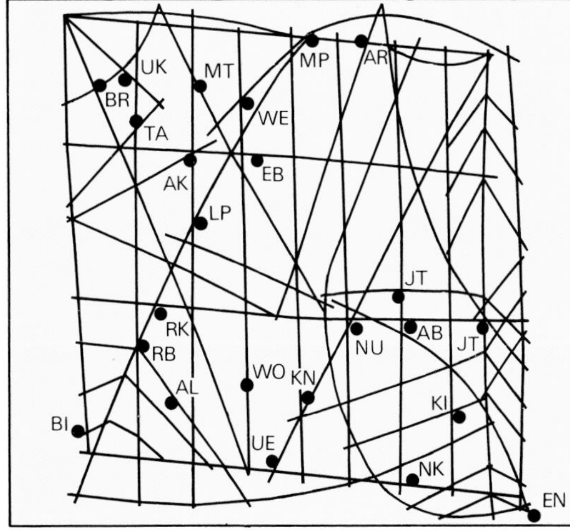

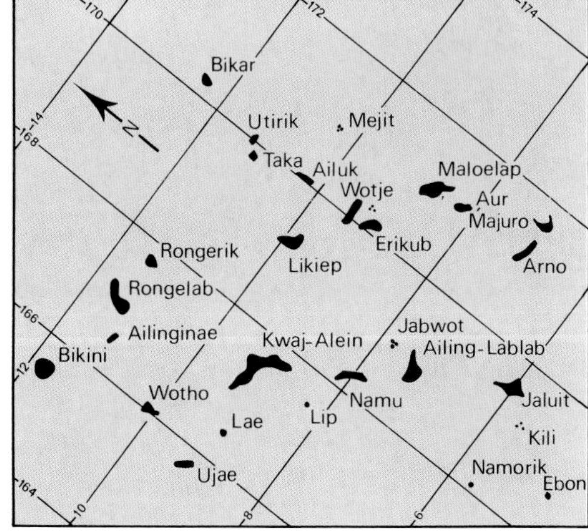

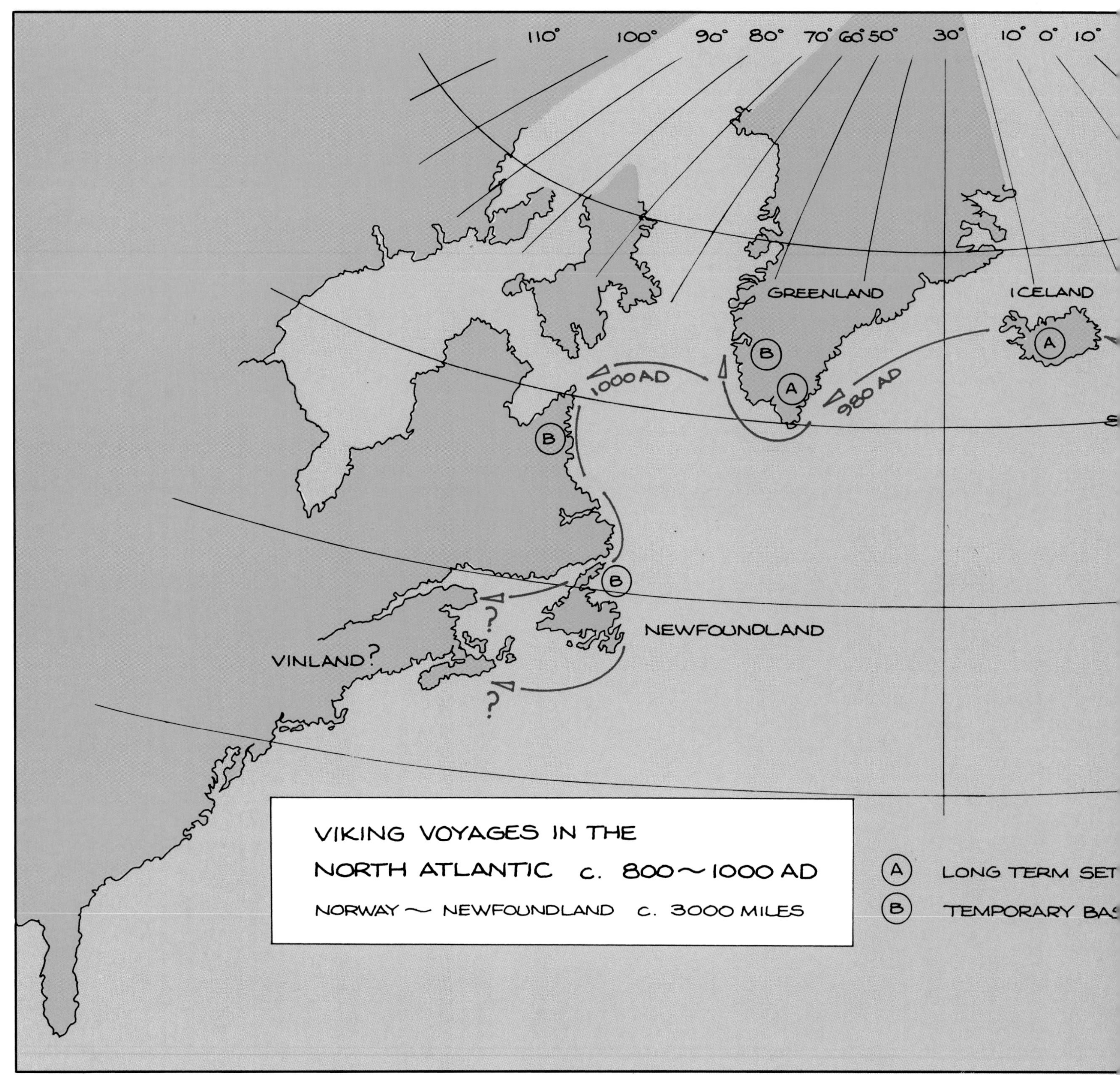

VIKING VOYAGES. Clear evidence of Viking settlements in Newfoundland around 1000 AD has confirmed the account of Norse voyages to America in *The Saga of Eric the Red*. However these colonies were soon abandoned, and whether the Norsemen penetrated the American mainland is still unknown. Drawing by Peter Sullivan.

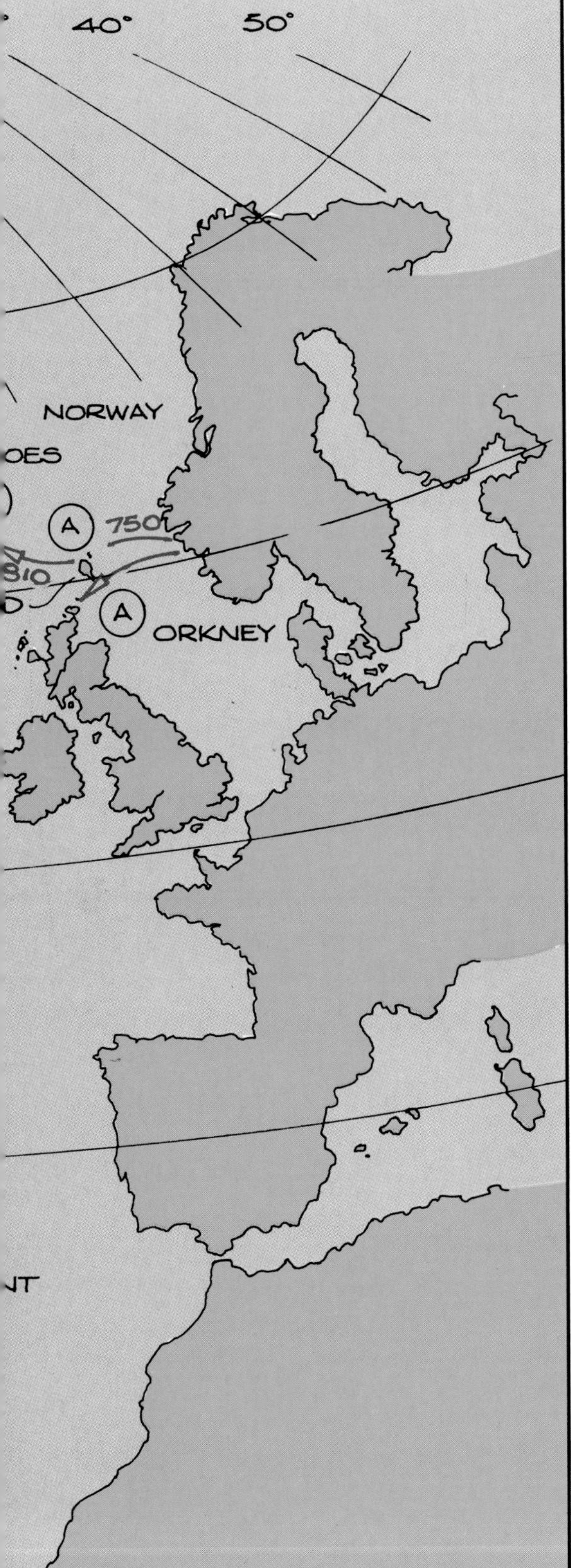

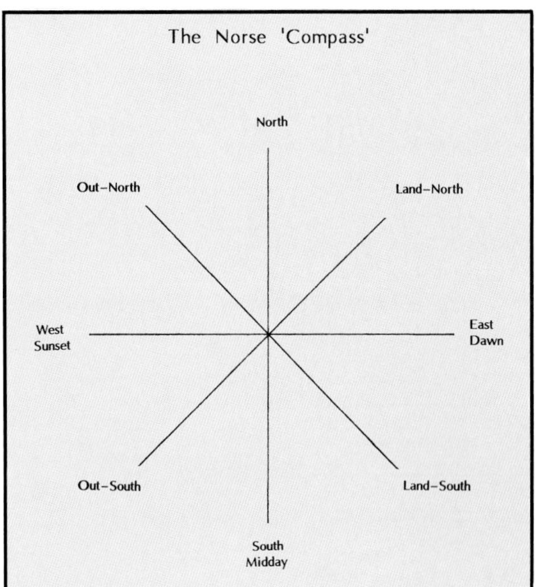

A NORSE NAVIGATIONAL COMPASS as described in Norse literature. Based on the cardinal points Out and Home, equated with sunset and sunrise, a dial such as this may have been mounted on board ship.
After Newby: *World Atlas of Exploration*, p.57.

The merchant ship had fewer oars, and relied on sail to make long voyages at a steady speed. The warship's great weapon was the ram: it must manoeuvre at close quarters, accelerate, ram and withdraw, hence oars proliferated. The naval battle of Salamis in 480 BC, in which the Greeks defeated the Persian fleet, is regarded as a crucial event in European history, turning back the threatened invasion of Greece by Persia. Five centuries later, as Rome progressed from city state to Empire, the sea was again crucial in supply and communication. Rome consumed vast quantities of corn, oil, minerals and luxury goods, most of it transported by sea from the east. All the great cities of the Empire were ports – Alexandria, Antioch, Corinth, Carthage. The battle of Actium in 31 BC between the Roman and Egyptian fleets paralleled that of Salamis as a moment when the centre of Mediterranean power might have shifted decisively eastwards.

Both trade and warfare clearly demanded a tradition of skilled seamanship among all the nations bordering the Mediterranean, yet much remains obscure, even mysterious in their navigational methods. This mystery is even stronger in the history of some other seafaring peoples, such as those of the Pacific. Somewhere around 2500 BC the inhabitants of New Guinea began a process of seaborne migration into the Pacific. By way of the Solomon Islands and Vanuatu, they had reached Fiji by 1300 BC, and soon afterwards they made their way to Tonga and Samoa. Around 200 AD a wave of Samoans made the 2,000-mile journey east to the Marquesas Islands, which then seem to have served as a dispersal centre for Polynesian culture. Between 400 and 800 AD these people settled Hawaii, Tahiti, the Society and Cook Islands, and Easter Island, and finally New Zealand itself by 900 AD. These voyages across thousands of miles of empty oceans must have occupied weeks or even months, and we have no real knowledge of how they were accomplished. These societies were pre-literate, and their navigational skills were transmitted by oral traditions long since lost. The primary role we assign to the compass must have been filled by the stars and the winds, as well perhaps as other skills in recognizing weather-features, birds or vegetation that might betray the presence of land.

It is equally difficult to penetrate the psychology of these ocean-wanderers. We are told that for thousands of years the Atlantic formed a barrier of fear to European sailors, forbidding and unassailable. Did the Polynesian migrant feel no such fear of the Pacific? How did they know they would find land across the seas? Were they seeking a specific

destination, and if so how did they know about it in advance? If the migrants from the Marquesas to Hawaii for example had steered a course one degree more to the north, they could have sailed on to Alaska. What instinctive ocean chart did they possess in their minds that made such voyages possible? There exists an ethnic sea-chart made by the people of the Marshall Islands, but it fails to answer these larger questions, remarkable though it is. It covers an area some 500 miles across and shows the relative positions and distances of the main islands in the group with surprising accuracy. But its nineteenth-century origin prevents its use as evidence of traditional skills of navigation. European contact with the Marshall Islands was made very early, and was renewed throughout the eighteenth and nineteenth centuries, and they were partly mapped by British and Russian expeditions. The possibility cannot be discounted that this chart was produced in imitation of European models; its orientation approximately 45 degrees from a North-South axis might be evidence of this.

Exactly contemporary with these Pacific migrations was another wave of non-Mediterranean sea-traffic – that of the Norsemen. The Viking voyages involved distances that were less vast than those of the Polynesians, but they were accomplished in a far

NORMAN SHIPS from the Bayeux Tapestry, late 11th century. The Vikings who settled in France became known as Normans, hence the ships which carried the invaders to England are identical to the Viking longships: open, deck-less, with a single square sail and an animal figurehead. Oars are omitted from this picture, but their sockets can be seen in the rail.

Bridgeman Art Library

harsher environment, the cold and stormy waters of the North Atlantic. In the years 750–1000 AD, setting out from the Norwegian coasts, the Norsemen sought first plunder then settlement. About 890, Ohthere of Norway, 'desirous to find how far that country extended north', sailed around the North Cape into the White Sea. But most Norsemen explored not east but west: to Britain, Iceland, Greenland and finally North America. The precise location of 'Vinland' described in *The Saga of Eric the Red* is unknown, but the remains of a Norse settlement on the Newfoundland coast have been dated to 1000 AD, and prove conclusively that the Vikings were the first Europeans to make contact with America. Their small colony failed, and although the story was not entirely forgotten in medieval Europe, the knowledge was not exploited in the way that it was to be five centuries later. It was not a 'discovery' because the eleventh century was not fired by the rage for discovery. The missing ingredient was the idea that the new land was the gateway to the east, to China and India, for it was this that lay behind the Renaissance voyages of discovery. The celebrated Vinland map, which came to light in the 1950s, is almost certainly a forgery, but it was in any case claimed to date from the fifteenth century and cannot be used as evidence of Norse geography or chartmaking.

We do know that the Vikings devised certain navigational aids which they used at sea. One was a type of compass based on the sun: at the higher northern latitudes the noon meridian each day could be used to set a pointer on a circular dial, which gave an axis running directly north-south. (It has been claimed that in bad weather the Norsemen used a natural polarizer such as Iceland spar to locate the sun, but this is not certain.) This axis could form the basis of a quasi-compass which also has elements of a chart. The coast of Norway runs roughly north-south, giving the Norsemen a base-line for their bearings. They spoke of north-east and south-east as 'land-north' and 'land-south', while 'out-north' and 'out-south' were the western bearings. To some extent they used natural phenomena to recognize the proximity of land: birds such as fulmars fly landward to roost at night; the presence of fish such as cod indicate the shallower waters of the continental shelf. Whether this kind of knowledge may be termed navigation is debatable, since it contains no certainty of position – that the nearby land is the land that is sought. Nevertheless the Norsemen succeeded in making themselves masters of these northern waters, voyaging as far as North America at least four times to our certain knowledge, and perhaps more. That the seafarers of this time felt deeply the challenge and the power of the sea is clear from the literature of Norsemen and Saxons:

> List how I, care-wretched on ice-cold sea
> Weathered the winter, wretched outcast
> Deprived of my kinsmen
> Hung with hard ice flakes where hail-scur flew,
> There I heard nought save the harsh sea
> And ice-cold wave . . .
>
> –*The Seafarer,* 10th century AD

The Vikings are the most famous seafarers of early medieval Europe, but in the years following the decline of Rome's power the sea carried other peoples, their culture and their wars. The Vandals crossed from Spain to North Africa, then launched a seaborne conquest of Sardinia, parts of Italy and, in 455 of Rome itself. It was by sea that the Byzantine reconquest of Vandal lands took place in the following century under Belisarius. In the north, the Saxons crossed the sea from Germany to possess England, pushing many Britons to migrate to Brittany. In the ninth century it was the turn of the Saracens to use the Tunisian coast to launch attacks on Italy and southern France; the islands of Sicily,

Neantmoins les trois chevalliers
dessus nommes se tindrent sur
leur place les trente iours tout
acomplis et oultre puis sen retour
nerent tout par loisir chascun en
son lieu. Quant ilz furent venus
a paris qui leur furent bonne chie
re ce fut bien raison car moult
vaillamment sestoient portes et
grandement avoient garde lhon
neur du royaume de france come
bien y parut aux ioustes.

THE WINCHELSEA SEAL, *c.*1300. Medieval town seals are important sources for our knowledge of ship design. Here we see the castles fore and aft which were added to the open longship, while the overlapping plank ('clinker') construction of the hull is very plain. On ships like this English merchant captains sailed the North Sea and the Channel, soldiers were carried to the wars in France, and pilgrims embarked for the Holy Land.

National Maritime Museum, Greenwich.

Sardinia, Corsica, and Crete were especially vulnerable and were occupied. When Moslem rulers came to occupy much of the Near East, they inherited the ancient trade routes from the Red Sea to East Africa and from the Persian Gulf to India. As early as 851 AD Sulaiman el-Tagir composed his account of a journey to India and China in which he describes the shipping of goods from Canton through to Basra and Jeddah. The Arab presence in the Indian Ocean is also witnessed by the phenomenal traveller Ibn Battuta who ranged from Mombasa to Sumatra. Arab sailors had developed some navigational aids unknown in the west. One of these was the Kemal, which determined latitude by sighting the altitude of the Pole Star; though simple in itself it shows an unmistakable basis in scientific astronomy. The Arab skill in astronomy was especially valuable in southern waters, when out of sight of the Pole Star. There is a persistent tradition that the compass itself was brought to the west from China by Arab seafarers but this has never been demonstrated.

In the middle ages the Mediterranean was still a great theatre of trade and conflict. Christian and Moslem, Venetian and Byzantine, Norman and Turk sailed the trade routes and harassed their rivals' ships. This was an age of privateering, of state-sponsored piracy, for all these groups were delighted to see their opponents suffer without resorting to open warfare. The great maritime adventure of the age was the crusading movement: between the years 1000 and 1300 some hundreds of thousands of men were transported from the ports of western Europe to Constantinople and the Middle East. These expeditions had an enormous impact on cities like Genoa and Venice, and they stimulated many changes in ship design. At the same time the nations of northern Europe were developing merchant navies and trading networks of their own stretching from London, Hamburg and Bergen into the Baltic. The characteristic ship here was the cog, a rounder, broader sailing vessel, often with raised castles fore and aft, essentially a merchantman design, dispensing with the oars and speed of the galley or longship. It was among these merchant ships that vitally important changes in ship design occurred between the twelfth and fourteenth centuries: the rudder hinged to the stern, the use of three masts, and the mounting of two sails on the same mast. These, with changes to the build of the hulls, created the caravel, a ship that was larger and stronger, yet more manoeuvrable and able to sail closer to the wind, all pre-conditions for ocean sailing. The great historical fact of Moslem occupation of the entire Middle East meant that when Europeans were ready to break out of their home continent, they took to the ocean south and west. But before that could happen a navigational breakthrough was needed. It was in the Mediterranean that the earliest recoverable phase of navigation history emerges: in the late thirteenth century comes the first evidence of the compass and the sea-chart. For the first time the mariner's skills and knowledge were transmitted and preserved in written form, and an objective basis for ocean navigation was established, without which the seafarer could not venture beyond the coasts and inland seas of Europe.

CRUSADERS EMBARKING, from a 15th-century manuscript. Thousands of Christian soldiers and pilgrims left the ports of France and Italy for Antioch, Tripoli or Acre, and this traffic brought a fortune to shipowners, stimulating Mediterranean ship design, away from the oared galley to the rounder sailing cog with raised decks.

The British Library, Harley MS 4379, f.60v.

PISAN CHART, late 13th century. The oldest surviving sea-chart is possibly Genoese in origin despite its familiar name. There are two networks of rhumb-lines, one centred near Sardinia, the other in the Aegean, and each forms a 16-point compass. The density of Mediterranean place-names contrasts with the gross inaccuracy in the drafting of Northern Europe. This chart is one of the most enigmatic in the history of mapmaking: did it appear *de novo*, or had this image of the Mediterranean been evolving for centuries?

Bibliothèque Nationale, Paris.

CHAPTER 2

The Sea-Chart and the Age of Exploration

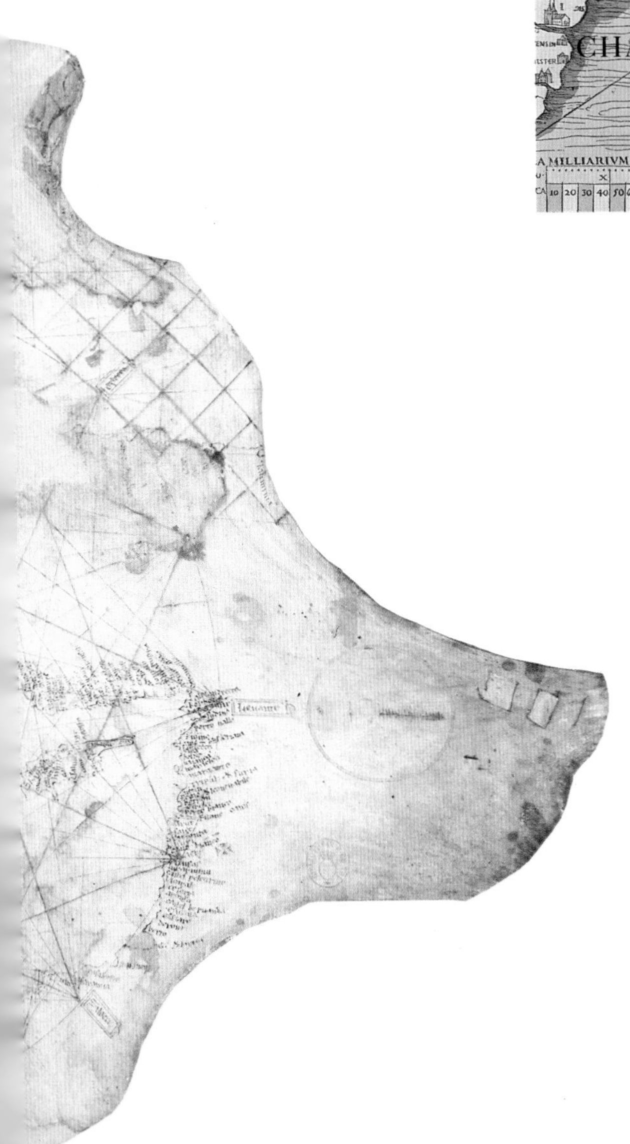

In the year 1270, the French king Louis IX – Saint Louis – was sailing for Tunis on his last, ill-fated crusade, when a storm arose. To re-assure the king of the ship's position, the captain produced a map, and they decided to make for harbour in Sardinia: this is the first recorded use of a chart on board a ship. Early in the following century, maritime ordinances in Spain and Italy were including a requirement for all ships to carry charts on board, and inventories from ships prove that this practice became standard. If the chart was one half of a radically new approach to navigation, the other was the compass, and the first evidence of its use also occurs in the thirteenth century. In 1218 Jacques de Vitry, a bishop who had travelled to the lands of the crusades, wrote: 'An iron needle after it had made contact with the magnet stone always turns towards the north star, which stands motionless while the rest revolve, being as it were the axis of the firmament. It is therefore a necessity for those travelling at sea.' Thus it was that the Pole Star became known as *Stella Maris* – the star of the sea. We do not have a ship's compass from this early date, but we know what kind of chart the French king must have seen because it is from exactly this period that the oldest extant sea-chart survives, the Pisan Chart of *c.*1290.

The appearance of this chart (and of the others which survive from the following century) is one of the most mysterious events in the history of mapmaking. A glance at the Pisan Chart immediately reveals two outstanding features: the coastlines of the Mediterranean are drawn with striking accuracy; and the map is covered with a network of lines radiating from two central points, which clearly impose the form of the compass over the whole map. How did this highly accurate map suddenly appear in medieval Italy, and how exactly was it linked to the compass? Was it the original work of a single individual, or was it descended from a line of much older charts which had been developing for centuries? The former is difficult to believe, but the latter cannot explain why there is no shred of evidence for the existence of such maps before 1270.

What did develop from the classical era into the middle ages was the book of sailing-directions: the *periploi* of the Greeks were known in the thirteenth century as *portolani*, lists of ports and the distances between them. One famous example entitled *Lo Compasso da Navigàre* was current among Italian mariners, and it would be tempting to suppose that the contents of a text such as this had been transformed with the aid of compass bearings into the Pisan Chart. Unfortunately, the places named in *Lo Compasso* differ sharply from those named on the map, even the names in Italy itself. Moreover the transition from a list of names and bearings to an accurate map is an enormous one, requiring not only a high degree of geometric and drafting skill, but also an imaginative leap to create a graphic form for which there was no parallel. Even if the Pisan Chart were based on some now-

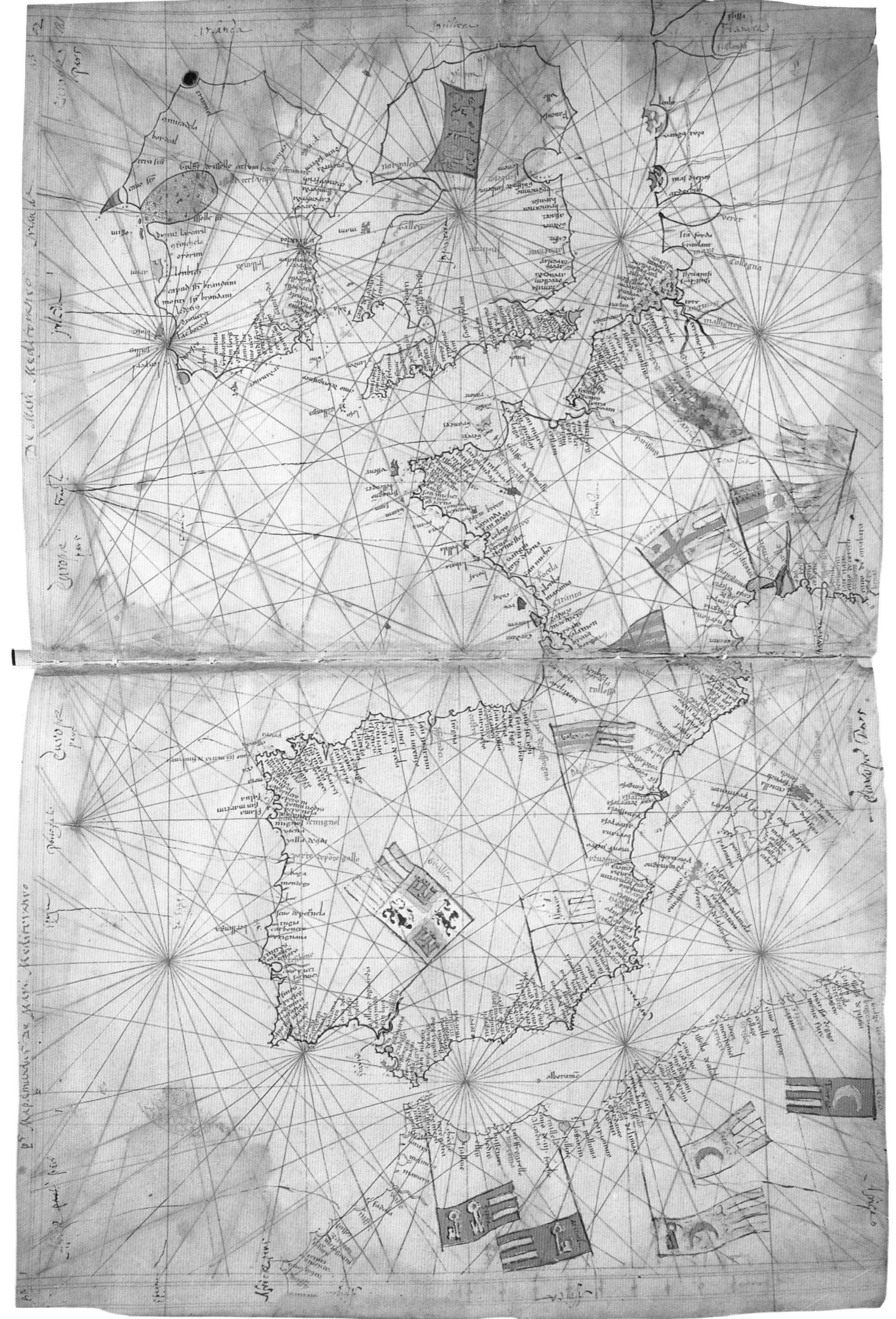

lost *portolano*, we have no real idea how it was done. Nor can we really answer the most fundamental question of all about the chart – how was it used? We have no independent description of its use, although we do know, from examination of the chart itself, that the compass lines were plotted *before* the map itself was drawn. We can only read back from later practice, and assume that a compass line on the map served as a line of bearing – a rhumb line. The extension of this line through the fore-and-aft line of the ship will give the course heading. To find a course from the chart, we assume that the navigator placed a straight-edge on the map joining his two ports, adopted whichever rhumb line was parallel to it, then kept his ship's head in that direction. This requires that some form of compass was mounted on deck, through which the direction of the ship was controlled. Techniques to correct the effects of winds and currents on this constant course must have followed very quickly from the first use of the compass. How were the accurate coastal outlines measured and drawn? Later practice was to make a running survey, in which coastal features – capes, bays, or islands – were sighted from two, three or four positions as the ship sailed by. Starting from the ship's course, the distances run and the angles of sight were used to build up a profile of the coast. This method was in use by the later sixteenth century, but we can only conjecture whether it was known at the time the Pisan Chart was drawn. If it was not, it is extremely difficult to account for the accuracy of some of the coastlines, which would scarcely be improved on at this scale until the eighteenth century.

Whatever the uncertainties surrounding the Pisan Chart, the advent of the chart and the compass bring a new dimension to the recorded history of seafaring. The making of portolan charts (so-called because of their supposed association with the *portolani*) gathered pace in the fourteenth century, first in the Italian maritime centres of Genoa and Venice, and then in the Catalan region, especially Majorca. Later charts originated from Sicily, Marseilles and Alexandria. Strangely, no comparable charts emerged in northern Europe. The North Sea and the Baltic formed an area of very active maritime trade from at least the thirteenth century, yet these waters remained uncharted until a distinctive type of coastal survey emerged late in the sixteenth century. This absence of northern charts is yet another aspect of the puzzle surrounding late medieval mapmaking. In Italy and Spain a number of early chartmakers pioneered mapmaking as both a business and an art, and some of them were evidently supplying an expanding chart market over many years: Vesconte and Pizigano in Venice, Dulcert and Valseca in Majorca – these are the first mapmakers known to us by name. The accuracy of the Mediterranean coastal outlines in these early charts is startling and precocious, the more so since they appear to be based exclusively on empirical knowledge, and have no basis in geometry or cartographic theory. No latitude or longitude is ever given, indeed around the year 1450 the very concept of terrestrial latitude and longitude was known to only a handful of European mathematicians. The portolan charts are not drawn on any projection, so it is evident that no thought has been given to the problem of representing the spherical earth in two dimensions. On that most fundamental of map requirements, the scale, the evidence is confusing. Many of these charts do show a graded line which may have been taken for a scale, yet no numerical key is ever given. These scales have been interpreted as representing the traditional leagues, but the value of the league was not standard among the Mediterranean nations, hence their appearance here is enigmatic.

The use of the word 'chart' at this early period, and for several centuries thereafter, should not be taken to imply any narrow or technical definition. The chart always showed a compass and a network of rhumb-lines, and in theory it could be used to take bearings. But compasses soon began to be drawn on land-maps too, and the mere fact of a compass appearing on a map does not mean that accurate bearings can be drawn: other factors such as projection are vital here. It would be tempting to say that a chart was a map designed

A CHART OF WESTERN EUROPE by Pietro Vesconte *c.*1325. Vesconte is the earliest professional chart-maker known to us by name. Although a Genoese, he was active in Venice between 1310 and 1330, producing a number of atlases of the Mediterranean and Black Sea in the classical Italian style: no inland features are shown, but flags distinguish the main nations and cities. The names in red are generally the more important ports and cities.

The British Library, Add. MS. 27376, ff.180v–181.

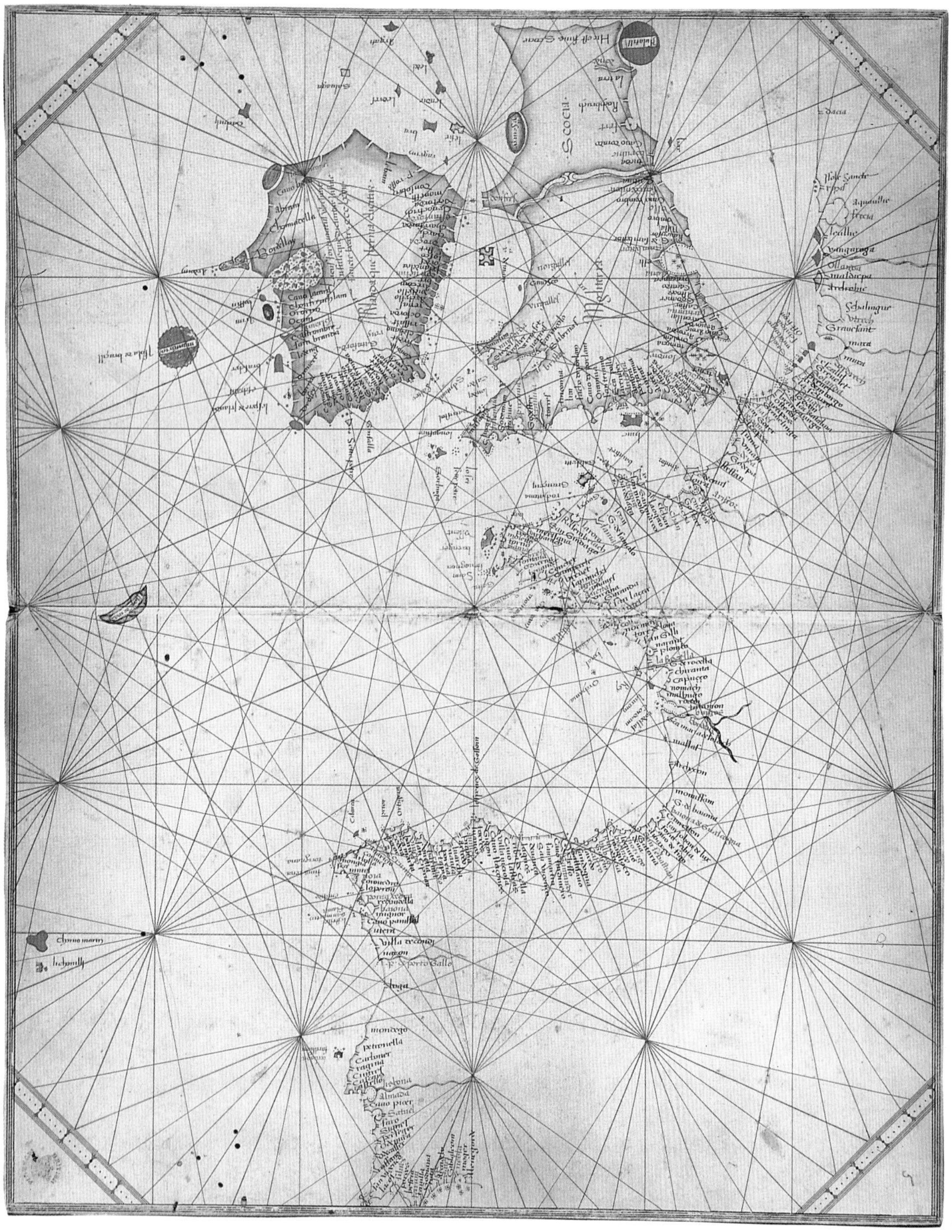

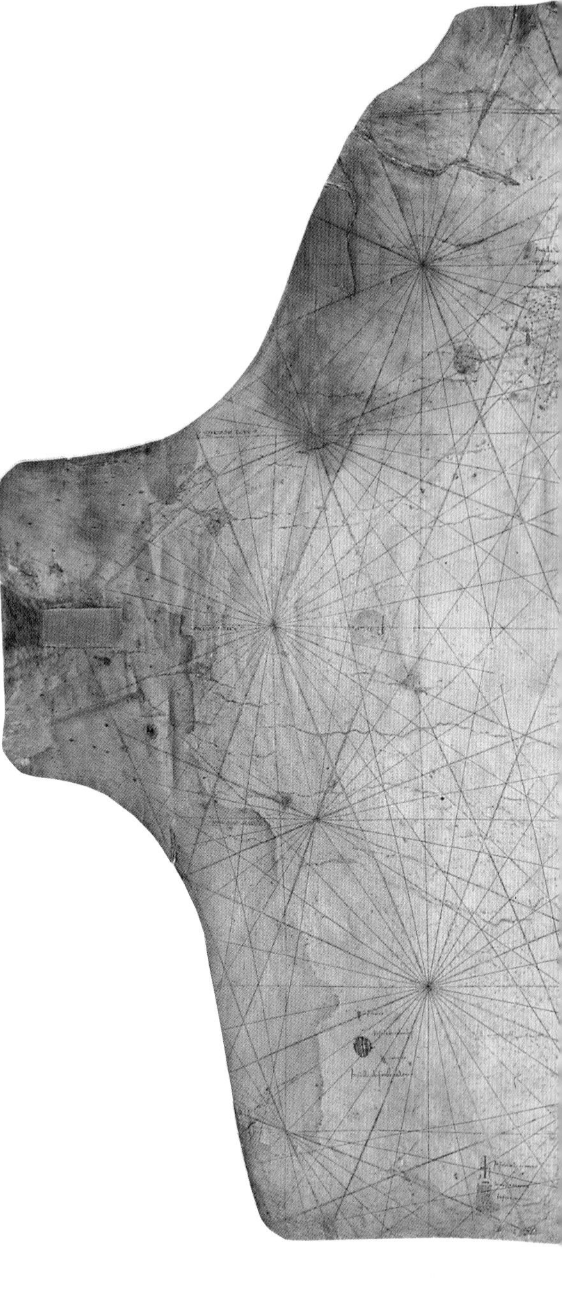

for use at sea; but many maps which show the characteristics of the sea-chart also showed many other features irrelevant to the mariner, and it is clear that they were never intended to be taken to sea. This lack of a precise definition is not surprising at this early period: land-maps and topographic maps had not yet developed a conscious specification or style, so why should the sea-chart? Perhaps all we can say to define the sea-chart is the most obvious fact that the chart is centred on the sea, and the land is on the margins, rather than vice versa. The sea-chart of this time was certainly not the precise technical instrument that it later became.

WESTERN EUROPE by Graziosa Benincasa, 1469. Benincasa was one of the most prolific of the early chartmakers. The maps he produced between 1461 and 1482 maintain a relatively stable picture of the Mediterranean, but show great changes in the mapping of parts of northern Europe and the African coast, the former derived from Italian trade with Flanders, the latter from Portuguese explorers.

The British Library, Add. MS. 31315, ff.4v–5.

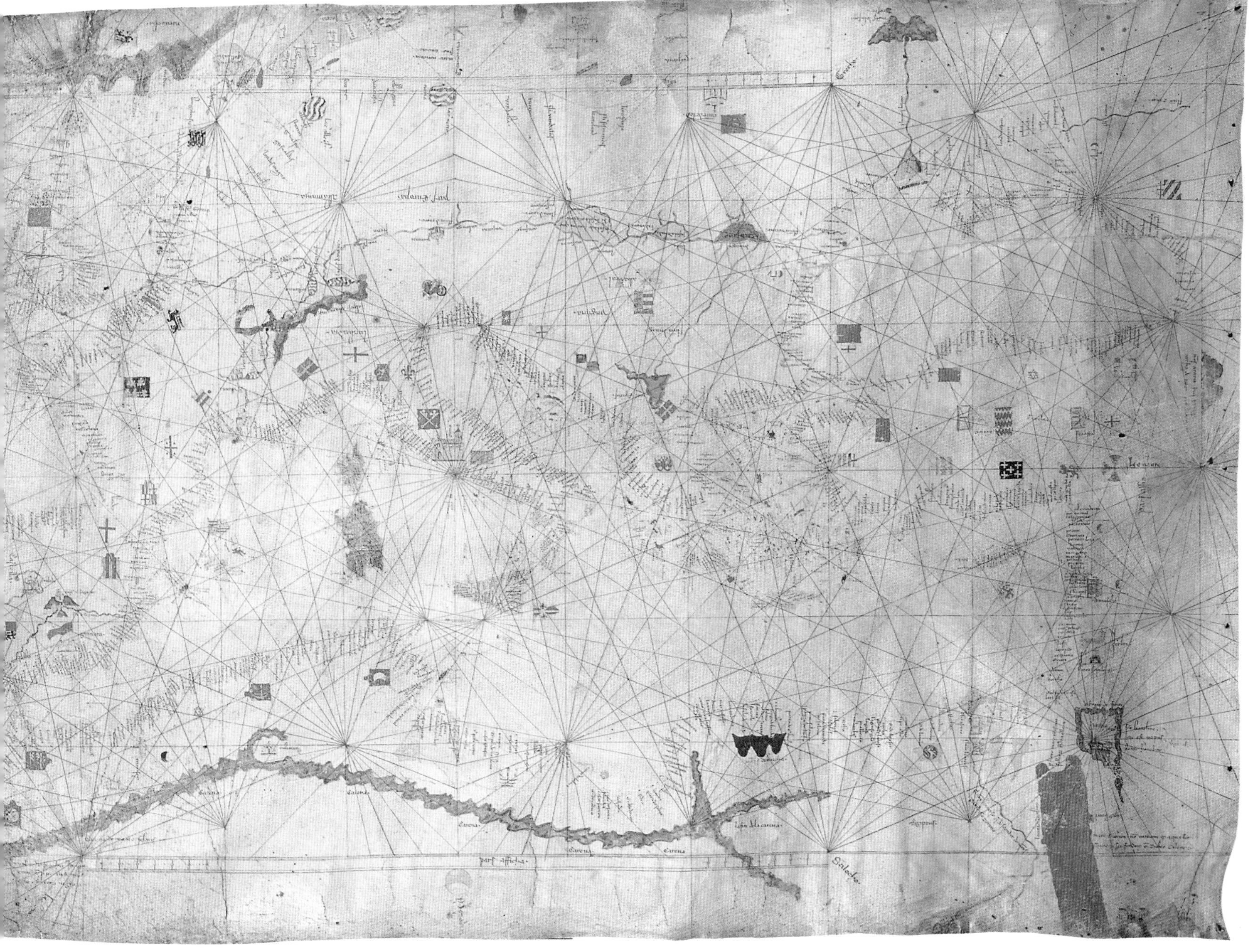

THE MEDITERRANEAN, mid-14th century, attributed to Angelino Dulcert. A typical early Catalan sea-chart: the entire Mediterranean region is shown on a single vellum skin at a scale of approximately 1:6 million. Inland features begin to appear – the Alps, the Atlas Mountains, the Rhine and the Danube – and pictorial symbols for cities, such as the church marking Rome.

The British Library, Add. MS. 25691.

Once the prototype chart had been drawn, a breakthrough to a new type of graphic representation had clearly been made, and new charts could readily be copied. Yet the portolan charts are by no means static, for they show significant developments in three main areas: geographical refinement, place-names, and style. The central or normal area of the portolon chart was the Mediterranean, from the Straits of Gibraltar to Constantinople and into the Black Sea, and no great changes in this area are observable between the years 1300 and 1500. By contrast the peripheral areas – Europe's northern coast, the British Isles, the Atlantic islands and the African coast – were steadily expanded and improved. This is especially noticeable in the work of Benincasa, whose series of portolan atlases,

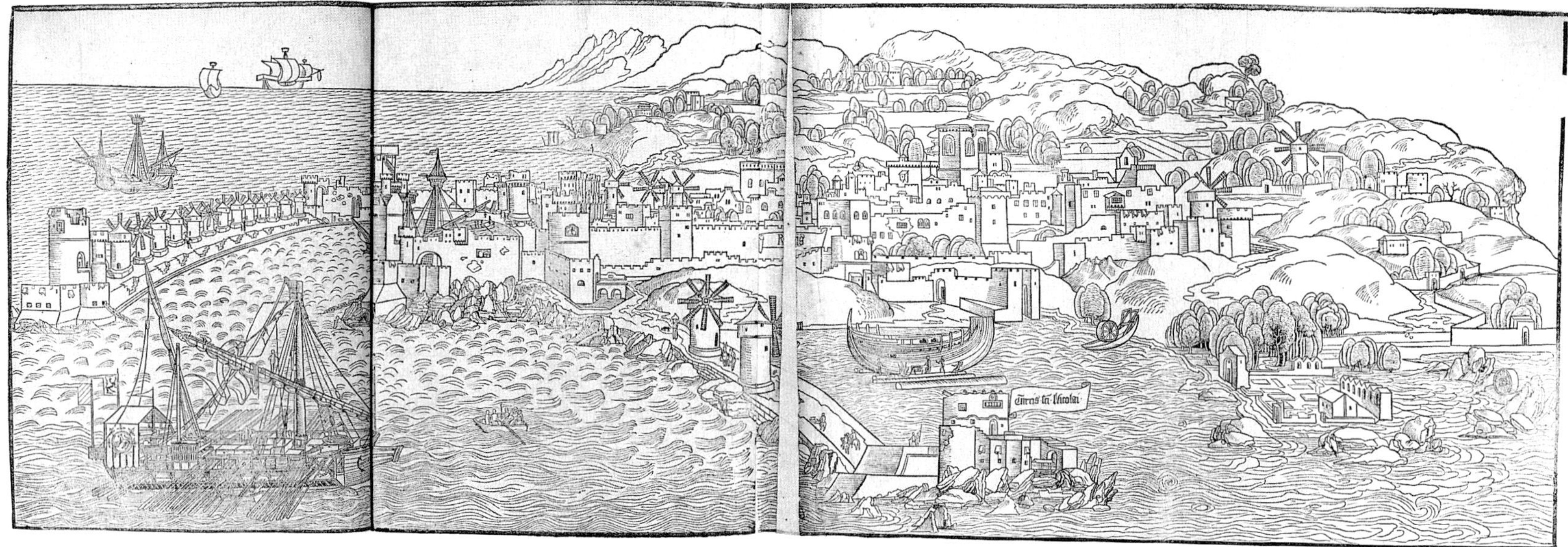

RHODES, 1486. The harbour on the island of Rhodes was an important base for pilgrims and crusaders. After 1309 the Knights of St John established a fortress there and operated a fleet which protected the Eastern Mediterranean sea routes against the Turks for two centuries. The island finally came under Turkish control in 1523. This view is from one of the earliest illustrated travel books, the *Pereginatio in terram sanctam* of Bernhard von Breydenbach, 1486.

The British Library, IB 41612.

produced between 1460 and 1480, display an evolving geographical knowledge. Likewise, the array of coastal place-names characteristic of these charts shows a process of development which must mean that the chartmaker maintained a constant dialogue with mariners, and perhaps with land-travellers too. At an early stage the Italians conceived the form of the portolan atlas, the group of small regional charts bound together between boards, a format that was certainly practical at sea and permitted concentration on particular areas. Although these chart-books were essentially sectional maps of Europe, the scale was not necessarily consistent, each chosen area – the Adriatic, the Aegean, or the Black Sea – filling a page. The Catalan school persisted with the larger chart of the whole Mediterranean, drawn on a single vellum skin, usually well over one metre broad.

Although originating, we assume, as simply a navigational aid, the portolan chart underwent a striking development in the years 1300 to 1500, and emerged as a comprehensive map of the known world. Generally the Italian school preserved a stricter approach to chartmaking, a functional but graceful style which emphasized the coastlines and the place-names. It was the Catalan school which moulded the early sea-chart into a world map. The key element is the inclusion of land detail. If the sea-chart is purely an instrument of navigation, then it is unnecessary to map the land surface, physically or politically, and this rule is strictly observed in the charts of Vesconte and Benincasa. In complete contrast, from the very beginning the Catalan chartmakers were drawn to display rivers, mountains and cities, including cities such as Paris, Florence and Toledo, that had no relevance to the sea. Religious shrines were often marked, and royal and national flags flew over the appropriate countries. Descriptive texts appeared on the Catalan maps, and the deserts are ornamented with picture of camels, the seas with ships. Finally, portraits of the world's rulers, the Arabs and Tartars seated within stylized tents, completed a vivid picture of the Mediterranean region. It is difficult to resist the conclusion that these charts began to assume the role of general maps of the known world. Were they really made for use at sea? Perhaps, but they were undoubtedly studied and used by landsmen too, and increasingly they were made for presentation, with highly-wrought decorations drawn by a specialist artist and not by the mapmaker. Another type of dual-purpose map of land and sea were the island maps which appeared in manuscript collections in the fifteenth century. One of the earliest and most influential was that of Cristoforo Buondelmonte,

MITILENA (Lesbos) by Cristoforo Buondelmonte *c.*1485. Buondelmonte's 'Book of Islands' first appeared *c.*1420, and described all the principal islands in the eastern Mediterranean. Although not strictly sea-charts, they must undoubtedly have been based on mariners' maps, and they in turn were used by seafarers. They developed a semi-pictorial style, showing mountains, rivers, forests, castles and harbours. Buondelmonte was a Florentine who lived for many years in Rhodes, gathering information from mariners.

The British Library, Arundel MS. 93, f.152.

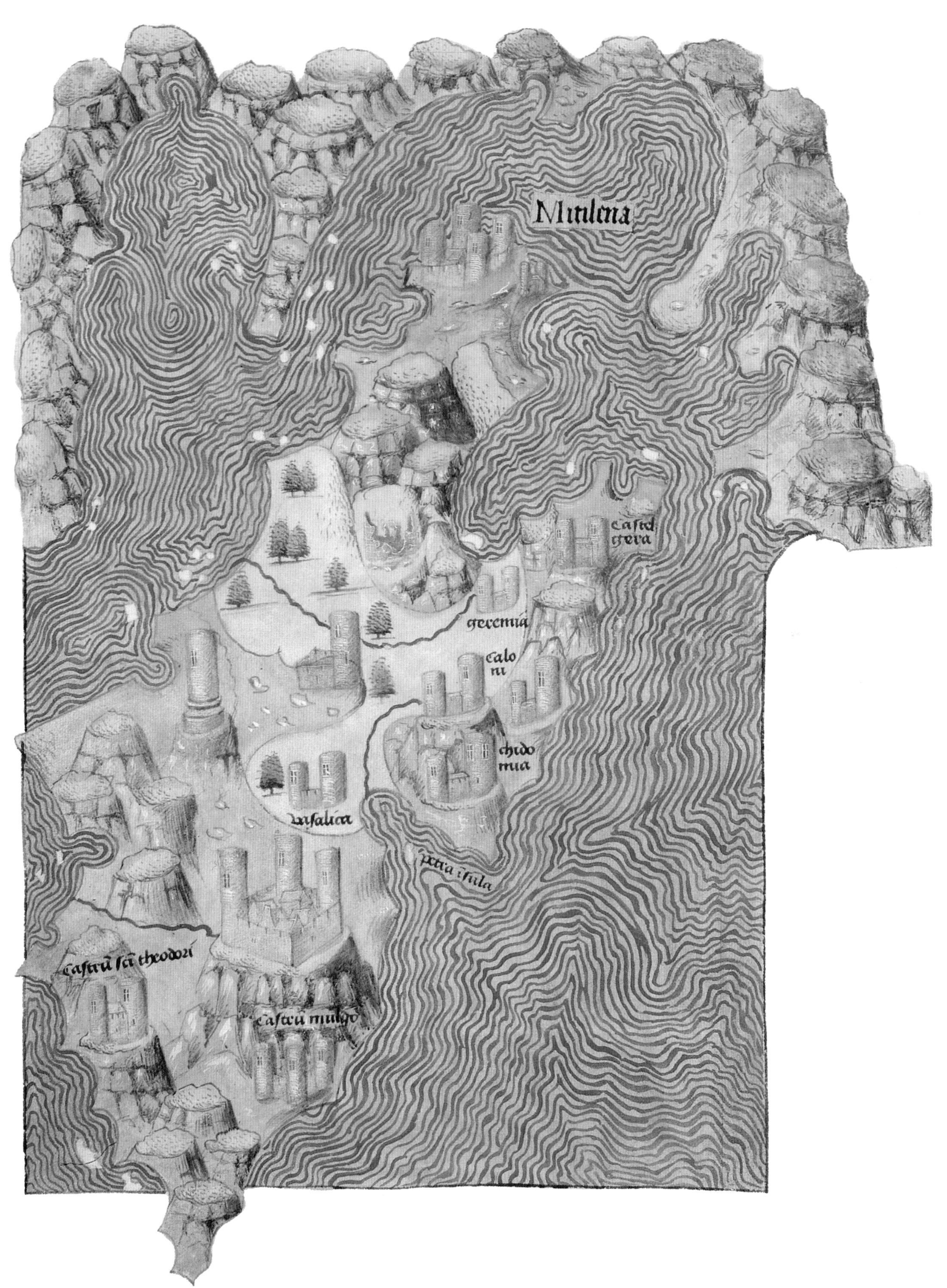
Mitilena
castel gera
geremia
calo ni
chido mia
basalica
petra isula
Castrū sci theodori
Castrū mulgo

COLUMBUS IN THE NEW WORLD, 1495. After Columbus's return an account of his voyage was published which included the first pictures and maps of the new world. The Spanish ship is seen here against a background of islands bearing the names 'Ysabella', 'Fernando' etc., but there is no attempt at a genuine map: this is an imaginative news-picture whose context is both geographical and political.

The British Library, IA 37918.

whose account of the islands of the eastern Mediterranean was written around 1420 and was accompanied by numerous maps. Although not strictly navigational in purpose, they contributed to the growth of map-awareness among European travellers and seafarers. Based largely on Buondelmonte was the later collection of Bartolommeo dalli Sonetti, which was printed around 1485 although manuscript copies are also known. This work is remarkable as being the only travelogue whose text is written in sonnet form – hence the author's surname. Sonetti's maps have a more authentic nautical appearance than Buondelmonte's with a compass rose, a scale bar and symbols for offshore rocks.

The importance of the early sea-charts to the wider history of mapping is enormous. The accurate European coastlines they displayed were incorporated into more and more world maps from around the year 1450. It was at this time too that the classical mapping of Ptolemy was rediscovered by Renaissance scholars, with its scientific approach to coordinates and projection. When the empirical accuracy of the sea-charts was combined with the mathematical structure of the Ptolemaic map, authentic mapmaking could begin to emerge.

But did the advent of sea-charts effect a revolution in navigation? In the context of the Mediterranean's 4,000-year history of seafaring, the answer must be no, if taken in isolation. The traditional skills of the mariner were so strong that any development would take the form of gradual evolution, not radical change. Nevertheless the chart and compass innovation of the thirteenth century stands at the beginning of a process where these traditional skills became codified and transmitted in objective form. Formal navigation depends on an understanding of formal geographic relationships, and the *visualization* of the Mediterranean region in an accurate map was clearly an essential step. As one of the great early writers on navigation, Pedro da Medina, would later explain: 'Among the instruments which are necessary to Navigation is the carde (*i.e.* chart) for without it good Navigation cannot be made, seeing that in it the Pilot or Sayler doth see the place wherein

A MARINER'S ASTROLABE.

National Maritime Museum.

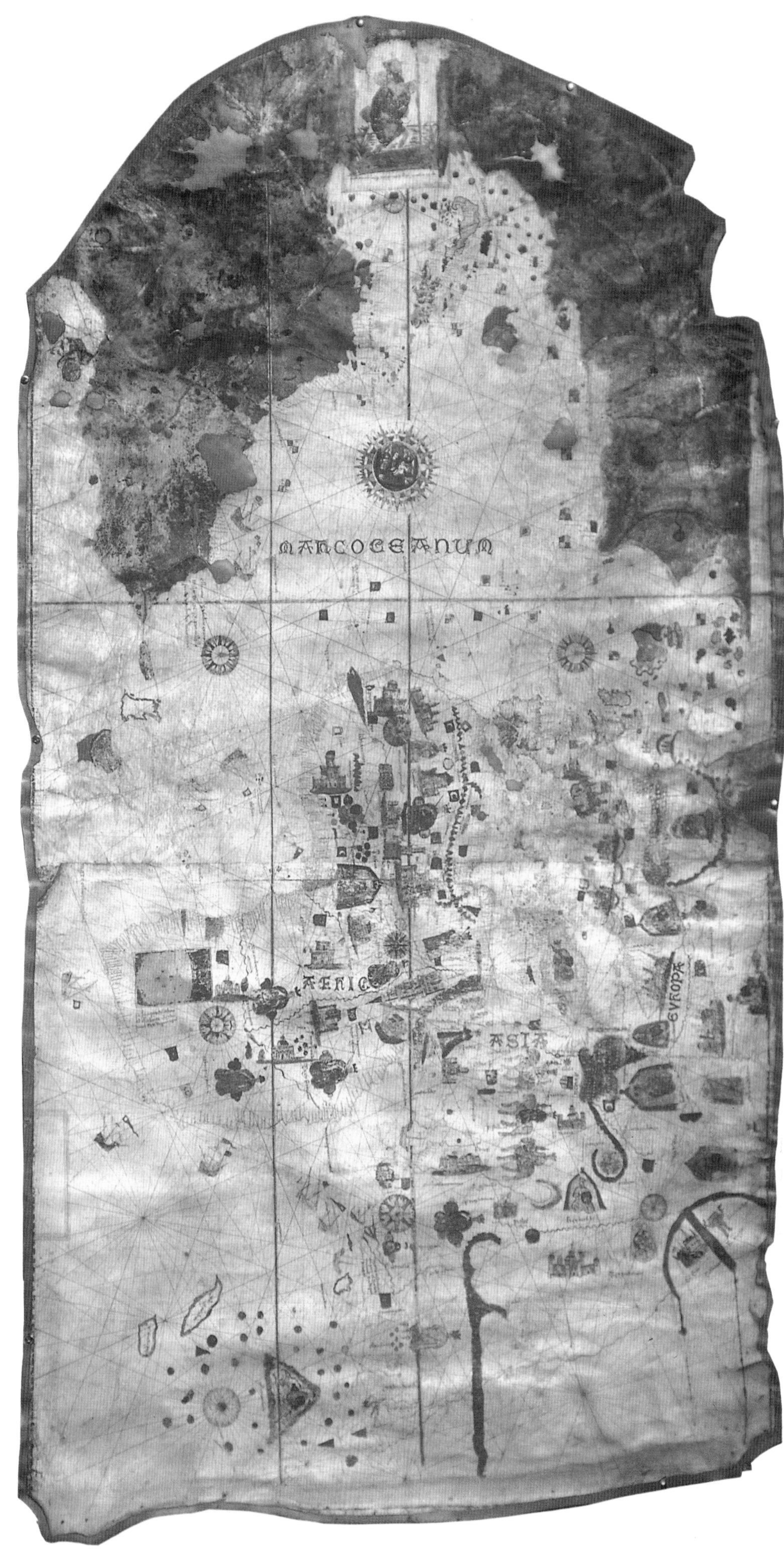

WORLD CHART, 1500 by Juan de la Cosa. Cosa was a Spanish pilot who had accompanied Columbus, and this is the first, historic depiction of the Americas on a world map. It is equally original in its picture of Africa, so recently circumnavigated by the Portuguese. The map's centre is the familiar Catalan sea-chart of Europe, but in this age of dynamic exploration, the Mediterranean sea-chart has become enlarged until it is transformed into a world map. The Spanish, Catholic context of the map is clearly visible in the figure of St Christopher, the saint of travellers, placed in the new world.
Museo Naval, Madrid.

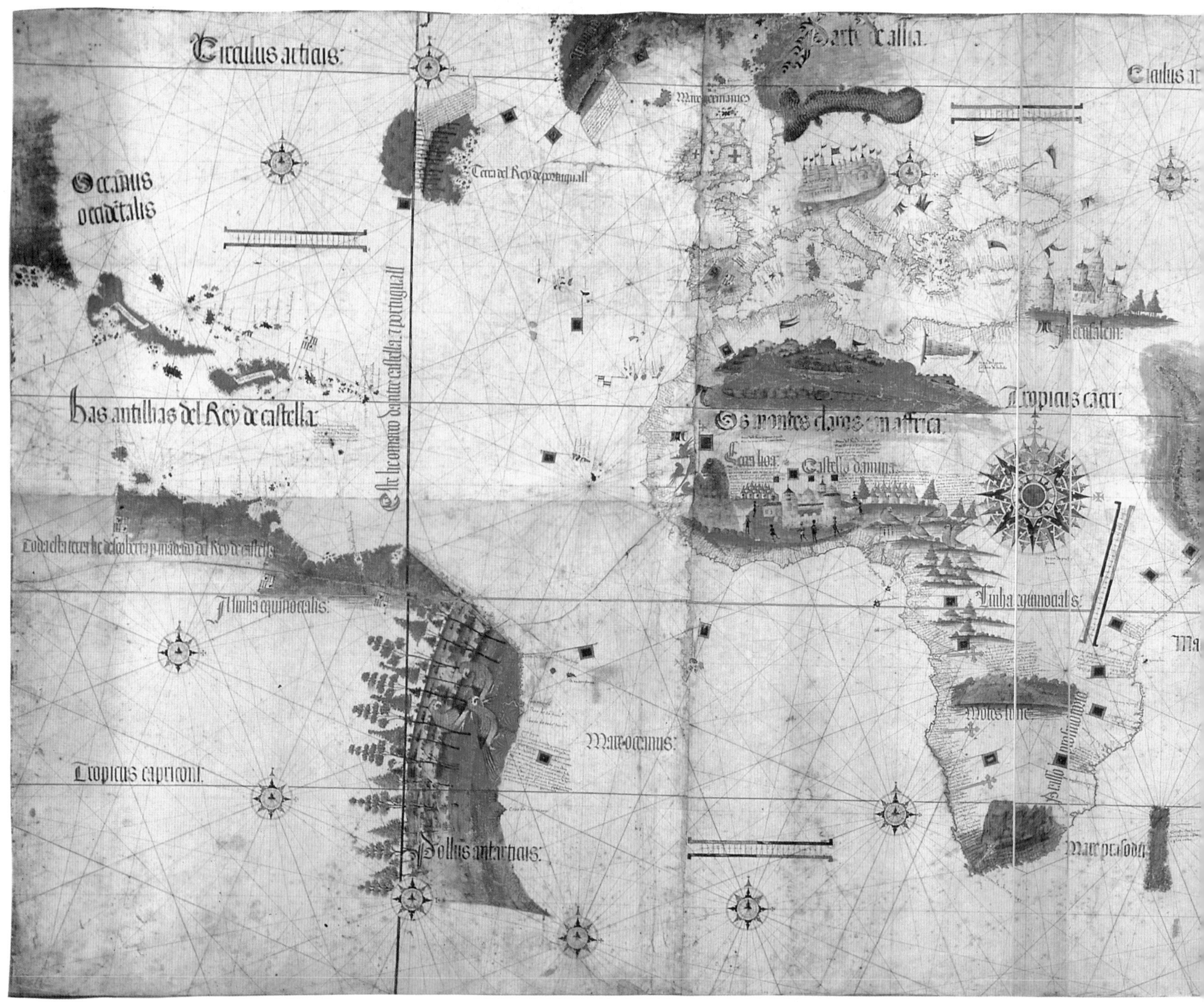

he is, and the place whither he pretendeth to go . . . he seeth also what winde or windes will serve him in his course . . . he also seeth the distance of the way which he shall goe . . .'. Development towards more precise navigation depended on mariners' becoming more literate and numerate. It cannot have been common for a medieval mariner to be highly literate, although he must have been able to read place-names on a chart. Chaucer's description of his Shipman, written around the year 1390, dwells on his *knowledge* of his craft, acquired through experience – creeks, tides, and harbours – but there is no mention of charts, instruments or formal navigation.

CHART OF THE WORLD, 1502. Known as the Cantino chart, this map may be dated just two years later than the Cosa chart. It shows the rapidly evolving knowledge of south America, following the Portuguese landfalls there. The clear vertical line through Brazil is the so-called Tordesillas line, allocating by Papal authority the land to the east to Portugal and that to the west to Spain.

Biblioteca Estense, Modena.

How much do we really know about navigation in this period? The first treatises on navigation were not published until the early sixteenth century. Long before that, scholars were writing on the mathematics, especially the spherical geometry, that underlies navigation. A work such as Sacrobosco's *De Sphaera* was the standard textbook of astronomy used in all the universities of Europe, and it certainly dealt with such matters as coordinate systems and the measuring of latitude by the altitude of the Pole Star. But before the year 1500 probably only a handful of European mariners were capable of applying such knowledge. What we have from the thirteenth and fourteenth centuries are

A TRAVERSE BOARD of the late fifteenth century.

National Maritime Museum, Greenwich.

WORLD CHART, 1516 by Martin Waldseemüller. This is the only printed version of the world sea-chart, the printed equivalent to the great manuscript maps of Cosa, Verrazzano and Ribero. The map's title refers explicitly to the Portuguese navigators, and the eye is drawn to the portrait of Portugal's king, Manuel I, astride a dolphin. The inland features, especially the texts and pictures in Asia, make it clear that this map functioned as a latter-day *mappa mundi*, a visual panorama of the known world.

Schloss Wolfegg. (With secondary colour.)

scattered references to navigation, and the existence of certain aids which acted as early position-finding instruments. The Traverse Board was a circular piece of wood marked out with all the compass points, each bored with eight holes to receive pegs. Each half hour a peg was moved along the direction the ship had travelled, and at the end of each four-hour watch, the mean course was noted on the chart, and the process repeated. The use of the rhumb lines on the chart to plot a course highlighted the great difficulty of dead reckoning: the sailing ship must tack with the wind, and the ship must be constantly brought back to its desired course. For this purpose Traverse Tables were drawn up which reduced angular differences in courses to rectangular coordinates. Both the tables and the board were in existence by the early fourteenth century. The use of such tables may be seen as an aspect of the spread of numeracy that followed the adoption of Arabic numerals credited to Leonardo of Pisa's *Liber Abaci* of 1202. The work of the navigator, like that of the surveyor, architect and accountant, became at once simpler and more sophisticated. Traverse Tables were included with some portolan atlases in the fifteenth century as was another type of table, the lunar calendar, whose purpose was to permit the calculation of high tides from the new moon. Perhaps the piece of information which the Mediterranean navigator of this time valued most was the distance between points, for this was the fundamental proof that he was following a true course. Obviously the old measure of a day's sail could not be transferred to a chart, hence the appearance of the league on the chart, and the use of measured lengths of line paid out from the stern to gauge the distance run and thus the ship's speed. The other fundamental which needed to be measured was depth of water: the lead weight on a measured line was in constant use in shoal water, on entering harbours and especially in darkness or bad weather.

The changes of navigational methods were observed with admiration by several landsmen of the time. A German priest, Felix Fabri, wrote in 1483 that mariners 'see

where they are even when they can see no land and when the stars themselves are hid by clouds. This they find out on the chart by drawing a curve from one line to another and from one point to another with wondrous pains.' The skill of the mariner in this age of new techniques is illuminated by an unusual statement on a chart of 1403 by Francesco Beccari: 'It was several times reported to me by many owners, skippers and sailors proficient in the navigational art that the island of Sardinia . . . was not placed on the charts in its proper place. Having listened to the aforesaid persons I placed the said island in the present chart in its proper place.' So the sea-chart was obviously but one aspect of

RIBERO'S WORLD CHART, 1529. Diego Ribero was a Portuguese who had sailed to India with Da Gama and Albuquerque. He entered the service of Spain and assumed responsibility for maintaining the *padron general* – the master chart which incorporated geographical reports from all incoming Spanish ships. It is outstanding as being the first map to show the true extent of the Pacific, as recorded by Magellan's survivors. It is also the first sea-chart to embody cosmographic information: a calendar, a quadrant, an astrolabe and a declination scale, all with texts explaining their use.

Biblioteca Apostolica, Vatican.

a slowly changing balance between new knowledge and inherited skill. Taken with the compass and with elementary astro-navigation, a revolution in navigation was possible, and indeed was imminent, but it could not happen yet.

In fact there were a number of reasons completely external to seafaring why the fourteenth century tended to produce an increased isolation in Western Europe, rather than a move to explore the seas. The first was the great outbreak of plague which between 1347 and 1350 swept ruthlessly in a vast arc from Constantinople to the Baltic. As many as 25 million people, one third of the population, may have perished. The effect on social life, on trade and travel, was catastrophic, as a great fear of human contact gripped all levels of society, and it would take many generations before the effects of this depopulation were overcome. At the same time another equally implacable force, but this time a human one, was advancing into Europe: the Ottoman Turks. Emerging from their

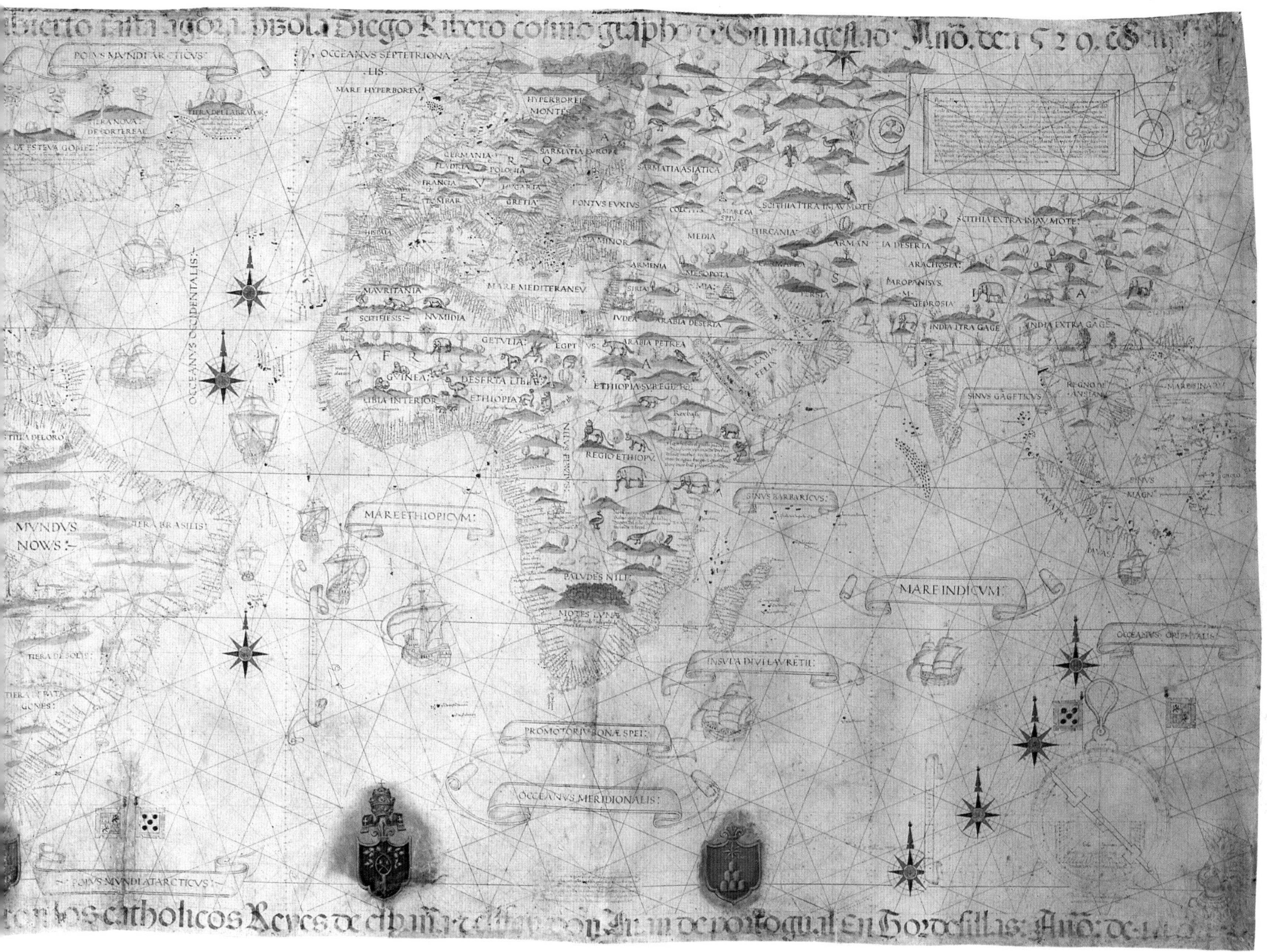

homeland in northern Anatolia around the year 1280, the Ottoman dynasty had by 1450 built an empire that embraced all Turkey, Greece and the Balkans, extinguishing Byzantine power in all but Constantinople itself until its fall in 1453. The impact on the fortunes of Genoa and Venice was extremely serious, since their vessels had received all the Black Sea trade from the east and shipped it onwards to the west. Syria, Palestine and Egypt had long been Moslem territory, so that this Ottoman advance had the effect of sealing the eastern Mediterranean. It is hardly surprising that the fourteenth century acquired a sense of crisis: the plague, the threat from the east, the divided papacy, all seemed to menace the stability of western Christendom. Earlier, in the thirteenth century, the Mongol conquests in central and western Asia had opened a temporary corridor between Europe and the east, and Marco Polo's account of the wealth and culture of the east acted as an enormous spur to European exploration.

ARE.SINAR
GEMINI
CANCER
IVNIVS
MAIVS
IVLIVS
TAVRVS
APRILIS
ARIES
MARTIVS
LINEA
EQVINOCTIALIS
PISCES
FEBRVARI
IANVARIVS
AQVARIVS
NOVEMBER
DECEMBER
SAGITARIVS
CAPRICORN
TROPICVS
ÇAPRICORNI
CIRCVLVS
ATARCT
ARCHIVIUM
S. CONG
DE PROP. FIDE

DETAIL OF THE Pacific Ocean area of Ribero's World Chart on the previous page.

MAGELLAN: an allegorical portrait of the great navigator entering the Pacific. He calmly studies his armillary sphere as the flames of Tierra del Fuego leap beside him, and the gods of air and sea protect him. (From De Bry's *Voyages*.)

The British Library, 579.K.14(4).

Intriguingly, it was at precisely this moment that the advanced but hitherto isolated civilization far to the east might at last have made decisive contact with Europe. There is evidence, in the form of coins, pottery and other artefacts, that the Chinese had been trading in East Africa since the tenth century. But in 1405 a major reconaissance and trading voyage was undertaken from China, under the command of the court eunuch Cheng Ho. If the contemporary record is to be believed, the expedition was on a colossal scale: 62 ships, some of 1,000 tons, bearing 37,000 men, laden with arms and merchandize. From Nanking the fleet visited Indo-China and Sumatra before turning west across the Indian Ocean to Bengal and south to Ceylon. Six more voyages followed in the next thirty years, to Ormuz and the Persian Gulf, to Aden and the Red Sea as far as Jedda, and to East Africa as far as Mombasa. One account has the Chinese reaching the Cape itself and sighting the Atlantic Ocean. The exact motive for these vast expeditions is obscure, but tribute to the Emperor was exacted at all ports of call, and Chinese knowledge of the world was greatly extended. With a change of Emperor and the death of Cheng Ho, these voyages came to an end. No charts remain from Cheng's great voyages, and there was arguably no permanent result from this episode: no colonies were established and no trading empire was founded. Yet it was an extraordinary moment in Chinese and world history. Had they so desired, the Chinese might have established a hegemony throughout the Asian and African coasts. It is not impossible that they might have sailed the Atlantic, north to Europe or west to America. Seventy years later when the tiny Portuguese fleets reached South Asia, they found no opposition to their activities. Had these regions been under Chinese domination, the entire history of European involvement in Asia and the Pacific might have been very different.

The emergence of Portugal, a minor player in the European theatre, as a sea-power destined to revolutionize the history of seafaring, is one of those caprices of history that

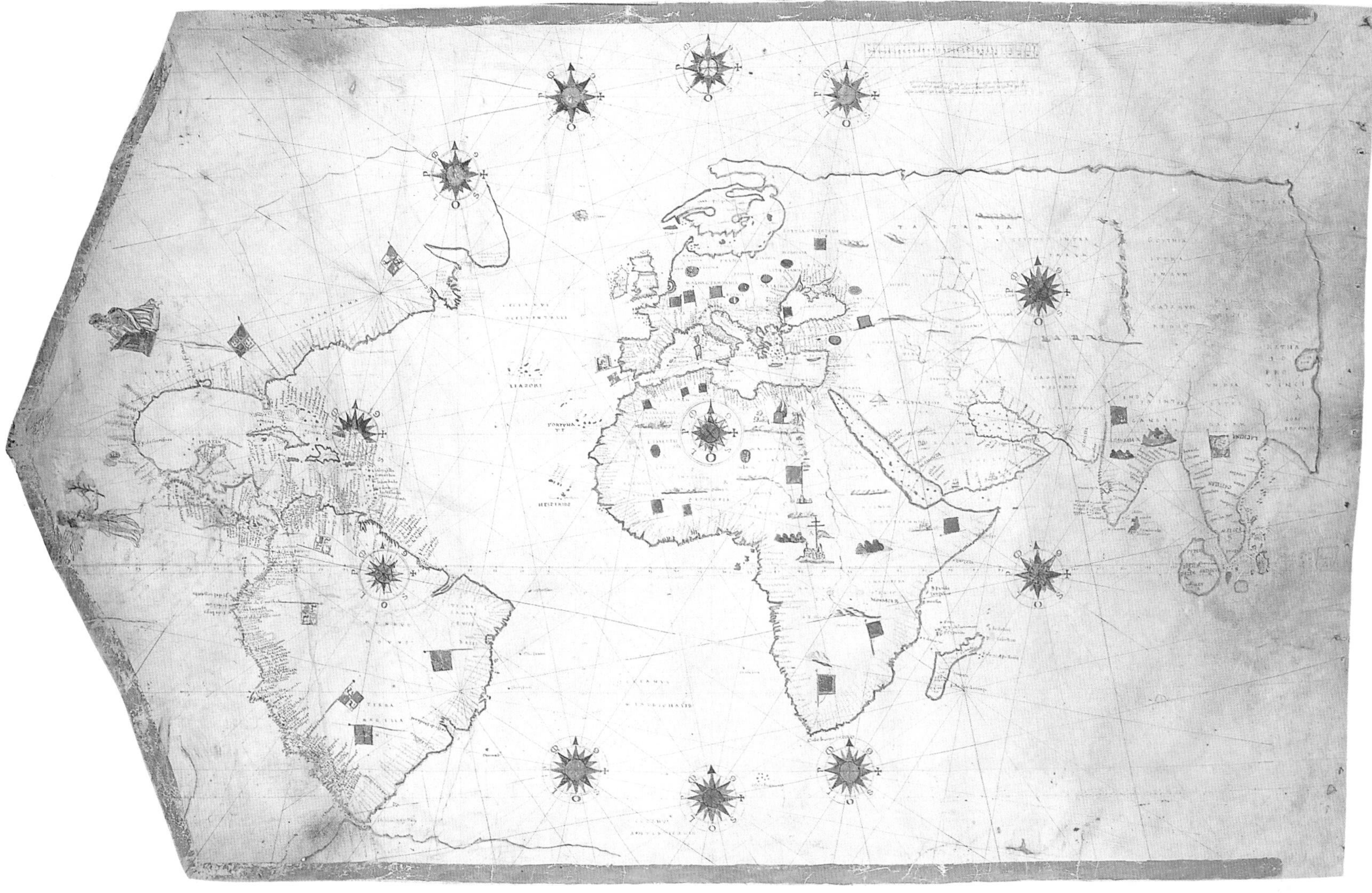

can never quite be explained. Permenently surrounded and overshadowed by a powerful neighbour, with the Mediterranean dominated by Italians in the west and by Moslems in the east, Portugal, when her moment came to awake and expand, had no outlet but the southern sea. The consequences were momentous, for, as one Portuguese historian later wrote, 'God gave them a small country as a cradle, but all the world as a grave'. In 1415 the Portuguese attacked and captured the Moorish seaport of Ceuta. The motives were mixed: a limited crusade against the Moslems, to put down the Moorish pirates who harassed the shipping of the western Mediterranean, and the hope of gaining control of a major caravan route which carried gold and ivory across the Sahara. These aims were accomplished, except the last, for the caravans moved to other centres such as Algiers. So there was born another ambition – to find the source of the African gold, and to continue the crusade south of the Sahara, both of which could be achieved only by sea. This challenge was taken up by the young prince of Portugal, Henry, later rather fancifully known as the Navigator. His motives were a curious mixture of intellectual curiosity, religious fervour, and avarice. He set up an academy of geography with an observatory, and embarked on a conscious attempt to inaugurate a new era in navigation, although curiously he himself never sailed beyond the Straits of Gibraltar. Astronomers, mathematicians, mapmakers and seafarers were brought together at Henry's court, and from 1420

WORLD CHART by Girolamo Verrazzano, 1524. Verrazzano was a Florentine pilot in command of a French expedition in search of a westward passage to Asia. While coasting the outer banks of North Carolina, he became convinced that the inner waters of Pamlico Sound were those of the Pacific. The 'Sea of Verrazzano' which he publicized on his return became a feature on a number of 16th-century maps. Its imagined coastline, roughly parallel to the Gulf of Mexico, can be seen here.

National Maritime Museum, Greenwich.

onwards there began the long series of voyages which opened the era of European expansion. This concentrated royal patronage may be thought of as shaping the first national navy, in an age when all shipping had been private. The Portuguese intention was undoubtedly to use a fleet to carry out distinct national policies of trade, and if necessary warfare. In addition to changes in ship design, the advent of firearms and small cannon which could be carried aboard ship gave confidence to seafarers venturing into unknown regions of the world. Cape Bojador, lying at 26 degrees north, was the first great obstacle, both nautical and psychological. Jutting 25 miles out from the African coast, it was a place of persistent gales and currents from the north, and thick fog. In medieval legend it had become the 'sea of darkness' from which the seafarer could never return, and many attempts were to fail before Gil Eannes succeeded in rounding it in 1433.

Thereafter one by one the great landmarks of Africa's inhospitable coast were passed: the Senegal River, Cape Verde, the Gambia River, Cape Palmas, Fernando Po, and the Congo, until finally Batolomeu Dias rounded the Cape in 1489 and advanced several hundred miles into the Indian Ocean before turning back. The Portuguese navigators had been taught to measure latitude, though longitude was a far more difficult matter, and their observations are of particular interest. At the Gambia River, which lies at 13 degrees north. Alvise da Cadamosto recorded in 1455 that 'the Pole Star sank so low that it seemed to touch the sea, standing only one third of a spear-shaft above the water'. To the south he saw 'six large and wonderful stars. We measured them with the compass. We believed them to be the Great Bear of the Southern Hemisphere.' The reference to six bright stars is puzzling, but it seems likely that Cadomosto had seen the four stars of the Southern Cross and the two brightest stars in the nearby constellation Centaur. The use of a spear-shaft as a rough-and-ready measure of altitude seems to indicate that the astrolabe was not yet in use at sea, although when Diogo Cao passed the mouth of the Congo in 1485 it certainly was. The mariner's astrolabe was a less sophisticated version of the astronomer's instrument, being simply a circular dial graduated with the degrees and equipped with a sighting device which read the elevation of a star above the horizon. Simple as it was however, it represented a breakthrough from inherited skill to formal science. The use of terrestrial coordinates in maps or instruments dates only from the mid-fifteenth century, and was largely attributable to the rediscovery of the classical geography of Ptolemy. Nevertheless seamen until the nineteenth century continued to measure direction by referring to the 32 points of the compass, not to the degrees of the circle. In southern waters mariners sought for a counterpart to the Pole Star, but finding none they turned instead to the sun. Determining latitude from the sun is more complex than using a fixed star since the sun's noon declination changes each day. It was necessary to consult tables giving that information, then to add or subtract the declination from the sun's altitude, depending on the season and the hemisphere. These rules, known as the Regiment of the Sun, had been formalized by the Portuguese by the 1480s, and they later appeared in all the manuals of navigation.

It is remarkable that only two or three fifteenth-century Portuguese sea-charts survive to testify to this period of exploration. It cannot be that this new knowledge was kept

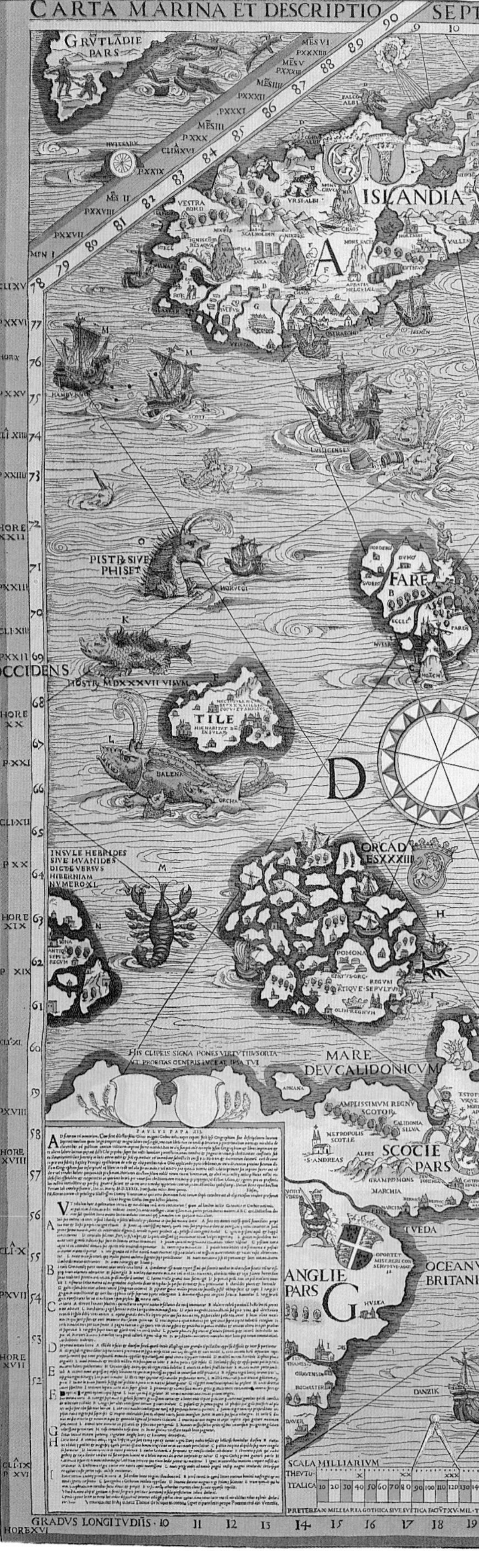

SCANDINAVIA, 1539. Published to accompany a 'Treatise on the Northern Peoples' by a Swedish priest, Olaus Magnus, this map forcefully illustrates the overlap between land and sea maps. The mapmaker's intention was clearly to show not only the nations of Scandinavia, but the seas and the maritime culture which they shared: their ice-sledges, seal-hunters and trading craft, and the nightmare sea-creatures which threatened them. Some of the land features here, and the latitude bar, are grossly inaccurate, but at this date no surveys of this region had ever been carried out, by sea or land.

Royal Library, Stockholm. (With secondary colour.)

LIVM ERRARVM·AC·MIRABILIVM·RERVM·IN·EIS·CONTENTARVM·DILIGENTISSIME ELABORATA
ANNO DÑI 1539
FINMARCHIA
SCRICFINIA
BIARMIA
LAPPIA
BOTNIA OCCIDENTALIS
BOTNIA ORIENTALIS
CARELIA
MARE BOTNICV
SCANDIA
NORVEGIA
SVECIA
FINLANDIA
MARE SVETICVM
MARE FINONICVM
MOSCOVIE PARS
RVSSIA ALBA
LIVONIA AQVILONARIS
MARE LIVOICVM
GOTHIA
MARE GOTICVM
DANIA
LIVONIA AVSTRALIS
SAMOGETHIA
LITVANIE PARS
FRISIA
MERIDIES

THE BATTLE OF LEPANTO, 1571. The great engagement between Christian forces and the Turkish fleet which for a time severely checked the power of the Ottoman navy.

National Maritime Museum, Greenwich.

secret, for the delineation of the coast of Africa became further and further extended in the Italian charts of this period, such as those of Benincasa. It has been suggested that the destruction of libraries and archives in the great Lisbon earthquake of 1755 was responsible for the disappearance of the Portuguese chart legacy.

The closing of the gap between mariners and scholar-scientists was crucial to the progress of exploration and to the new maps that emerged from it. The revived Ptolemaic map may have been archaic in some of its geography, but it presented an objective method for locating places on the earth, just as astronomers had measured celestial positions for centuries. The revived interest in the mathematics and geometry of the earth led to the construction of the earliest globes in the 1480s, and it clearly underlay Columbus's conviction that the east could be reached by sailing west. Under the twin influences of Ptolemy and Marco Polo, the mariners of the late fifteenth century set out to find new ways to Cathay. Ptolemy proved that it was geographically possible, and Marco Polo promised that the rewards would be great. Columbus was an excellent navigator in the use of dead reckoning, but he foresaw that ocean sailing would create a challenge of a different order. To determine longitude accurately was an insoluble problem at this date, for there was no means of measuring local time and comparing it with a standard time at an agreed meridian. Instead Columbus focussed closely on the art of latitude-finding, reasoning that if he could steer a course south-west from Spain on the north-east trade winds, but remain certain of his latitude, he must strike the east coast of China on the same latitude as the Canaries. Of course he greatly underestimated the longitudinal distance involved, but his landfall in the Bahamas was indeed at 24 degrees north as planned.

In the course of his voyages, Columbus experienced two phenomena which some sailors had already noticed and which were to be of great importance to future ocean navigators: magnetic variation, and the rotation of the Pole Star. He was much exercised to explain the apparent eastward shift in stellar positions, for he believed that the compass needle must always be true. It would be many years before the difference between magnetic north and true north was understood. However he was correct in identifying that the Pole Star, although a good approximation to the north celestial pole, was not precisely on it, so that it too appears to rotate like the other stars. In 1492 it was less close than it is today, due to precessional movement: it lay about 3·5 degrees south of the

AN ELIZABETHAN WARSHIP sailing in the English Channel. From Christopher Saxton's Map of England and Wales (1583).

The British Library, Maps C.7.d.7.

THE NILE DELTA, *c.*1540 from Piri Re'is's *Kitab-i-Bahriye* ('Book of Maritime Matters'). Piri Re'is was the most famous Turkish sailor of his time. He was first a corsair then a high officer in the Ottoman fleet. Between 1515 and 1525 he produced his book of Mediterranean charts and sailing directions, which were more detailed than anything contemporary in the west. He is known to have worked on a large world map, of which only a fragment survives, showing the discoveries of the western navigators. He was executed in 1554 after a failed Turkish attack on Portuguese-held Hormuz.

Walters Art Gallery, Baltimore.

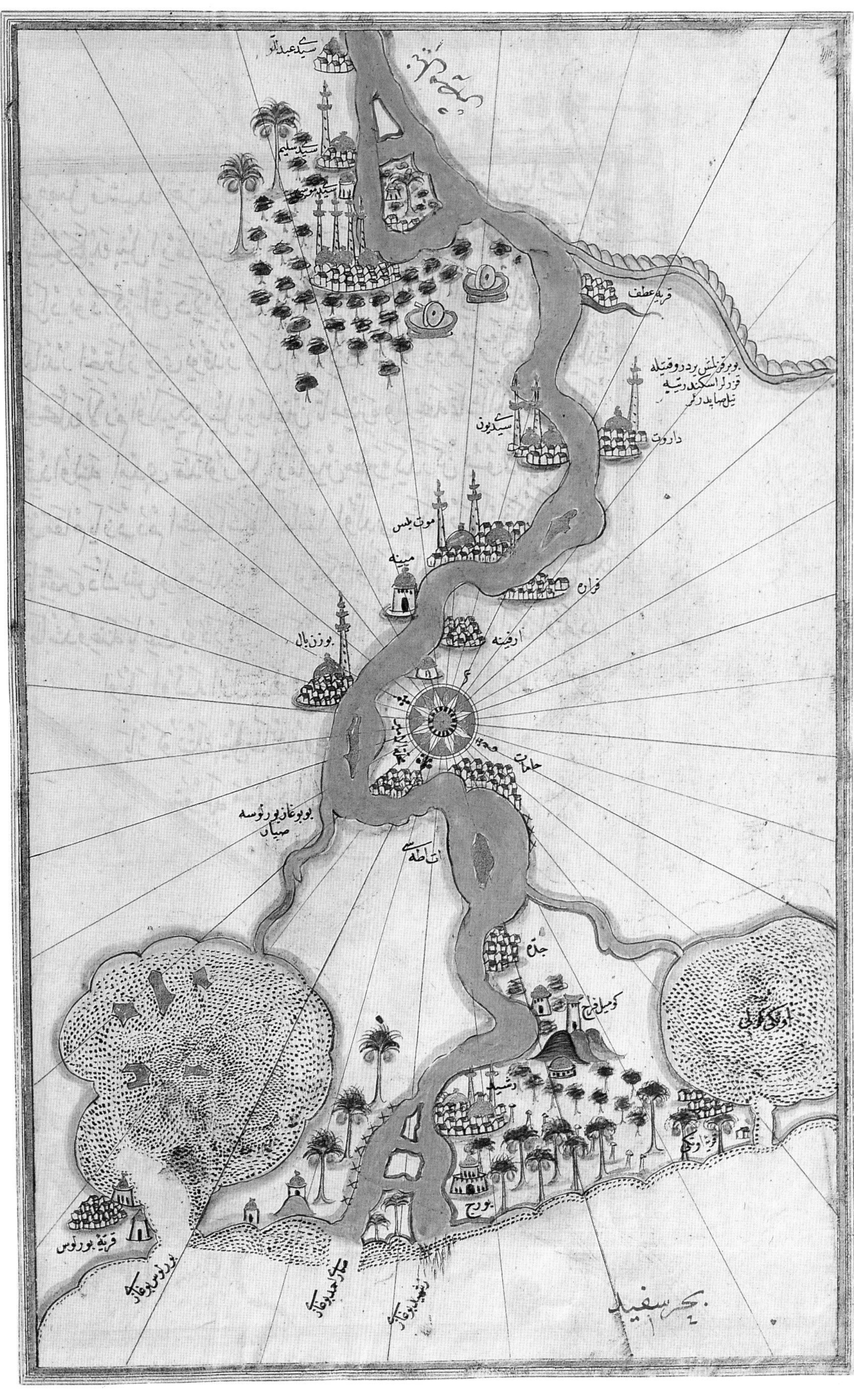

CORNWALL (Mount's Bay), *c.*1540. Part of the earliest survey of England's coasts, commissioned by King Henry VIII, fearing possible invasion from France and Spain. At this time England possessed neither topographic maps nor charts of her seas; this type of pictorial view was the only form of mapping currently understood.

The British Library, Cotton MS Aug.I.I.35.

WESTERN EUROPE from an anonymous Turkish sea-atlas of the late sixteenth century. The artistic quality of these Turkish charts is exquisite – evident especially in the miniature views of the ports of London and Marseilles. Accurate as far north as the Flemish coast, the chart then becomes wildly unreliable – note the separation of Scotland from England. Clearly the Turkish mapmaker had no information for this area, nor perhaps any great interest in it.

Walters Art Gallery, Baltimore.

celestial pole. This raised the problem of determining its true altitude at any given time of night. Fifteenth-century mariners devised a diagram known as the 'Regiment of the North Star', in which the configuration of the Pole Star in relation to the two bright stars α and β Ursa Major are memorized at eight different points. These two stars were known as the Guards of the Pole Star, and they pointed to the invisible north celestial pole, and incidentally gave the hour of the night to those who memorized them.

The importance of positioning is acknowledged by the appearance of the latitude bar on sea-charts from around the year 1500. A measure of longitude, though not unknown, was far less common and was necessarily very approximate. The merging of two traditions – of the mariner and the scholar-scientist – resulted in the production between 1490 and 1530 of a series of innovative charts and maps in which the new worlds revealed by the Spanish and Portuguese were announced to the European audience. The massive form of Africa, the Indian Ocean and the Spice Islands, the New World in the West with its uncertain relationship to Asia, and the vastness of the Pacific – all these took shape in the Cosa, Cantino, Waldseemüller, Verrazzano and Ribero maps. Appropriately in an age of dynamic exploration, the sea-chart had evolved into the world map. The culmination of

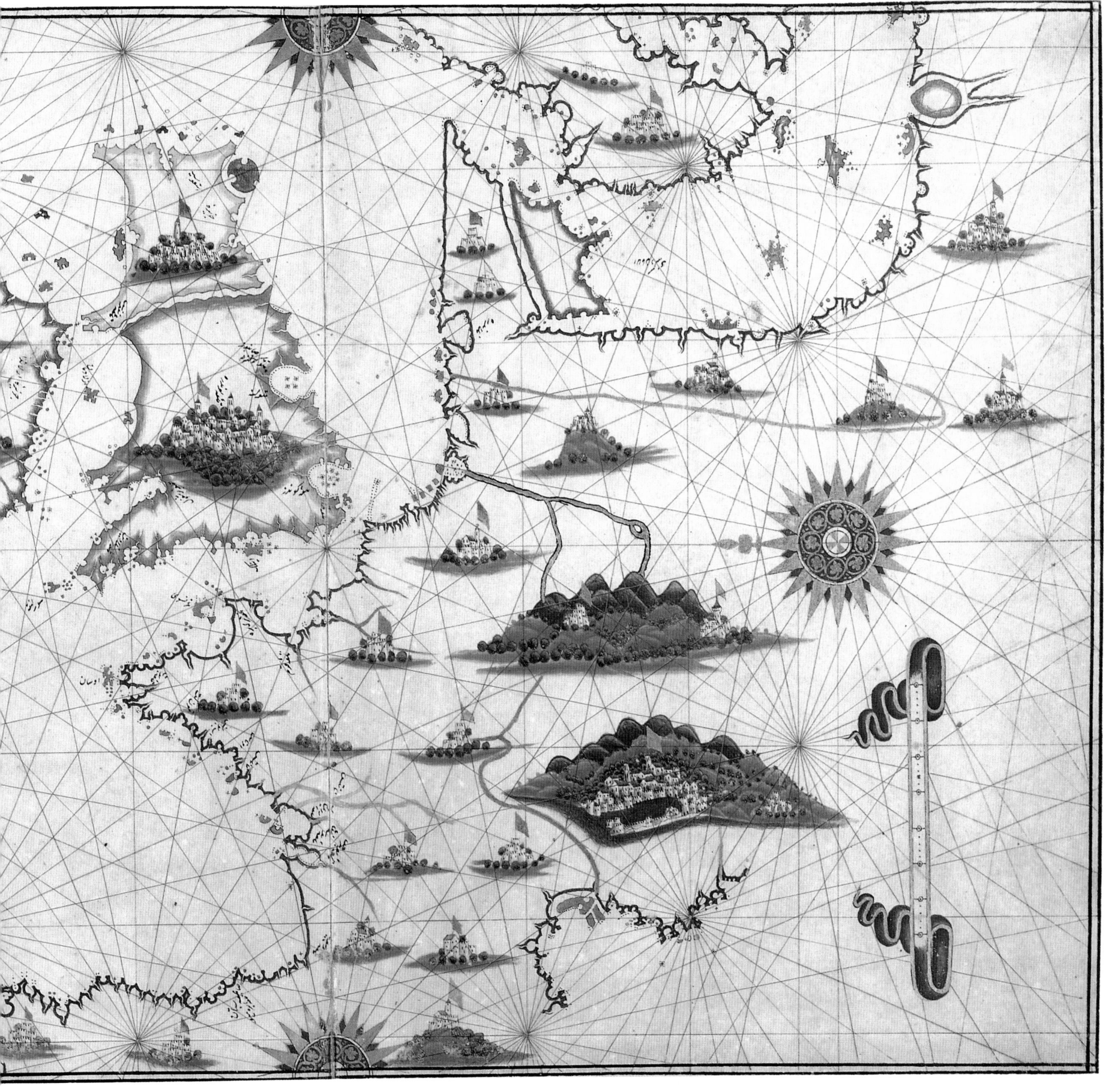

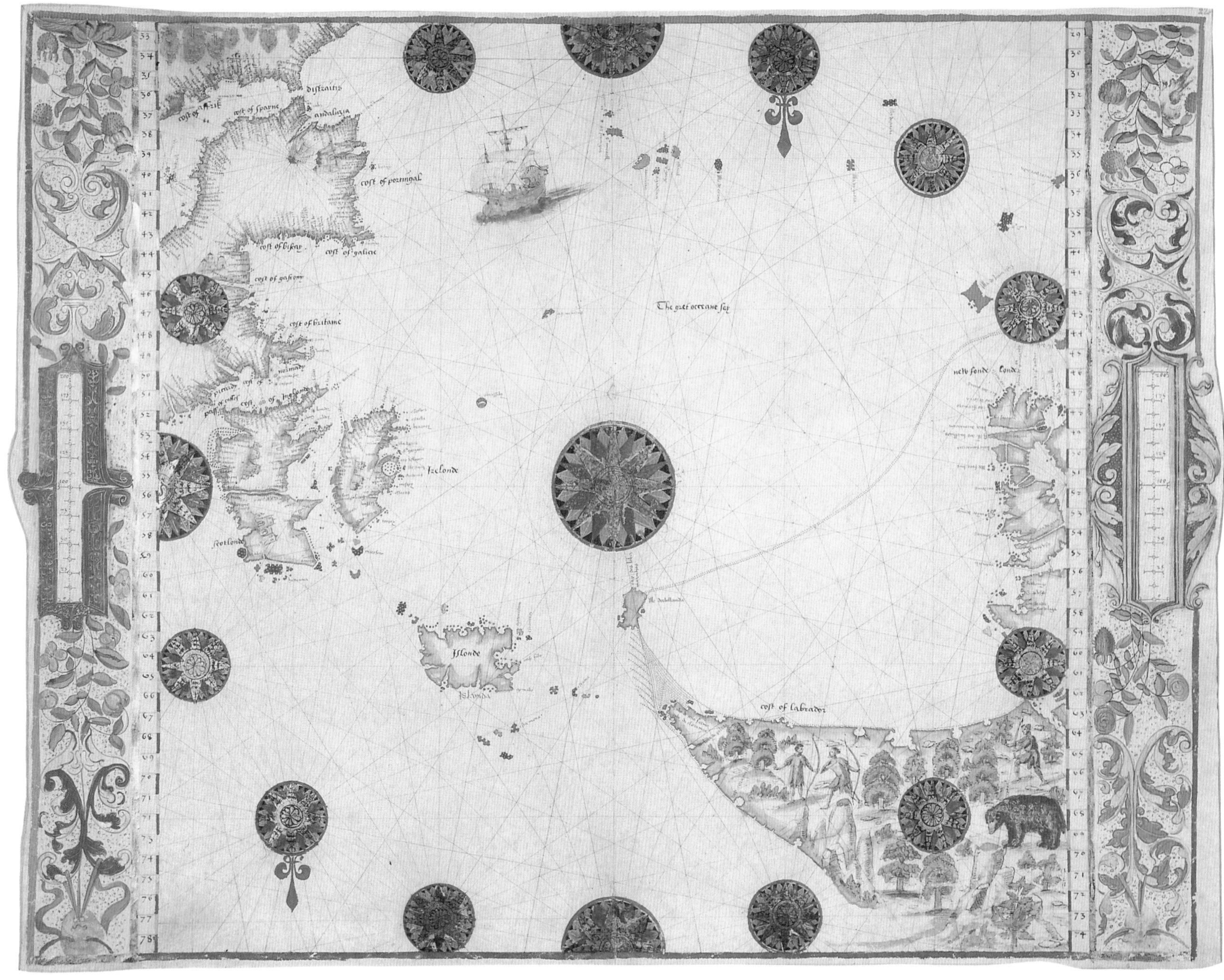

this dramatic development came with the return of Magellan's crew – sadly without their captain, for he was dead – in 1522 after the first circumnavigation of the world. The immensity of the Pacific was first displayed on Ribero's great chart of 1529, but for decades thereafter mapmakers would place it on the edges of the map, fading into emptiness.

Even after Magellan's epoch-making voyage it is hard to assess methods of navigation, or how precise and scientific they had become. Elementary rules of astro-navigation to determine latitude would be introduced by mathematicians, but they might thereafter be used on an empirical level by mariners who had no real understanding of their theoretical basis. One of the early Portuguese writers on navigation, Pedro Nuñez, made this point in 1537: 'These pilots, they do not know the Sun, Moon or Stars, neither their

THE NORTH ATLANTIC by Jean Rotz, 1542. Rotz was a leading chartmaker of the school of Dieppe, much of whose work took the form of highly-finished manuscripts for presentation rather than for use at sea. These maps combined the latest information on areas of special interest, such as Canada for the French, with startling inaccuracies elsewhere: in this map Scotland is shown as an island separated from England. Where the Mediterranean charts had almost invariably faced north, the Dieppe charts might be orientated in any direction, north being given by the compass-rose.

The British Library, Royal MS. 20 E IX, ff.21v–22.

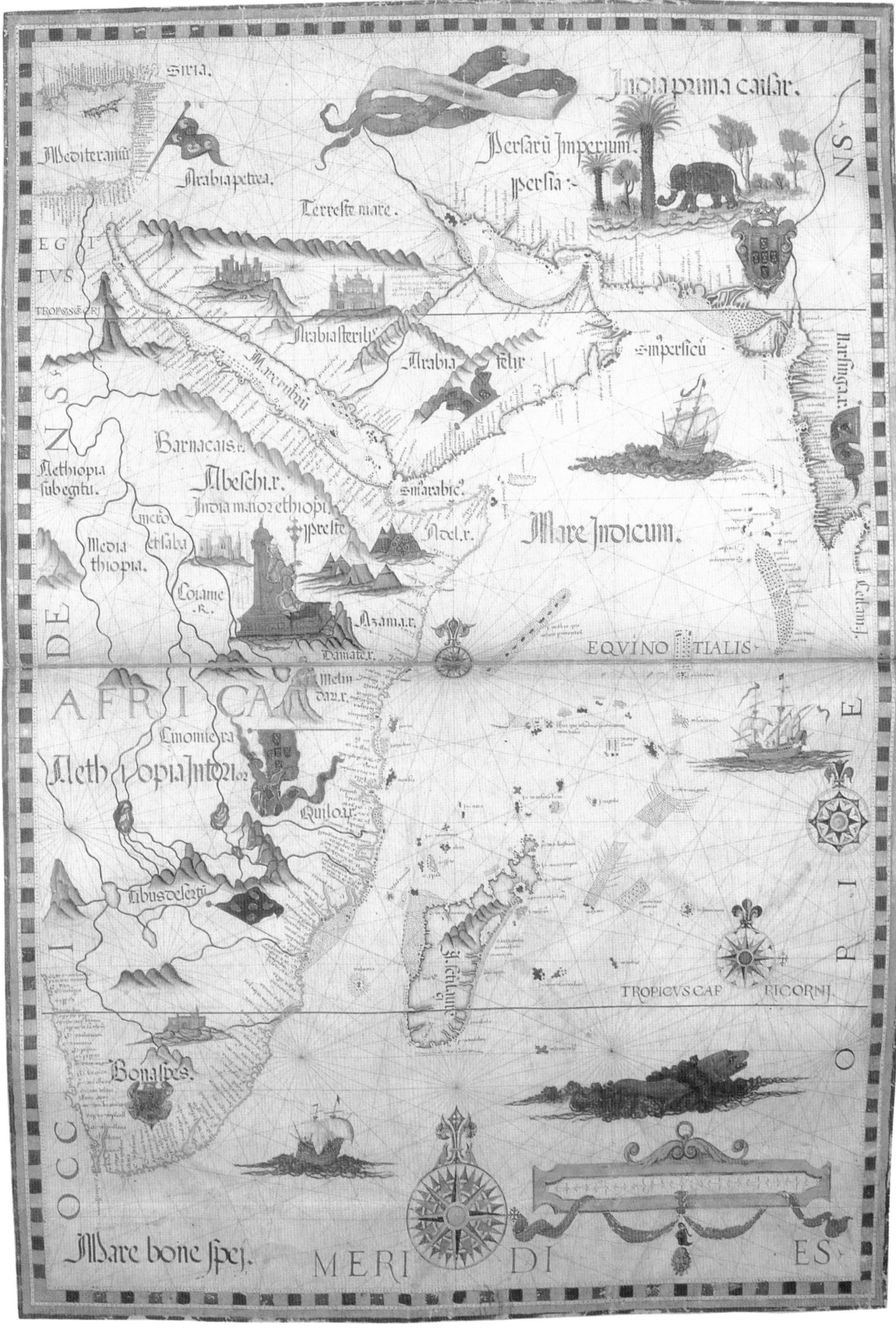

EAST AFRICA 1558 by Diogo Homem. Part of a highly artistic atlas made for Queen Mary by the leading Portuguese chartmaker of his time. Although drawn in the style of a chart, the many cultural icons betray the map's true function as a visual panorama of the world. Africa is dominated by the Christian king Prester John, a mythical figure whom medieval Christendom believed would be an ally against Islam.

The British Library, Add. MS. 5414.

PORTUGUESE CARRACKS and a galley, about 1580.

National Maritime Museum, Greenwich.

THE ATLANTIC, 1558, by Sebastien Lopez, a typical Portuguese chart of its time, with its images of the natives and wildlife of Brazil, and in North Africa a battle between the Portuguese and the Moors.

The British Library, Add. MS. 27303.

courses, movements nor declinations.' Nuñez was a mathematician of a very high order, and his work *De Arte Atque Ratione Navigandi*, 1546, is full of spherical geometry that must have been out of reach of most seamen. By contrast the very title of John Davis's navigational treatise of 1595, *The Seaman's Secrets*, suggests that navigation was an esoteric skill passed from master to disciple. Davis's book was modelled closely on that of Pedro da Medina, another seminal Portuguse writer, and it noticeable that both begin with a description of the Ptolemaic universe, permissible perhaps for Medina whose work appeared in 1563, but far less so for Davis in 1595. This use of traditional craft rather than true science is underlined by the great defect of the sea-chart which had gone uncorrected for centuries: the problem of map projection.

Just as the mariners' advance from the Mediterranean into the open waters of the Atlantic raised new problems of direction-finding, so the extension of the world map meant that the problem of map projection could no longer be ignored. The earlier portolan charts had not indicated latitude or longitude, and they must be described as projectionless. In the waters of the Mediterranean, limited in north-south extent to twelve degrees, and bounded by familiar coasts, this was tolerable. But in a latitude chart of the Atlantic, or still more of the entire world, the question of how the location of places had been determined within the coordinate system became all-important if a true course was to be steered from that chart. In fact the maps such as those of Cosa, Waldseemüller and Ribero, crucial historical documents as they are, would have been useless for navigation precisely because their makers were unable to depict the spherical earth on a two-dimensional surface. These maps, and the sea-charts drawn throughout the sixteenth century, are what are known as 'plane charts', although a better description might be 'squared charts'. The plane chart was a map which treated the latitude and longitude degrees as forming rectangles whose sides are in a constant ratio. The most natural ratio would be 1:1, with

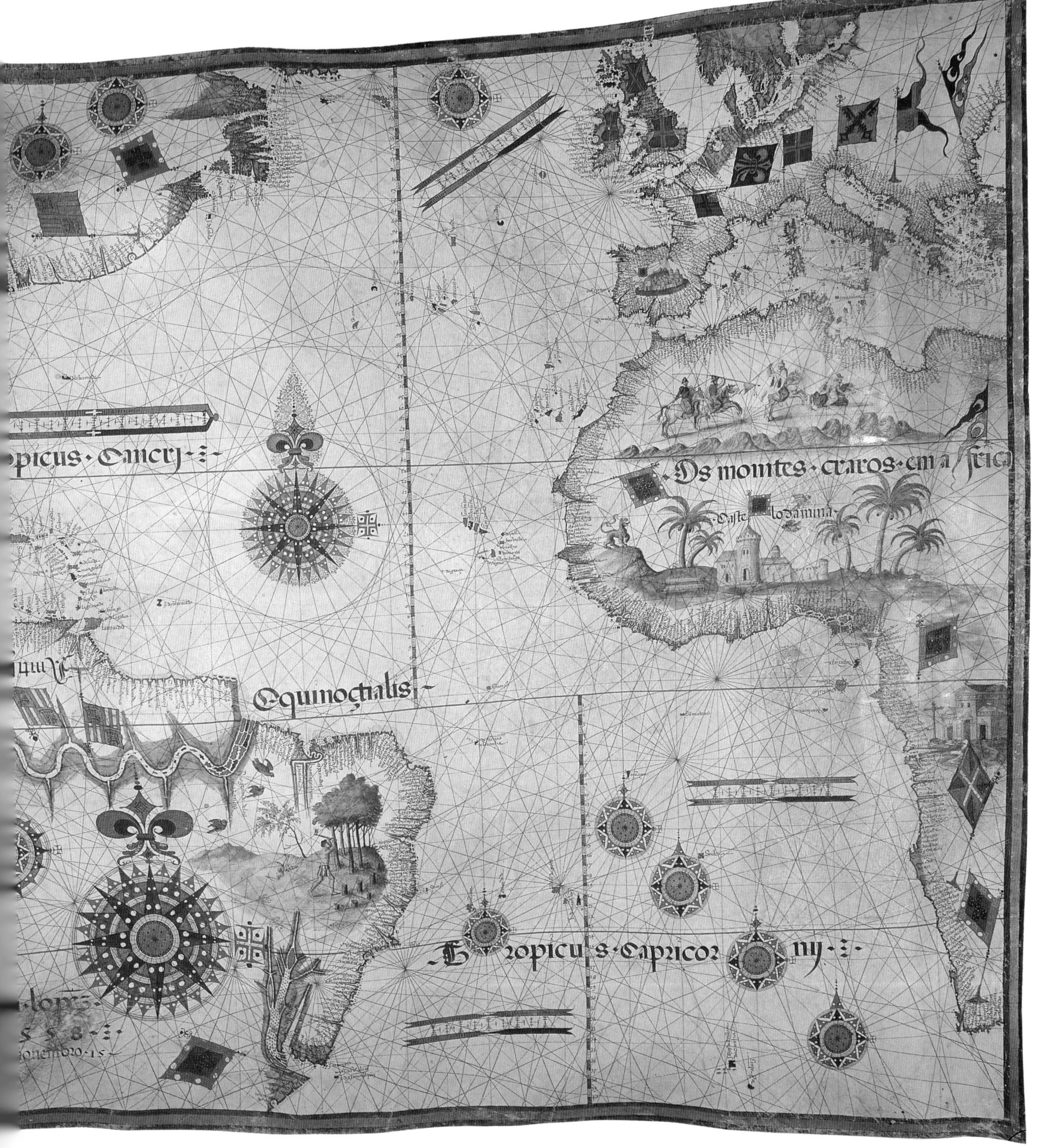

opicus · Cancrj
Equinoctialis
Os montes · claros · em africa

the map plotted by simply squaring the surface, one degree by one degree and entering all the places by their coordinates. But bearing in mind the shape of the Mediterranean and the shape of the vellum skin on which the chart was drawn – both rectangles – graphic convenience dictated that the ratio adopted was around 1:2, one latitude degree equalling two degrees of longitude. This ratio was applied over the whole chart, but it was of course a completely fallacious way of drawing a map. The sphericity of the earth means that in reality the ratio between latitude and longitude is not constant. The value of one longitude degree at the equator is around 66 miles; at 60 degrees north or south it is around 32 miles. The value of a latitude degree is, practically, constant, since meridians are all great circles, tracing the whole circumference of the globe. In failing to represent the changing value of the longitude degree, the plane chart effectively ignored the fact that the earth is a sphere. The result of this for the navigator was a wildly inaccurate chart. On the surface of the earth a line of direct bearing, a rhumb line, is the shortest distance between two points, and it cuts the meridians at slightly different angles. On the plane chart, the supposed line of direct bearing cuts all the meridians at the same angle, and spherical geometry shows that such a line is not a straight line but a curve, leading eventually to one of the poles. Put another way, if a triangle formed by any three places on the surface of the earth is transferred to a flat map, it is impossible that the three points should be correctly plotted: if the latitudinal distance is correct, the longitudinal distance cannot be, and vice versa. The supposed line of direct bearing on the chart that should have rendered navigation so precise, transpired, especially in the context of ocean navigation, to be useless. There was to be no solution to this problem until Mercator devised his clebrated map projection in 1569, and even then it was not widely understood by mariners. Knowledgeable mariners of the time certainly appreciated this problem and it is commented on in manuals of navigation such as that by John Davis. But they were convinced that the defect could be allowed for by applying certain rules, and they emphasize strongly that on each wind a degree has a different value in leagues, so that for example crossing twenty latitude degrees on a course North-North-East will be shorter than on a North-East course. Much attention was paid in the manuals to tabulating the value of the league on the different winds, but in practice the accumulation of errors as the ship moved from course to course can well be imagined, and this confidence in the traditional plane chart was completely misplaced.

If the mariner's understanding and use of charts was less than perfect at this time, he had another more comprehensible type of guide to rely on: the 'Rutter' or illustrated book of sailing directions. The archetype was Pierre Garcie's *Grand Routier et Pilotage* of 1483, a pilot guide to the west coast of France filled with advice on tides and anchorages. It was translated into English and printed versions appeared illustrated with woodcut views of coasts and harbours. It served as the model for numerous other rutters over the next two hundred years, such as Richard Proude's *New Rutter of the Sea for the North Partes*, a pilot of British waters. In the seventeenth century, the Spanish equivalent, the '*Derreterro*' was commonly used in the Caribbean, and they were known to have been taken and used by buccaneers. The rutters continue the tradition of the *periploi* and the *portolani* and they have their descendants in the Sailing Directions of the nineteenth century.

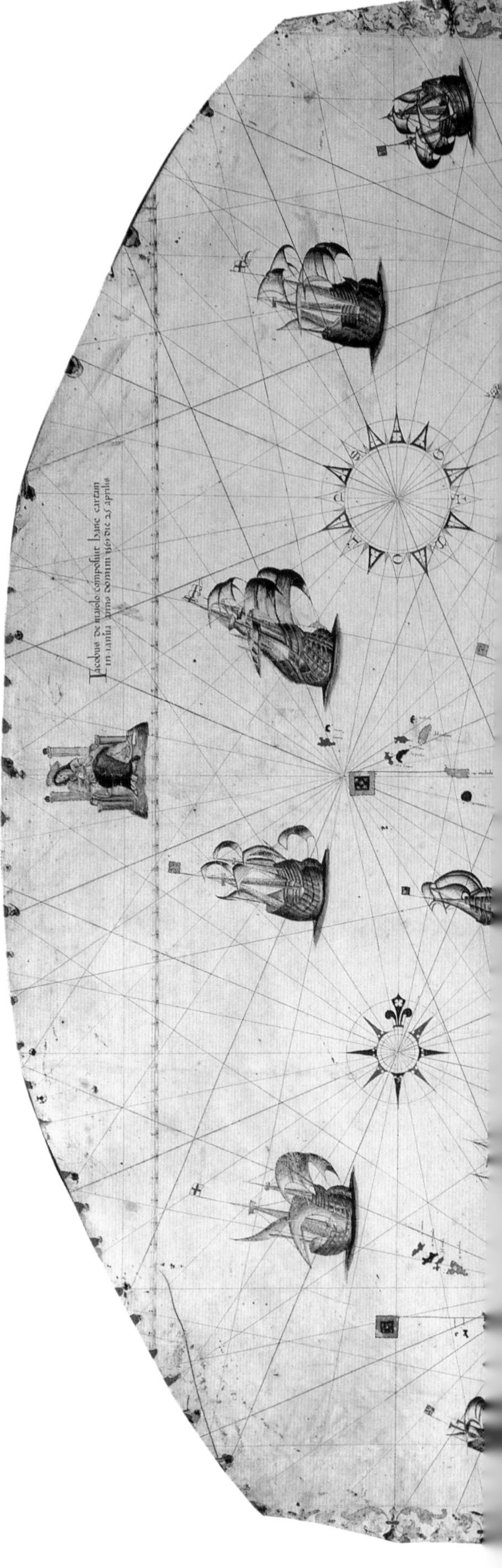

EUROPE, 1564 by Giacomo Maggiolo. This chart has at its heart the traditional highly-detailed of the Mediterranean, but it is more significant for its imagery: the Islamic Sultans in their tents, the galleons in the Atlantic and the Christian icon. The depiction of northern Europe is inaccurate and outdated, and the mythical island 'Fixdanda' appears in the north-west, which became in later maps 'Friesland', almost certainly a duplication of Iceland. The Red Sea is a survival from medieval tradition.

Archivio Scala

E V ROPA
A F R I C HA
ASSIA
ETIOPIA
GOTIA
EVROPA

DETAIL FROM MAGGIOLO'S CHART OF EUROPE. The mapmaker has filled the empty space of the Sahara with a small world map, in order to extend the usefulness of the traditional portolan chart of Europe. The array of forts around the entire coast appears to transform the whole of Africa into an Islamic stronghold, with the exception of the mythical kingdom of Prester John in the east. The dramatically shortened river Nile is simply a graphic convenience here, since it is shown in its full extent in the world map. More seriously, the southward bend of the African coast at the Gulf of Guinea is placed much too far west, an error which is difficult to account for since it is more correctly shown on the world map.

IVDEA
EVROPA
ASIA
AFRICA
ETIOPIA
AFRICHA

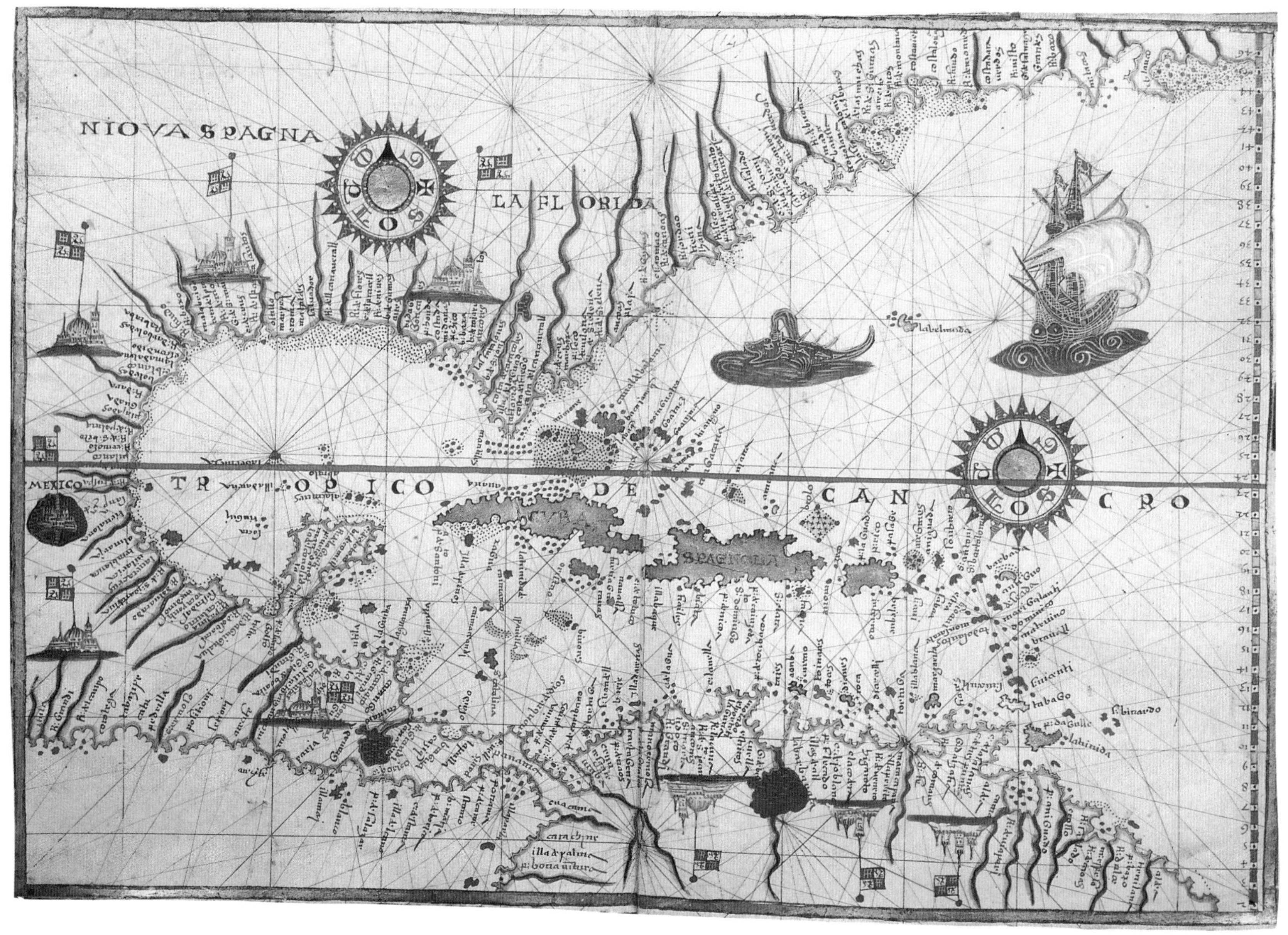

THE CARIBBEAN *c.*1578 by Joan Martines. A prolific Spanish chartmaker working in Messina, Sicily, Martines produced scores of highly-finished manuscript sea-atlases between 1550 and 1590. It is clear from the high degree of inland detail shown, that these maps functioned as world atlases rather than as strictly navigational charts, a role that was soon to pass to the printed atlases of the dominant Flemish map-makers Ortelius and Mercator.

The British Library, Harley MS. 3450, f.14.

printed maps which had grown out of the Ptolemaic tradition, published from the 1470s onwards. The Ptolemaic maps were derived first and foremost from the text of Ptolemy's *Geographia*. This was supplemented by later literary sources, such as Marco Polo's description of China, and the map itself became much extended from Ptolemy's original conception. This tradition produced the *Cosmographia Universalis*, the image of the whole world, usually shown on an oval projection extending to 360 degrees of longitude and 180 degrees of latitude. In practice it was not possible in the mid-sixteenth century to complete such a map empirically, and many features were added which were purely theoretical. It served in fact as a conceptual model of the globe, while the chart-based map was taken as representing the world as far as it was known. It was this kind of map of the real world, the world of sailors, merchants and adventurers, that appealed to European rulers and financiers.

For thousands of years sea-power had been defined entirely in terms of the Mediterranean; in the three decades between Columbus and Cortes, European sea-power moved out into the Atlantic and Indian Oceans. The first wave of exploration undertaken

EUROPE 1570, by Diogo Homem. The traditional portolan chart – the large, single-sheet, hand-drawn map of the Mediterranean region – still flourished a full century after the advent of map-printing. It marked latitude but not longitude, was almost always drawn at a scale of 1:6 million, and lacked any interest in northern Europe; Britain and Scandinavia are inaccurately mapped, and the Baltic fades into emptiness.

The British Library, Egerton MS.2858.

by the Spanish and Portuguese was swiftly transformed into a culture of rapacious trade. Building on Dias's success in first rounding the Cape of Good Hope, da Gama reached India in 1498, to be followed by the ruthlessly successful Albuquerque, Almeida, Varthema and Serrao, who by force of arms secured the great bases of Goa, Ormuz, Macao, Malacca and Timor. Spices, silk and other precious materials were shipped back to Lisbon, while from the West African coast the slave trade developed rapidly. Most slaves taken by the Portuguese were sent to Brazil, which had been discovered, apparently by accident, by Pedro Cabral in 1500. To circumvent the south-east trade winds in the south Atlantic, the Portuguese learned very early to sail far to the south-west from the Cape Verde Islands before turning east to the Cape, and it was on such a course that Cabral touched Brazil. This route demonstrates clearly the navigational confidence of the Portuguese: they had established the latitude of the Cape first by coasting western Africa, with its contrary winds and currents. Now armed with that knowledge they could seek an easier passage even if it were far longer, confident of still finding their goal. Cabral's landfall was of special political significance for Spain and Portugal. In 1494 Pope Alexander VI had issued a series of edicts dealing with the jurisdiction over newly-discovered

territories. The most important decision was to draw an imaginary line in the Atlantic 100 leagues west of the Azores, to the west of which all land would belong to Spain, that to the east being assigned to Portugal. This division of territory was agreed by Spain and Portugal at the Treaty of Tordesillas. The value of the league was not standardized, but the intention was clearly to allow Portugal the eastern sea-route to India, while Spain could take the west. The interesting question as to what would happen on the opposite meridian when it was reached, was not faced at this stage. The eastward trend of the South American coast was unknown in 1494, but Cabral's landfall at 16 degrees south of the equator undoubtedly fell within the Tordesillas line, and so enabled a huge area of the New World to fall under Portuguese control. The principal motive of Magellan's great voyage was to demonstrate, by sailing west, that the wealth-giving Spice Islands lay west of the line of demarcation, that is within Spain's hemisphere, not Portugal's; for Magellan, though a Portuguese, was in the service of Spain.

The Spaniards meanwhile had conquered Mexico and began immediately to ship out gold and silver, first back to Spain by the Atlantic, and then from the 1520s west to the Philippines, where it was used to buy silk and spices. Using the overland route across Mexico, the Spaniards effectively connected the Atlantic and the Pacific and were thus able to build an almost worldwide trading empire. The exception was their lack of direct access to Africa for slaves, and these the Portuguese supplied. Ports and fortress towns were founded in the New World, Asia and Africa which were to become famous in the history of seafaring trade and war: Veracruz, Havana, Manila, Luanda, Elmina and many more. Many of the trans-ocean routes required years of experiment to discover, sailing well away from the obvious course in order to master the winds and currents which made the direct routes impractical. These great barriers to ocean sailing were not to appear on any charts for three hundred years, for the concept of this kind of thematic mapping did not emerge until the nineteenth century. The Spanish charts that record this era are numerous, especially the works of Joan Martines, a Catalan who worked principally in Messina, Sicily, and produced more than thirty outstanding manuscript chart atlases between 1550 and 1590. Many Spanish ships of the sixteenth century crossed and re-crossed the Pacific without making a landfall, while others discovered islands that were subsequently lost, rediscovered and re-named; such uncertainty was natural when longitude was unfindable.

The Spanish and Portuguese had almost half a century's start in the quest for overseas territory and trade. Italy provided many of the key figures among the pioneers, but the Italian cities and states as such played no part, and it remained for France and England to embark on the maritime enterprise. Just four years after Columbus, John Cabot, a Venetian, landed in Newfoundland and took possession of it in the name of the king of England. Probably no pioneer has left so little trace of his achievement. He found nothing and left nothing, returned to England, and two years later sailed into oblivion. No English explorers followed him for half a century, and the next deliberate reconnaissance of North America was in 1524, again by an Italian, this time sponsored by the French crown. Giovanni da Verrazano was the first to conceive the idea of circumventing Spanish America by finding a northern route into the Pacific. Verrazano coasted and charted from North Carolina to Newfoundland, and imagined that in Pamlico Sound, seen from beyond Cape Hatteras, he had sighted the Pacific. A decade later Jacques Cartier was pursuing the same goal when he discovered the mouth of the St Lawrence, and opened up a northern *Terre Neuf* for France. To serve French maritime needs there was established by 1540 a school of chartmakers in Dieppe who were to produce some of the most highly-wrought maps ever drawn. The Dieppe chartmakers, among whom the most famous are Rotz, Desceliers and Le Testu, drew functional maps for the mariners of France, but they also designed highly artistic charts and atlases for wealthy patrons which were never intended for use

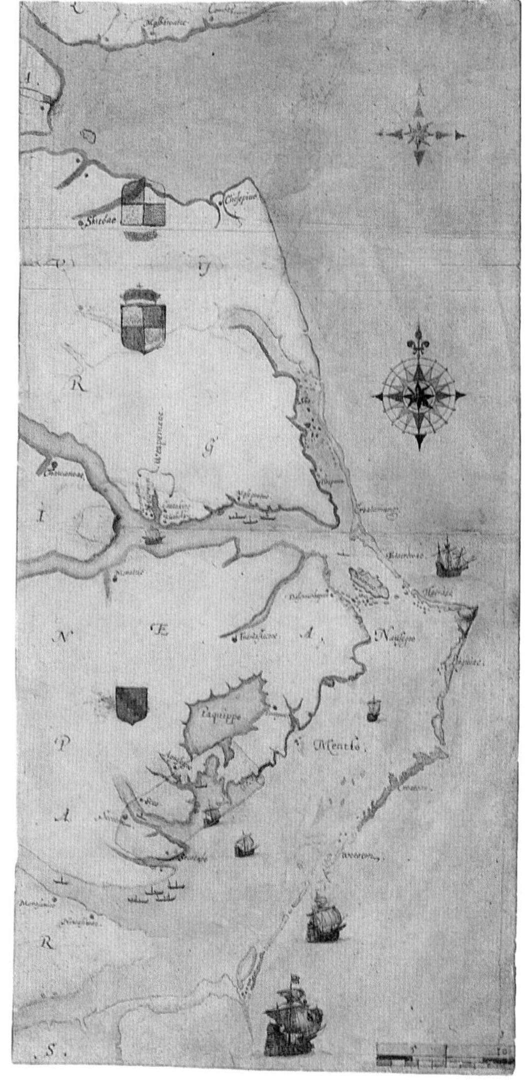

VIRGINIA, *c.*1585, by John White. White was a professional artist who participated in both the English colonies at Roanoke. Through his absence in England, he escaped whatever mysterious fate it was which overtook and destroyed the colony. His grand-daughter, Virginia Dare, was the first English child born in the Americas. White made several fine maps of the east coast, drawn after surveys by Thomas Harriot, and a number of watercolour paintings that were of historic importance in shaping the European image of America and its peoples. They were published as illustrations in several books, most notably in de Bry's 'Voyages'.

British Museum, Dept. of Prints & Drawings LB.1.(1).

THE EAST INDIES, 1587 by Pastoret. In this late, unfinished, atlas of the Dieppe school, artistic imagination has overwhelmed geography. Despite the presence of a latitude bar it is almost impossible to identify the intended location of some of the charts, while fantastic animals and plants fill the land. Stemming as they do from an age of exploration, when world geography was of supreme importance, the motive and the function of these fantasy-maps are quite mysterious.

The British Library, Egerton MS. 1513, f.51.

WORLD CHART by Joan Oliva, 1599. Oliva was a member of a Spanish family of chartmakers settled in Messina, Sicily. His work shows the persistence of a traditional Catalan-style chart in the Mediterranean – its accurate centre, and its formalized periphery which was used to place images of monarchs, religious figures and animals. The small world map appears almost as a concession to the pressure of new knowledge of the world beyond Europe.

The British Library, Add. MS. 24943.

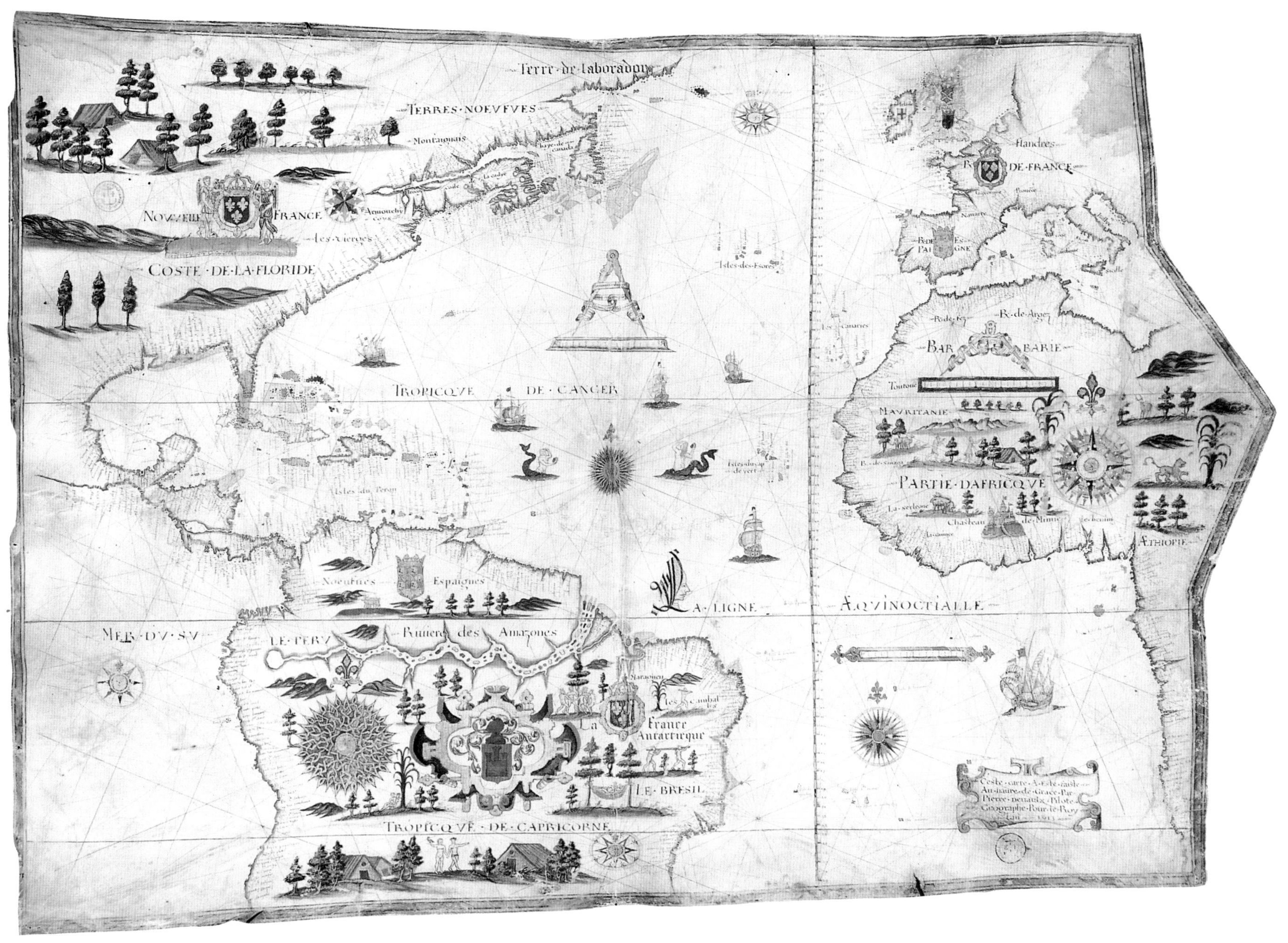

THE ATLANTIC, 1613, by Pierre de Vaulx. A late product of the Normandy group of chart-makers, this chart's title proclaims that it was drawn in Le Havre 'pour le Roy'. It may have been made specifically to flatter the monarch's sense of power, for the whole of North America is claimed as 'Nouvelle France', while the French settlement in Guiana is strangely entitled 'La France Antarctique'. It is tempting to think that the face visible in the ornate letter L on the equator is a portrait of de Vaulx himself.

Bibliothèque Nationale, Paris.

at sea. In their elaboration, these charts blurred the distinction between map and artistic manuscript, between empirical knowledge and imagination. While preserving the nautical apparatus of compass roses, rhumb-lines, and latitudes, the land interiors are now filled with a fantastic array of birds, beasts and flowers which serve as a background for visions of primitive peoples, noble or savage, in America, Africa or Asia. This decoration was clearly a function of the map's social role: they presented images of the newly-revealed lands which appealed to the European mind. But the restriction of the chart to empirical knowledge was also abandoned, and lands appeared whose origin lay in legend and imagination rather than in discovery. A special favourite of the Dieppe school was the vast southern continent which was made to extend across the entire globe, reaching to 20 degrees south in places. Variously named 'Terra Australis', 'Terra Incognita', 'Java Major', or 'Magellanica', it seems to have been compounded from many sources: Magellan's sighting of Tierra del Fuego, Marco Polo's accounts of lands south of China, and the classical Ptolemaic belief in a great southern land-mass counterbalancing those in the north. In certain Dieppe maps, such as those of Pastoret, fantasy outweighs reality, both in the geography and the artistic decoration; in their departure from the strict form and content of sea-chart, the Dieppe school represents the temptation towards the mannerism that was always present in mapmaking before the late eighteenth century.

Equally remarkable for their artistry were the Ottoman charts of the Mediterranean. No charts from the Turkish tradition pre-date 1400, and their essential similarity to western charts suggests a high degree of interraction between Christian and Moslem seafarers. The most obvious means of contact was the capture of vessels by one side or the other, and Islamic science would have been easily able to interpret the compass-lines and latitude bars. The persistent tradition that the compass was introduced from China into the Mediterranean by the Arabs has never been demonstrated, and all the documentary evidence points to the primacy of the western charts. The most famous name in Turkish charting is Piri Re'is, an admiral in the navy of Suleyman the Magnificent, who drew at least one large world map that showed the coasts of the New World, probably through an indirect connection with Columbus. Piri Re'is was also the author of a book of detailed regional Mediterranean charts with sailing directions, the *Kitab-i-Bahriye*, many manuscript copies of which circulated in the sixteenth and seventeenth centuries. The Turkish charts of this period are exquisitely drawn, more in the Italian style than the Catalan, without excessive ornamentation. Turkish power in the Mediterranean reached its height in 1571 with the capture of Cyprus from the Venetians, and Christian Europe moved swiftly to deal with the threat. The great battle of Lepanto, fought in October 1571 between Christian and Turkish galley fleets, had echoes of Salamis as a decisive European defeat of a hostile fleet from the east. It is said that among the Christian fleet was a representative of every noble house in Italy and Spain. Also among the Spanish was the writer Cervantes, who lost an arm in the fighting, and one of the English volunteers was Sir Richard Grenville, later the hero of the *Revenge*. It was the last great 'crusading' encounter between Christians and Moslems.

It was in the 1550s that English mariners turned seriously to overseas exploration. Like the French before them the English convinced themselves that they could circumvent Spanish America and Portuguese Africa, and establish their own trading routes to the east. The North-East and still more the North-West Passage attracted a series of courageous explorers who were ill-prepared for the hostility of the arctic waters into which they sailed. Frobisher, Davis, Hudson and Baffin left their names on the seas and coasts of North-East Canada, but the passage which they sought eluded them. The problem of longitude was a vital factor in their failure, for they had no real idea of the scale of the task they had set themselves, believing that any strait or inlet might lead west into the Pacific. A number of famous narratives resulted from these voyages, and Davis made a real contribution to navigation, especially with the invention of his quadrant which permitted the sighting of the sun's altitude without the need to look at the sun direct. It is striking that it was only in 1553 that the North Cape of Norway, the northernmost point of Europe, was passed, a full half-century after the first voyages to India and America. The attempts on the North-East Passage resulted in contact not with India and China but with the Muscovites, although no great trade ensued through such a forbidding passage, deep inside the arctic circle. No charts remain from this heroic phase of arctic exploration, for English mariners were remarkably slow to adopt charts as a new part of their professional equipment. Half a century after the first voyages across the Atlantic and Indian Oceans, Britain's coasts were first surveyed to assess their defensive character, in anticipation of invasion from Catholic Europe. The results of this survey cannot be termed

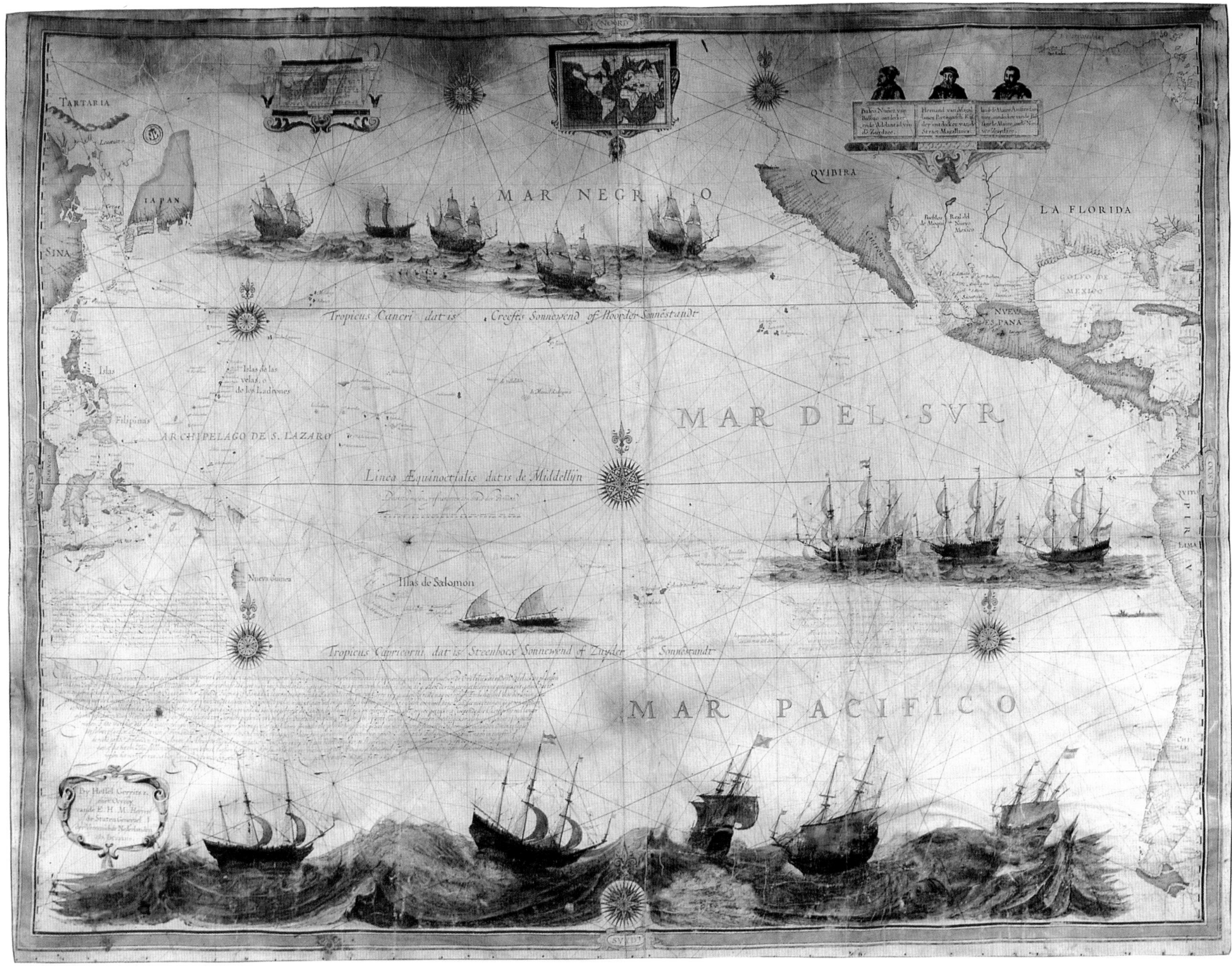

THE PACIFIC OCEAN, 1622, by Hessel Gerritz. This monumental map commemorates the newfound Dutch dominance in the Pacific, in particular the voyage in 1615–16 of Willem Schouten and Jacob Le Maire, in which they discovered and named Cape Horn. Le Maire's portrait appears beside those of Balbao and Magellan, the first Europeans to see the Pacific. Squadrons of ships flying the Dutch flag dominate the entire ocean. Gerritz was hydrographer to the Dutch East India Company, and this chart was part of its secret archive.

Bibliothèque Nationale, Paris.

sea-charts, but they provide an intriguing glimpse of Britain's coastal towns in the 1540s.

The years 1250–1550 had seen enormous changes in the maritime world, as in every aspect of European life, and the maps drawn by Europe's scholars and seafarers are a vivid index of these changes. The medieval world map was diagrammatic, with Jerusalem at its centre, a location that was fitting geographically and intellectually for Christian Europe. Over several centuries this map became elaborated with imagery from the Bible, Christian history and popular culture, but it did not become geographically more accurate. This world image was revolutionized during the years 1480–1530. First the emergence of the Ptolemaic map and of the sailor's portolan chart had produced a far more accurate picture of Europe; and then the discoveries to the east and still more to the west of Europe stretched the known world almost beyond recognition. But there was one further important effect, namely that Europe itself and not Jerusalem now filled the centre of the map. Once again this was both geographically justifiable and historically fitting, as Europe entered a period of world domination that was to last for four centuries.

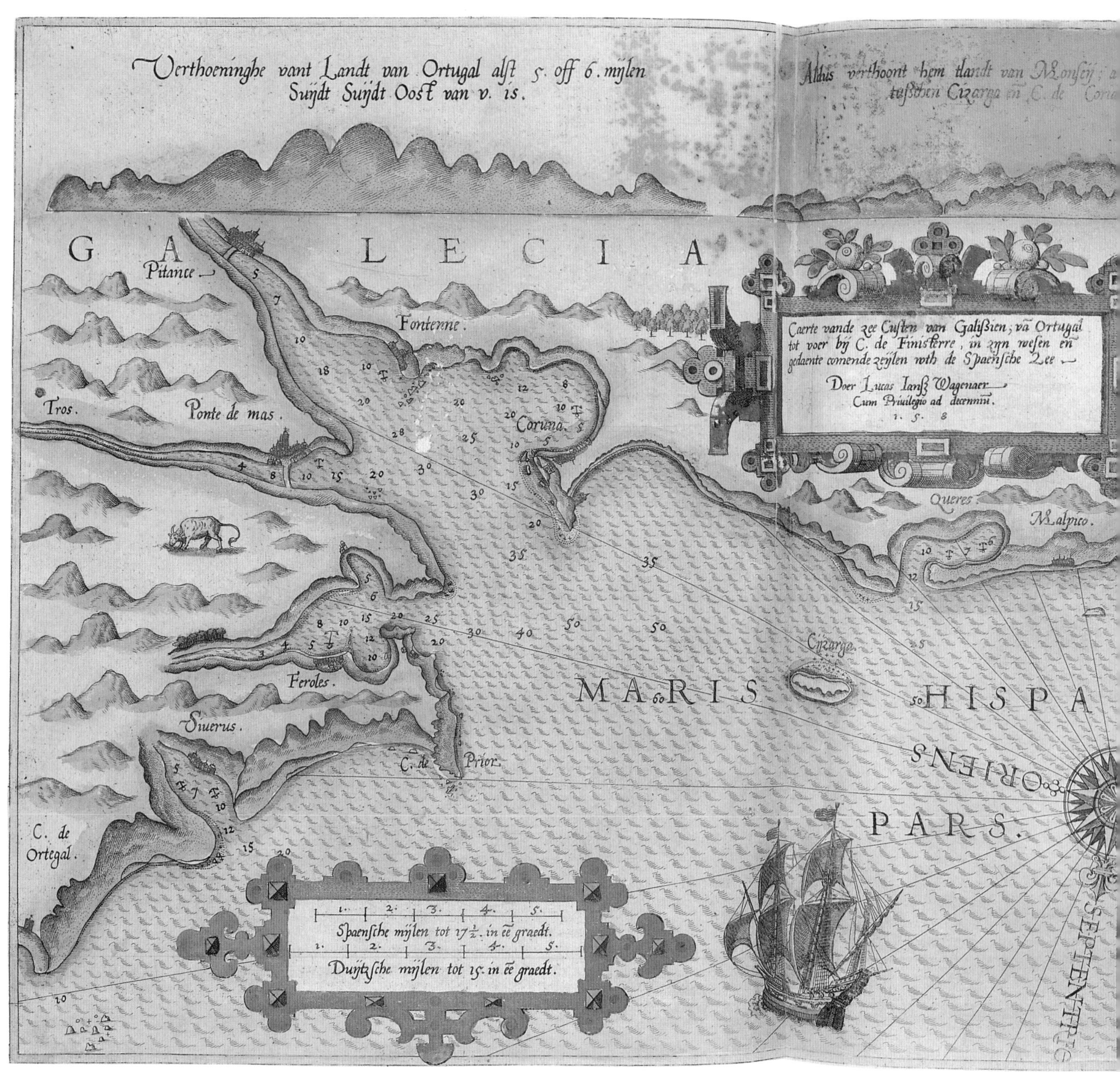
Verthoeninghe vant Landt van Ortugal alst 5. off 6. mijlen Suijdt Suijdt Oost van v. is.
Aldus verthoont hem tlandt van Monseij
tusschen Cizarga en C. de Coru
GALECIA
Pitance
Fonterne.
Tros.
Ponte de mas.
Coruna.
Caerte vande zee Custen van Galißien; vā Ortugal tot voer bij C. de Finisterre, in zijn wesen en gedaente comende zeijlen wth de Spaensche Zee
Doer Lucas Ianßz Wagenaer
Cum Priuilegio ad decennui.
Queres.
Malpico.
Cizarga.
Feroles.
MARIS
HISPA
Siuerus.
C. de Prior.
ORIENS
C. de Ortegal.
PARS.
Spaensche mijlen tot 17½. in ee graedt.
Duijtzsche mijlen tot 15. in ee graedt.
SEPTENTRIO

The Sea-Chart in Europe's Maritime Age

'Whoever has mastery of the high seas exercises great power on land. Look at the King of Spain: when he obtained mastery of the sea he conquered so many kingdoms that now the sun never sets on his territories.' So wrote the French admiral de Launay-Razilly to Cardinal Richelieu in 1626, urging the building of a French navy to surpass that of other nations. At the time he was writing the balance of power had shifted decisively northwards, and the years 1600–1800 saw interminable conflicts between England, France and the Netherlands, conflicts that were waged not in their respective homelands but throughout the oceans of the world. Other nations played subsidiary parts – Spain and Portugal, Sweden and Denmark – but the three principal antagonists competed for supremacy in the Atlantic and Indian Oceans. This northward shift of power lessened the drive to find new arctic sea-routes, for the enemies of Spain and Portugal seized every opportunity to attack them overseas and break the monopolies they had built up. The concept of colonization succeeded that of mere exploitation and the French, English and Dutch founded their New France, New England and New Amsterdam. This was the age in which Hakluyt promoted, with almost evangelical fervour, the special destiny of the English to explore and settle the new lands beyond Europe. Portugal's power crumbled in the years 1600–1620 as the Dutch captured their bases in South Asia, while Spain was irrevocably weakened by the Armada catastrophe of 1558. The golden age of both these nations had been founded entirely on their sea power: their history *was* maritime history, and this was to be no less true of the northern European nations to whom maritime supremacy now passed.

Underlying the quest for naval supremacy was the economic theory of mercantilism which dominated European thinking for two hundred years. Its central tenet was that a nation's wealth is expressed by the amount of gold and silver it possesses, and that colonies existed to feed the mother country with precious metals and other raw materials. That Spain's Golden Age had occurred while she was reaping her harvest of gold and silver from the new world was taken as proof of this doctrine. The Spanish fleet system had concentrated all legal trade with the new world into two great flotillas per year, the outgoing ships bearing manufactured goods, while on their return they carried gold and silver. In accordance with this theory, naval strategy was the key to both imperial policy and economic growth. The wealth derived from overseas was used to increase still further

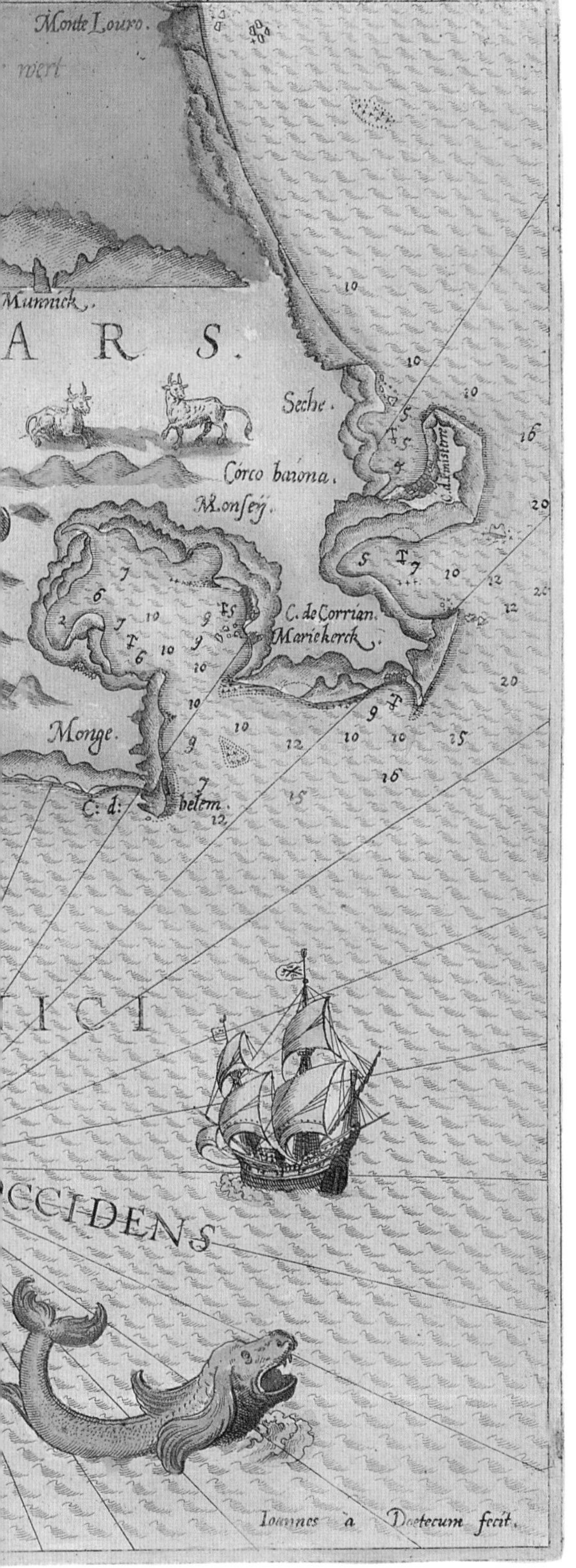

CAPE FINISTERE, 1584, from Waghenaer's *Spieghel der Zeevaerdt*. In the later 16th century the Dutch devised a new form of marine survey in which relatively small sections of coast were shown in detail, with frequent depth-soundings. Waghenaer's was the first printed book of sea-charts, covering these European waters from the eastern Baltic to the Straits of Gibraltar. These charts were not tied to any topographical surveys, so the coastlines were often inaccurately drawn, but capes, river-mouths and harbours were heavily emphasized.

The British Library, Maps C.8.b.1.

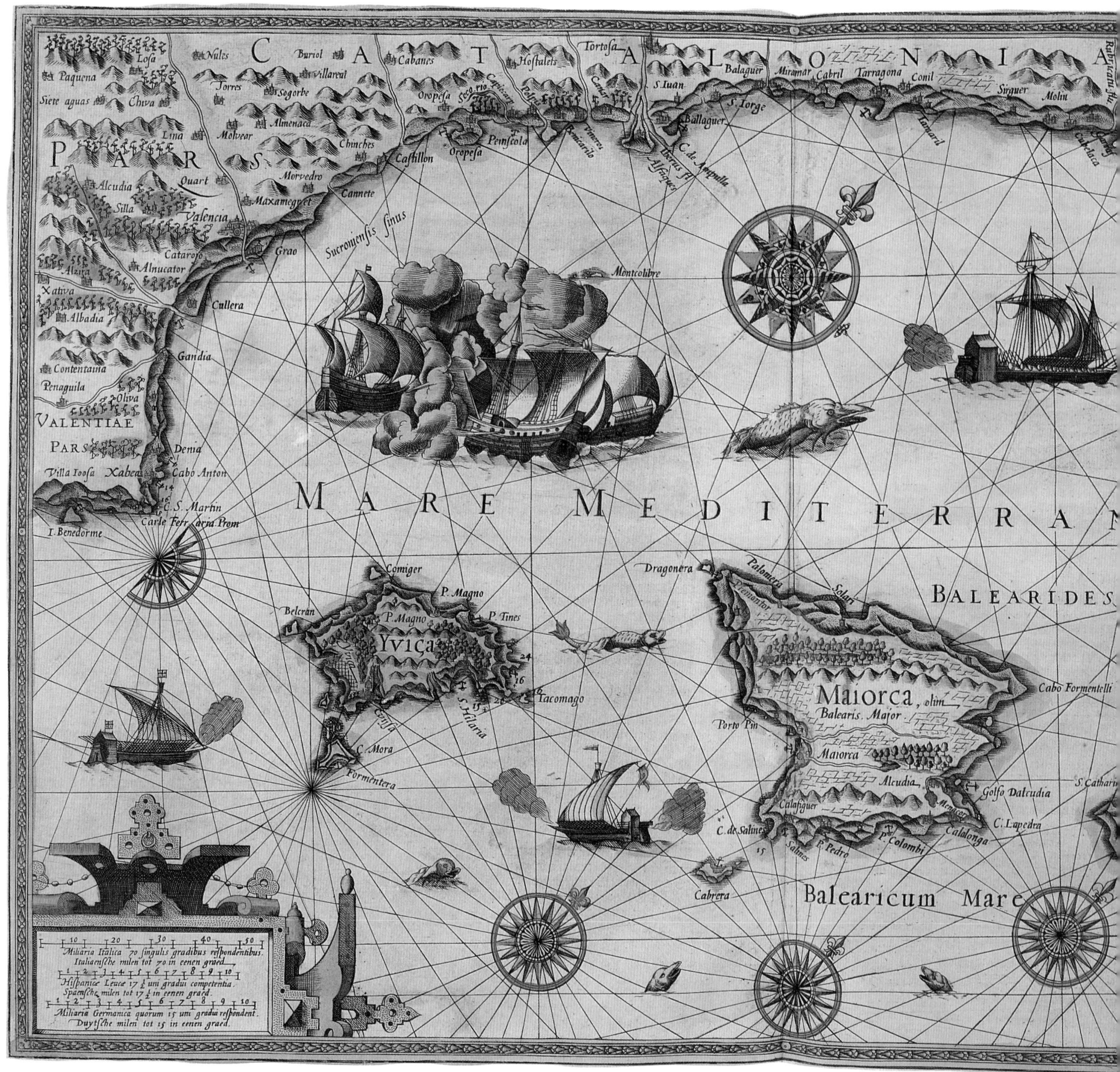

C A T A L O N I A
P A R S
VALENTIAE PARS
Valencia
Sucronensis sinus
M A R E   M E D I T E R R A N
BALEARIDES
Yviça
Maiorca, olim
Balearis Major
Balearicum Mare
Formentera
Cabrera
Dragonera
Tortosa
Tarragona
Castillon
Peniscola
Cullera
Gandia
Denia
Cabo Anton
I. Benedorme
Alcudia
Porto Pin
Cabo Formentelli
Golfo Dalcudia
Miliaria Italica 70 singulis gradibus respondentibus.
Italiaensche milen tot 70 in eenen graed
Hispanicæ Leucæ 17½ uni gradui competentia.
Spaensche milen tot 17½ in eenen graed.
Miliaria Germanica quorum 15 uni gradui respondent.
Duytsche milen tot 15 in eenen graed.

MAJORCA AND MINORCA, 1595, from Willem Barentsz' *Caertboeck van de Midlandtsche Zee.* This atlas of charts extended the new Dutch approach to charting throughout the Mediterranean. However Barentsz shows no depth soundings, and more topographical detail than Waghenaer. The scale of these charts is much larger than that of the traditional sea-charts drawn in Italy. Barentsz later turned his attention to the North-East passage, and died off Novaya Zemlya in 1597.

Rijksarchief, The Hague.

TITLE PAGE of van Keulen's Chart Atlas published in Amsterdam, 1682.

The British Library, Maps 7. Tab 126.

Europe's technical superiority over the rest of the world. The need for strategic overseas bases led to yet more acquisitions of territory. To the gold which was the first gift from the new world, were added the luxury goods which became part of European life – sugar, coffee, tea, tobacco, furs, spices and medicinal drugs. The drive to secure these goods had, by the late eighteenth century, created a worldwide economic network linking Europe with America, Africa and Asia in a system that could not function without the merchant ship and the navy's guns. In the first phase of Europe's age of discovery, Spanish and Portuguese mariners had always sought royal authority, lands were occupied in the name of the king, and the monarch secured the revenues for himself. In the more egalitarian countries of northern Europe, the joint stock company was evolved as the vehicle for a more general participation in the imperial venture. As early as 1555 the Muscovy Company had been formed in London to exploit a North-East Passage and trade with Russia, and numerous others followed, among the most famous being the East India Company, chartered in 1600, and the Hudson's Bay Company of 1670. These companies held the right to all legal navigation and trade in their respective regions; they made treaties with local rulers and established bases or garrisons; occasionally they waged war; sometimes they founded colonies, and they represented to all intents and purposes the nations who sponsored them.

The process of European expansion had an incalculable influence on navigation, shipbuilding and the maritime economy, and of course it was a two-way relationship: European technology permitted overseas adventures, while the lure of the new worlds stimulated further advances in ship design, weaponry and navigation. The three-masted ship had been a pre-condition of ocean sailing, and its design had undergone many changes during the sixteenth century as the maritime nations sought to gain the advantage in carrying-capacity and manoeuverability. But it is in the nature of the seaman's trade that there could be few secrets in ship design, so that the development of craft was international. One of the great forces working for change was the carrying of heavier and heavier weapons on board ship. The mounting of large cannon in the castles – the raised decks fore and aft – caused a dangerous instability in the ship and made them slow to respond in the water. Medieval naval warfare had consisted simply of filling a ship with armed men and boarding other craft for hand-to-hand fighting. The advent of firearms and canon revolutionized naval combat, so that the aim was now to out-manoeuvre the enemy and attack with cannon-fire. By the later sixteenth century, for example among the English at the time of the Armada, ships had reduced their superstructures, were longer in proportion to their beam, and had their cannon mounted on a lower gun-deck for stability. The need for the gun-ports to remain well clear of the waterline produced further refinements of hull and sail, resulting in the classic form of the galleon which dominated this period. The ship had become in fact a floating weapon. This European superiority in ships and weaponry meant that they could always overawe their opponents, in spite of being heavily outnumbered on their voyages of exploration and conquest.

This new sophistication of ship design was paralleled by improvements in instrumentation and a new approach to chartmaking. The contribution of the Dutch was paramount

EAST COAST OF ENGLAND, 1608, from Blaeu's *Licht der Zeevaerdt*. Blaeu's chart-atlas superseded that of Wagnenaer. The coasts were more accurately drawn, charted from more careful running surveys, and more depths were given. Moreover Blaeu undoubtedly had access to the earliest surveys of England by Saxton. Four scales are given corresponding to the changing value of the mile in Holland, France, England and Spain.

The British Library, Maps C.8.a.1.

THE ENGLISH man-of-war *Royal*. A print published in Amsterdam by Pierre Mortier.

The British Library, Maps 147.d.26.

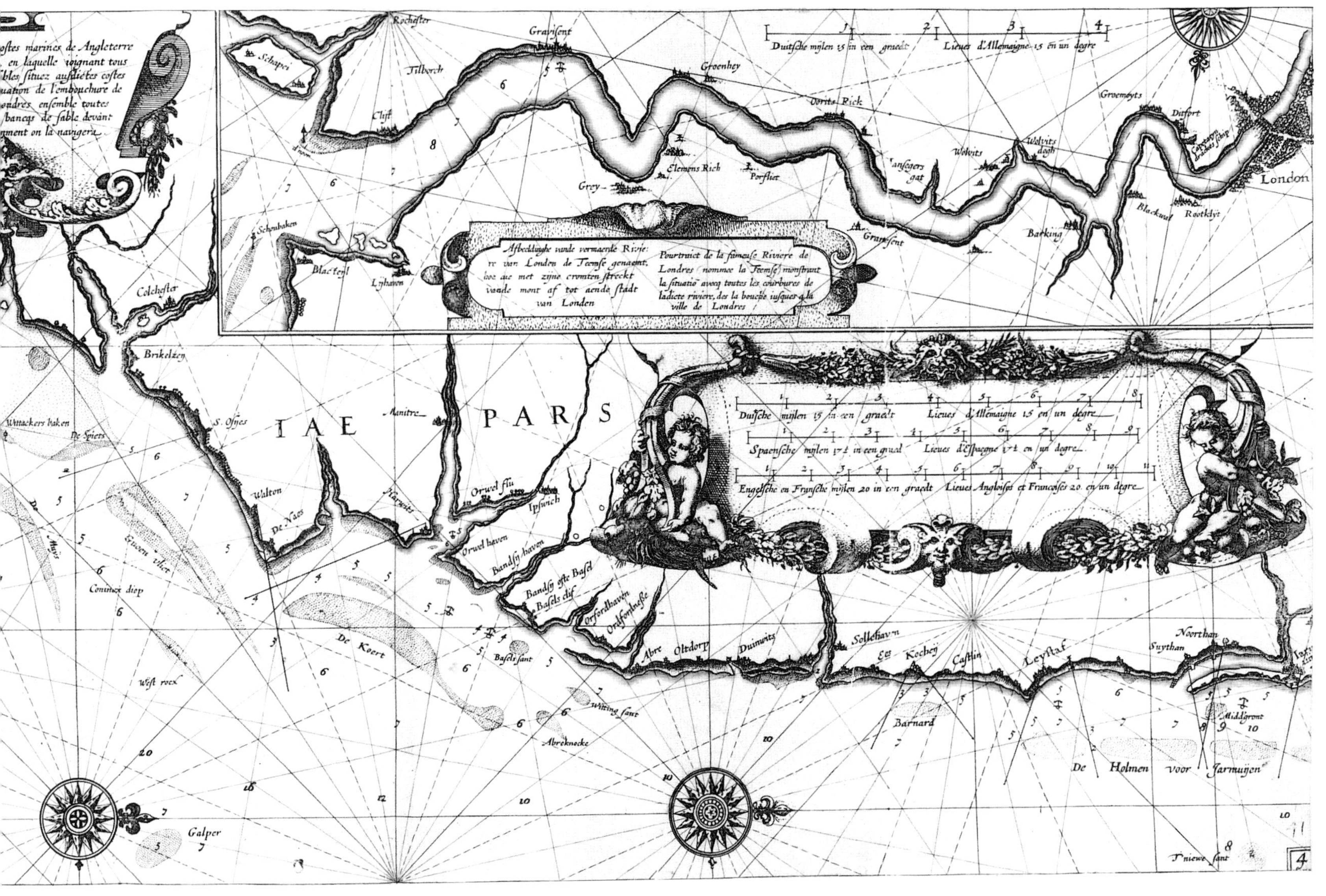

here. By 1590 Amsterdam and Antwerp were centres for navigators, engravers, instrument-makers and cartographers, and in this climate it was natural that the sea-chart should make the transition from hand-drawn manuscript to printed map. The sixteenth century had indeed seen some sea-charts emerge in printed form. As early as 1485 Bartolommeo dalli Sonnetti's island maps had been published as woodcuts, their form much simplified but retaining the large compass. The compass and the network of rhumb-lines so characteristic of the sea-chart also appeared on a small number of land-maps of the period which might be described as dual-purpose maps. The most important of these was the famous *Carta Marina* of Scandinavia, 1539, which was prepared by Olaus Magnus, a Swedish priest living in exile in Italy, to accompany his *Treatise on the Northern Peoples*. The rich artistry of this map was to be enormously influential on all future mapmakers. Whether it deserves its title of sea-chart is doubtful – for example its latitude bar is grossly inaccurate – but what is clear is that the mapmaker has endeavoured to portray the northern peoples as maritime nations, showing the seas as uniting the nations of Norway, Iceland, Denmark, Finland, Scotland and England. There are only two maps which consciously transfer the sea-chart tradition to the medium of printing: the great world map of 1517 by Waldseemüller, and Paolo Forlani's 1569 engraving of a Mediterranean portolan

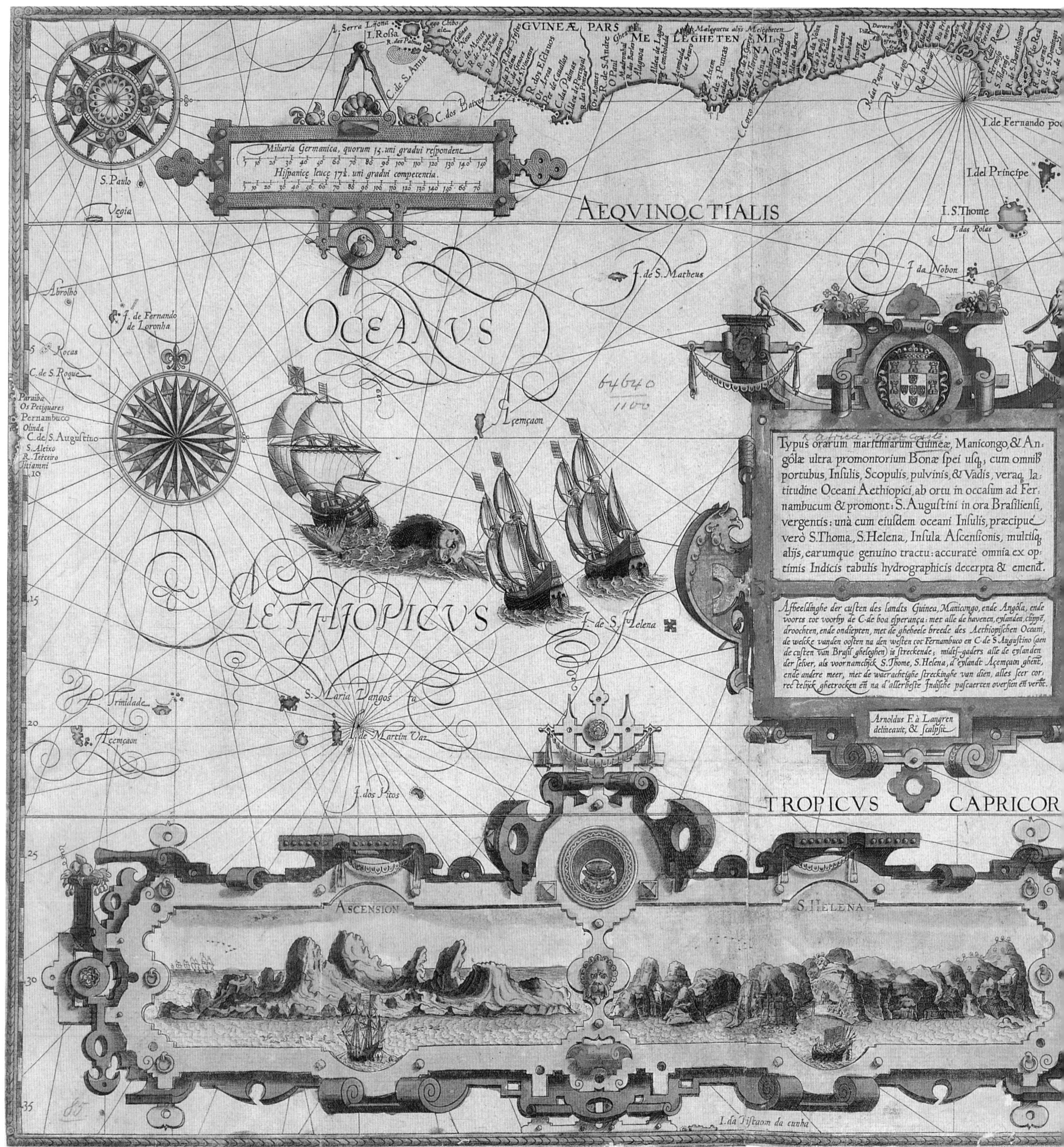
GVINEÆ PARS
MELEGHETEN
AEQVINOCTIALIS
OCEANVS
AETHIOPICVS
TROPICVS CAPRICOR
Miliaria Germanica, quorum 15. uni gradui respondent
Hispaniœ leucœ 17½. uni gradui competentia.
I.de Fernando po
I.del Principe
I.S.Thome
I.das Rolas
I.da Nobon
I.de S.Matheus
I.de S.Helena
Açemçaon
S.Maria Dangosta
I.de Martim Vaz
I.dos Pitos
Trimidade
Açemçaon
Abrolho
I.de Fernando de Loronha
Rocas
C.de S.Roque
Paraiba
Os Petiguares
Pernambuco
Olinda
C.de S.Augustino
S.Aleixo
R.Terteiro
S.Paulo
Vegia
C.de S.Anna
C.dos Baixos
I.Roßa
Typus orarum maritimarum Guineæ, Manicongo, & Angolæ ultra promontorium Bonæ spei usq; cum omnib' portubus, Insulis, Scopulis, pulvinis, & Vadis, veraq; latitudine Oceani Aethiopici, ab ortu in occasum ad Fernambucum & promont: S. Augustini in ora Brasiliensi, vergentis: unà cum eiusdem oceani Insulis, præcipue verò S.Thoma, S.Helena, Insula Ascensionis, multisq; alijs, earumque genuino tractu: accuratè omnia ex optimis Indicis tabulis hydrographicis decerpta & emend.
Afbeeldinghe der custen des landts Guinea, Manicongo, ende Angola, ende voorts tot voorby de C·de boa esperança: met alle de havenen, eylanden, clippē, droochten, ende ondiepten, met de gheheele breede des Aethiopischen Oceani, de welcke vanden oosten na den westen tot Fernambuco en C·de S Augustino (aen de custen van Brasil gheleghen) is streckende; midts-gaders alle de eylanden der selver, als voornamelijck S.Thome, S.Helena, d'eylandt Açemçaon ghent, ende andere meer, met de waerachtighe streckinghe van dien, alles seer correctelijck ghetrocken ēn na d'allerbeste Indische pascaerten oversien ēn verbt.
Arnoldus F. à Langren delineauit, & scalpsit
ASCENSION
S.HELENA
I.da Tristaom da cunha

chart. Waldseemüller's map bears the explicit title 'A Portuguese Navigational Sea-Chart' and it is clearly modelled on the Cantino chart. It shows only the coasts thus far explored by European navigators, yet the wealth of land-detail in Africa and Asia shows that the map was also intended to function as a *mappa mundi*, a visual encyclopedia of the world. These details are both historical and legendary – the depiction of Asia is heavily dependent on Marco Polo, while the fabulous king Prester John (the subject of persistent medieval romance) is shown enthroned in Ethiopia. Forlani's chart of Europe was designed by Diogo Homem, a leading Portuguese chartmaker, and except for the rich ornamentation that marks Homem's manuscript work, it is exactly an engraved portolan.

Why is it that only a handful of sea-charts were printed in the years 1480–1580, when map printing in general had become so well-established? One practical reason is that printing generally requires paper, and a paper chart would be too fragile for use at sea compared with the much tougher vellum on which manuscript charts were drawn. It was possible to print on vellum, but it was a troublesome and costly medium and its use was soon discontinued. There must have been commercial reasons too; perhaps the market demand for charts was insufficient. This would be surprising since the number of ships leaving such ports as Genoa, Palma, Rhodes or Lisbon numbered hundreds each year; if demand were small, this suggests that many seafarers had still not learned to use and value charts. Perhaps it was simply conservatism on the part of the chartmaker: he was a manuscript artist, not a publisher; and the mariner too was a conservative craftsman: the chart he knew was a hand-made instrument not a printed paper.

The new factor that changed this was the desire on the part of the Dutch to chart for the first time the waters of northern Europe. The manuscript chart had become rather formalized, both the general chart of the whole Mediterranean, and the portolan atlas of eight, ten or twelve regional charts. Their outstanding features were the compass lines and the coastal place-names, otherwise the amount of hydrographical information they carried was small. When the Dutch turned their attention to chartmaking, they had before them as models the foremost makers of land maps in the world, Ortelius and Mercator, and the Dutch were drawn at the outset to the concept of larger-scale sectional charts showing more hydrographical information, and printed from engraved plates to allow unlimited access by all mariners. In the sixteenth century Dutch sailors had already printed written sailing directions called *leeskarte*, which resembled the *portolani* of the Mediterranean, and the step was now taken of transferring these into visual form as coastal maps. The publication of Lucas Janszoon Waghenaer's atlas *Spieghel der Zeevaert* ('Mirror of Navigation') in 1584 opened a new era in the history of the sea-chart. It contained 44 charts of European waters, extending from the eastern Baltic to the Straits of Gibraltar. They are coastal charts, and their role in pilotage is complemented by the inclusion of detailed sailing directions for each region, and profile-views of coastlines. They display a compass and sixteen lines of direction, but omit the network of rhumb-lines, which were relevant to passages across open sea rather than coasting. The Waghenaer charts are the first to show soundings, measured in fathoms and reduced to mean half-tide values. Another innovation was the use of a range of conventional signs to represent anchorages, landmarks, rocks and shoal water. All these features combined to create a novel and

WEST AFRICA, 1596, by Linschoten. Through his book *Itinerario*, Jan Huygen van Linschoten stimulated Dutch interest in the East Indies, which led eventually to their takeover of the Portuguese bases. In the book Linschoten included a series of maps to illustrate the sea-routes to the East. Ascension Island and St Helena were important maritime bases, the West African coast itself being notoriously inhospitable and fever-ridden.

The British Library, Maps 64640(4).

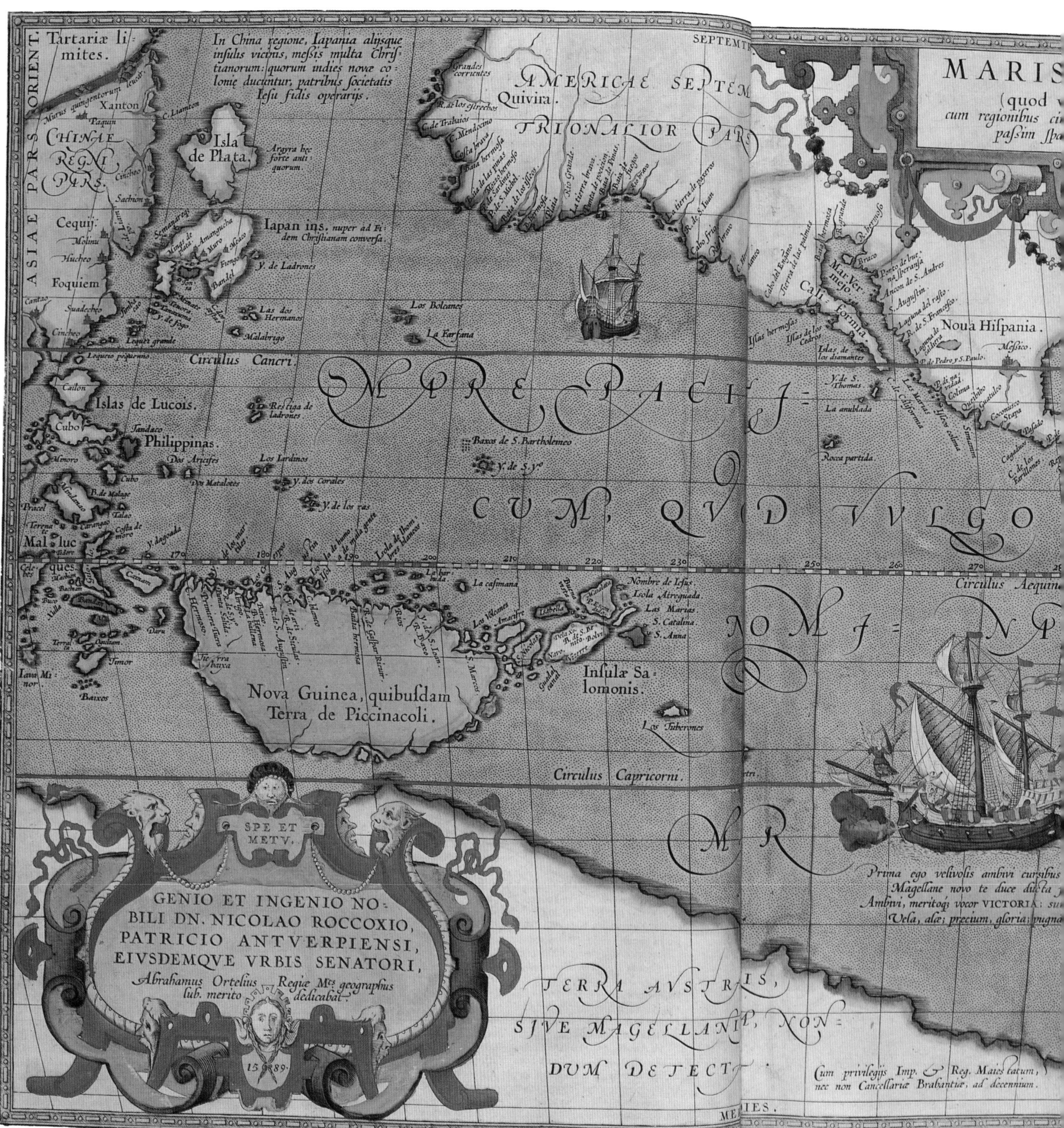

Tartariæ limites.
ASIAE PARS ORIENT.
In China regione, Iapania alijsque insulis vicinis, messis multa Christianorum: quorum indies novæ coloniæ ducuntur, patribus societatis Iesu fidis operarijs.
CHINAE REGNI PARS.
Isla de Plata.
Iapan ins. nuper ad Fidem Christianam conversa.
AMERICAE SEPTEMTRIONALIOR PARS
Quivira.
SEPTEMTR
MARIS
(quod
cum regionibus
passim
Noua Hispania.
Los Bolcanes
La Farfana
Circulus Cancri.
Islas de Lucois.
Philippinas.
MARE PACIFICUM, QUOD VULGO
Circulus Aequin
NOMINA
Nova Guinea, quibusdam Terra de Piccinacoli.
Insulæ Salomonis.
Circulus Capricorni.
SPE ET METV.
GENIO ET INGENIO NOBILI DN. NICOLAO ROCCOXIO, PATRICIO ANTVERPIENSI, EIVSDEMQVE VRBIS SENATORI,
Abrahamus Ortelius Regiæ Mtis geographus lub. merito dedicabat.
1589.
TERRA AVSTRALIS, SIVE MAGELLANICA, NONDUM DETECTA.
Prima ego velivolis ambivi cursibus
Magellane novo te duce ducta
Ambivi, meritoq; vocor VICTORIA:
Vela, alæ; precium, gloria; pugna
Cum privilegijs Imp. & Reg. Maiestatum, nec non Cancellariæ Brabantiæ, ad decennium.
MERIDIES.

THE PACIFIC OCEAN, 1589, by Ortelius. The earliest printed map of the Pacific is dominated by the picture of Magellan's ship, the *Victoria*, guided by an angel, its guns blazing. The sixty years that followed Magellan's historic voyage had done little to unravel the mysteries of the Pacific. A great southern continent existed in the European imagination, but Australia itself was still unsighted. The Spanish crossed the northern Pacific regularly from Mexico to the Philippines, carrying gold in exchange for spices and silk. On these voyages, many islands were touched, wrongly charted, lost and re-found, so that their identification is now all but impossible.

The British Library, C.23.e.12 (6).

TITLE PAGE of volume II of de Hooghe's Maritime Atlas published in Amsterdam by Mortier.

The British Library, Maps 147.d.26(2).

practical working chart, indeed the measurement of depth against position in coastal waters came to be seen as the fundamental mark of the hydrographic chart. The imagery of the Waghenaer charts – full-sailed ships dwarfed by spouting whales – is distinctive and immediately recognizable; it descends from the *Carta Marina* via Ortelius, and it gives these charts a strongly traditional maritime character. Yet despite their virtues the Waghenaer charts have some distinct oddities as geographical documents. There is no indication of latitude and longitude, so that once again the problem of projection is ignored. Since each covers a coastal strip, this is excusable, although it shows that one hundred years after the Ptolemaic maps revived the concept of coordinates, sailors were still ignoring them. More serious perhaps is that, although a scale bar is given, the charts depart wilfully from scale in the way they treat coastal topography. Important features such as bays, harbours and estuaries are clearly enlarged while stretches of plain coast are compressed. The whole effect is panoramic, and the Waghenaer chart is undoubtedly closer to a visual portrayal of an area than it is to a measured survey. No doubt this was deliberate in order to give the pilot more information on important features, but the effect can be highly distorting, and some of the coasts outside the Netherlands itself are simply unrecognizable.

Nevertheless Waghenaer's work was a huge success, and versions appeared in English, Latin and French to satisfy international demand. The term 'Waggoner' entered the English language to describe a collection of sea-charts. Its influence was felt among some manuscript chartmakers, who began to show depth soundings on their charts. Waghenaer stopped at the Straits of Gibraltar, but a similar chart atlas covering the Mediterranean was published in 1595 by Willem Barents, who was later to achieve fame for his attempts on the North-East passage. He died on his third attempt to round Novaya Zemla in 1597, his name being perpetuated in the Barents Sea.

The spectacular rise of Dutch maritime activity prompted other publishers to enter the field of sea-charts. In 1608 Willem Blaeu published his *Licht der Zeevaart* ('Light of Navigation'), containing forty-two charts of northern and western European waters.

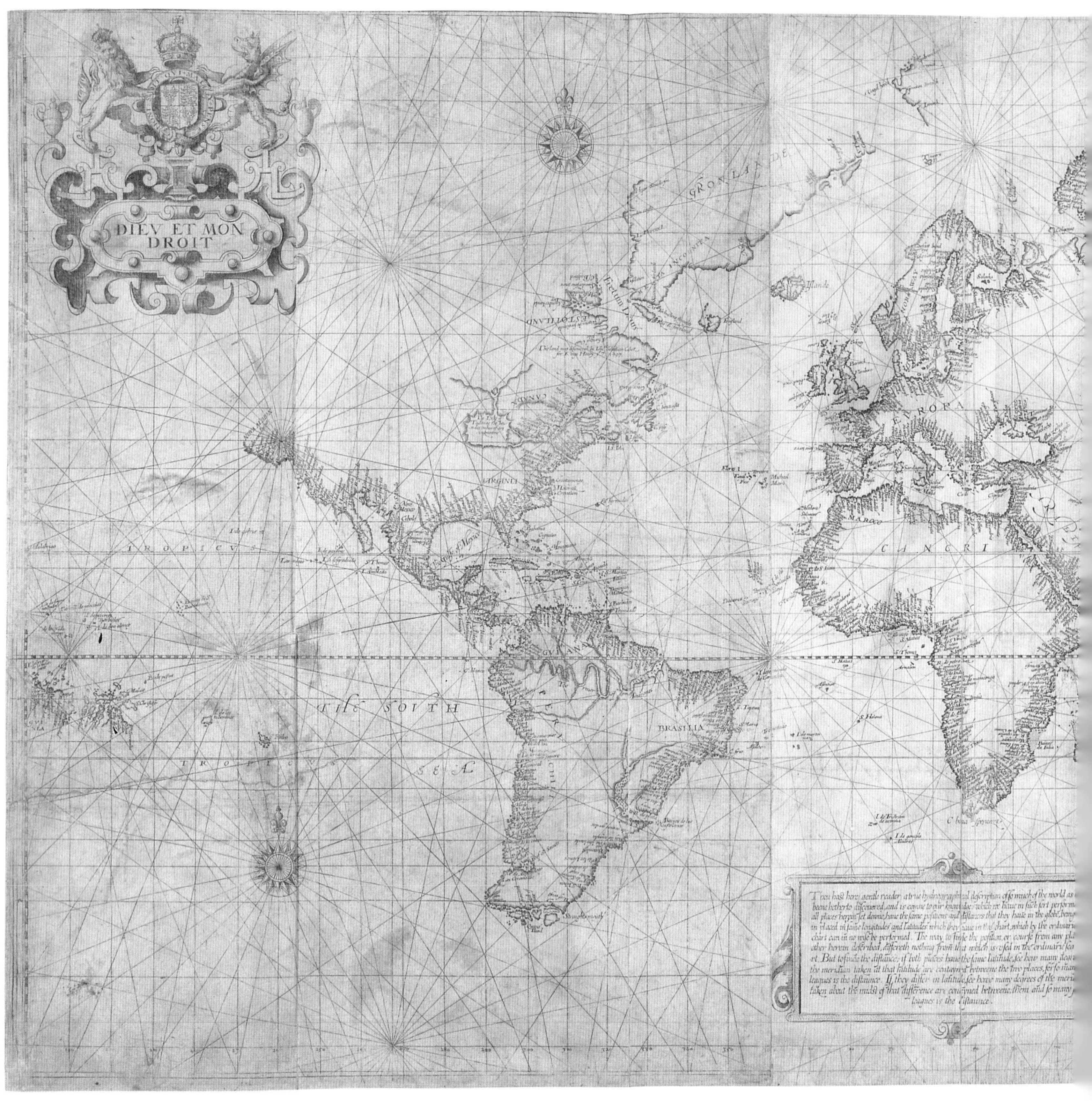

DIEV ET MON DROIT
GRONLANDE
ESTOTILAND
Fretum Davis
Islande
CANADA
VIRGINIA
EVROPA
MAROCO
TROPICVS
CANCRI
Gulfe of Mexico
GVYANA
THE SOVTH
SEA
BRASILIA
PERV
CHILI
TROPICVS
Tou hast here, gentle reader, a true hydrographical description of so much of the world as
beene hetherto discouered, and is come to our knowledge: which we haue in such sort performe
all places herein set downe, haue the same positions and distances that they haue in the globe, being
in placed in same longitudes and latitudes which they haue in this chart, which by the ordinarie
chart can in no wise be performed. The way to finde the position, or course from any pla
other herein described, differeth nothing from that which is used in the ordinarie sea
rt. But to finde the distance; if both places haue the same latitude, see how many degr
the meridian taken at that latitude are contayned betweene the two places, for so man
leagues is the distaunce. If they differ in latitude, see howe many degrees of the meri
taken about the midst of that difference are conteyned betweene them and so many
leagues is the distaunce.

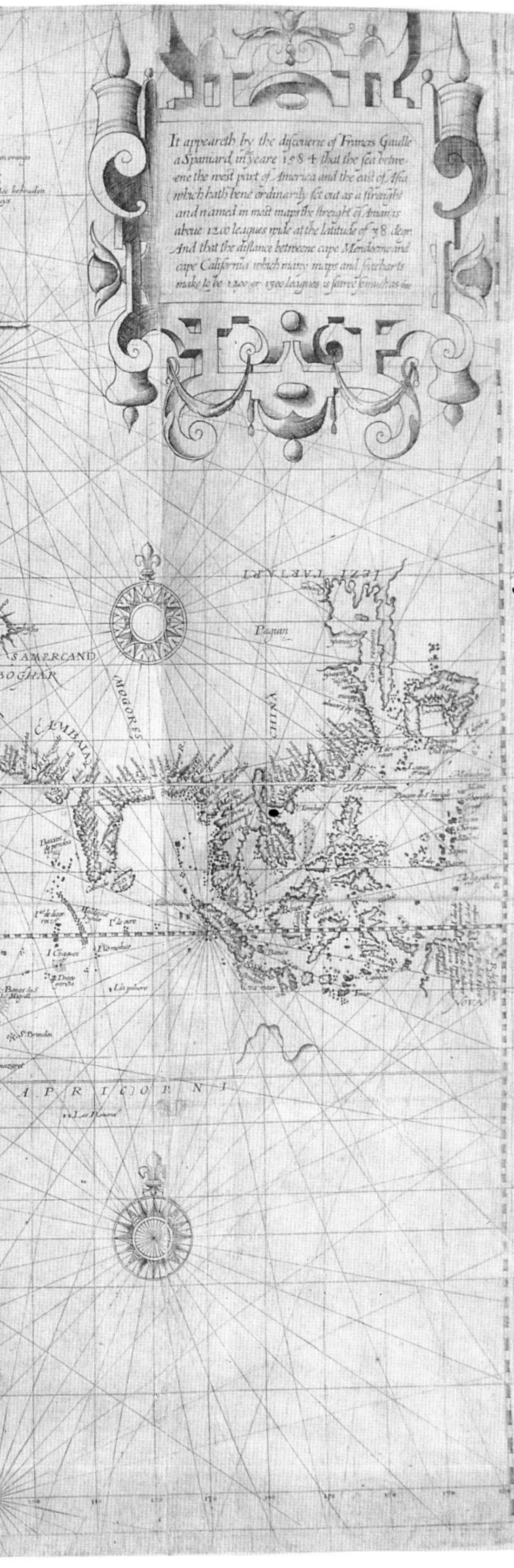

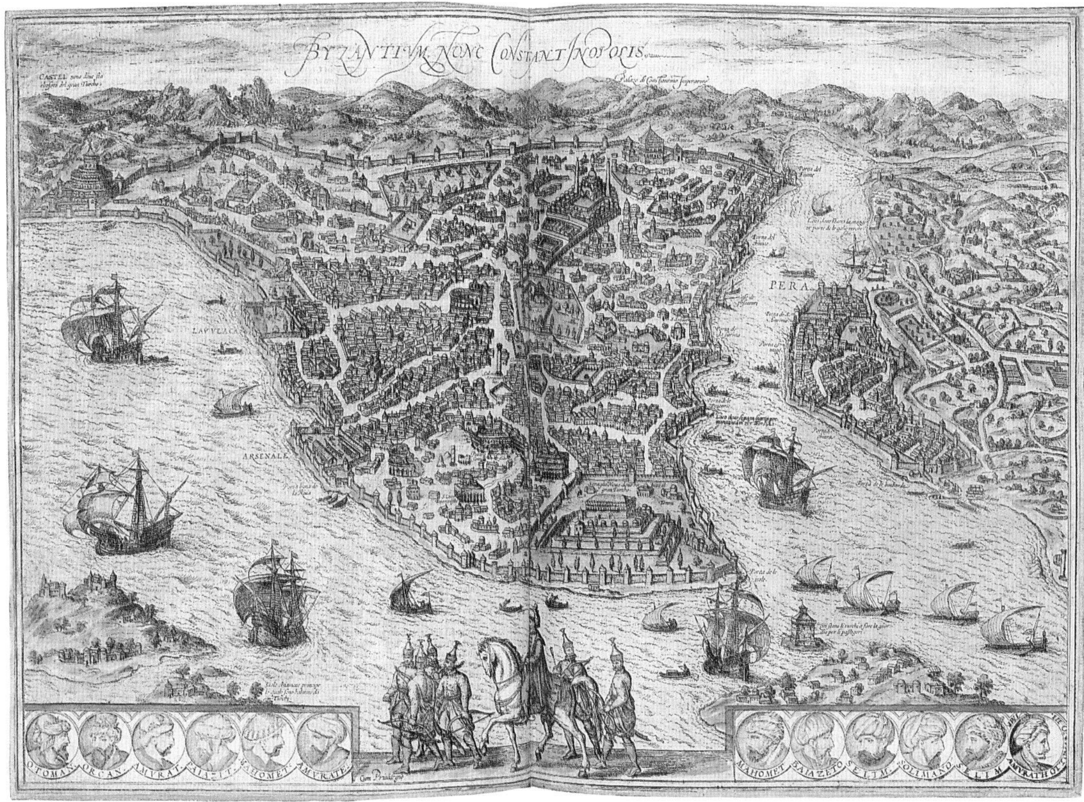

MERCATOR WORLD CHART, 1599. Although it is strictly impossible to represent latitude and longitude accurately on a flat map, there are some ways of doing so that are more useful to a seaman than others. On the Mercator chart, a straight line on the map is a line of constant bearing which the navigator can follow throughout his voyage. It is not a line of true direction, and will often lengthen a voyage slightly, but it is highly practical for the navigator. Mercator introduced the concept with his world map of 1569, but it was not widely understood by mariners. This version, by the English mathematician Thomas Wright, accompanied a treatise on navigation, and helped to popularize it.
The British Library, C.212.d.2.

CONSTANTINOPLE, 1572, by Braun and Hogenberg. From a vast collection of urban maps drawn in the style of panoramic views. They are especially evocative of the great maritime cities such as Genoa, Venice, Constantinople and Amsterdam, showing their harbours and approaches crowded with shipping, their fortifications and lighthouses.
The British Library, Maps C.29.e.1.

Although owing a great debt to Waghenaer, Blaeu improved considerably on his model. The coastlines are more accurate and he abandons Waghenaer's method of enlarging ports and harbours. The rhumb-lines are restored and a latitude bar appears, although not longitude. The atlas included sailing directions and coastal views, and the whole was prefaced by an essay on current methods of navigation. The 'Light of Navigation' was swiftly translated into English and French, and Blaeu's pre-eminence was recognized by his appointment as Hydrographer to the Dutch East India Company, in which post he was succeeded by his son Joan.

We have no precise knowledge of how Blaeu improved the hydrographic standard of these charts, how he gathered and edited his data. He must have commissioned mariners to make running coastal surveys, and to correct the Waghenaers which they were using.

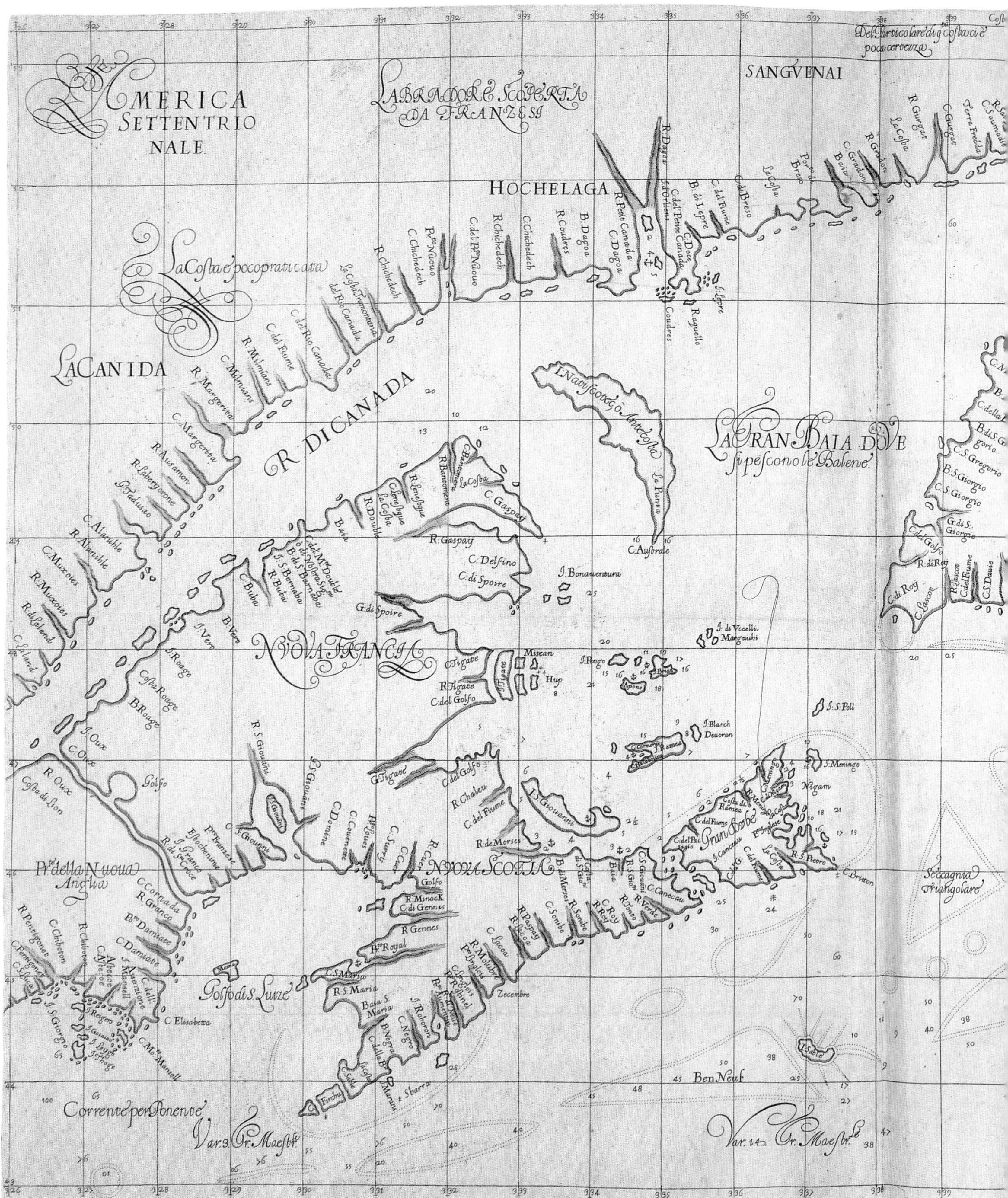
America Settentrionale
Labradore Scoperta da Franzesi
Sanguenai
Hochelaga
La Costa è poco praticata
La Canida
R. di Canada
La Gran Baia dove si pescono le Balene
Nuova Francia
Nuova Scotia
Pr. della Nuoua Anglia
Golfo di S. Luize
Corrente per Ponente
Ben Neuf
Var. 3 Gr. Maestr.
Var. 14 Gr. Maestr.

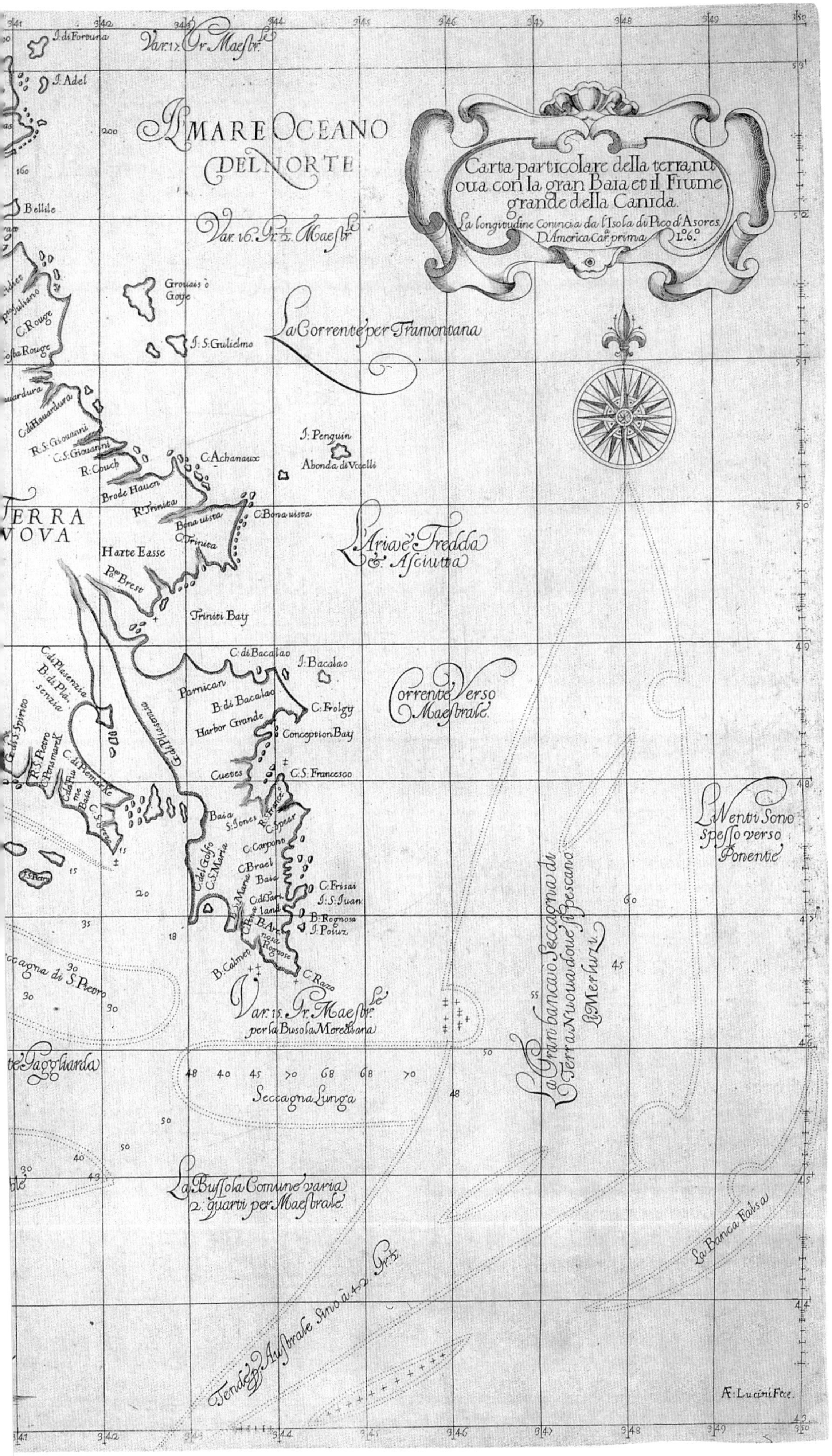

ROBERT DUDLEYS illustration of the use of the quadrant.

The British Library, Maps C.8.d.9(1).

THE NORTH-WEST ATLANTIC, 1661, by Robert Dudley. Dudley was an English exile living in Florence who produced *Dell'Arcano del Mare*, an innovative atlas of printed sea-charts consisting of almost 130 maps giving worldwide coverage. Dudley was an experienced mariner who spent almost two decades collating hydrographic information from Spanish, French and Dutch sources, which he replotted on Mercator's projection. The general level of geographical accuracy on this chart is good, and there is an array of notes on shoals, fishing-grounds, reefs and compass variations.

The British Library, Maps C.8.d.9.

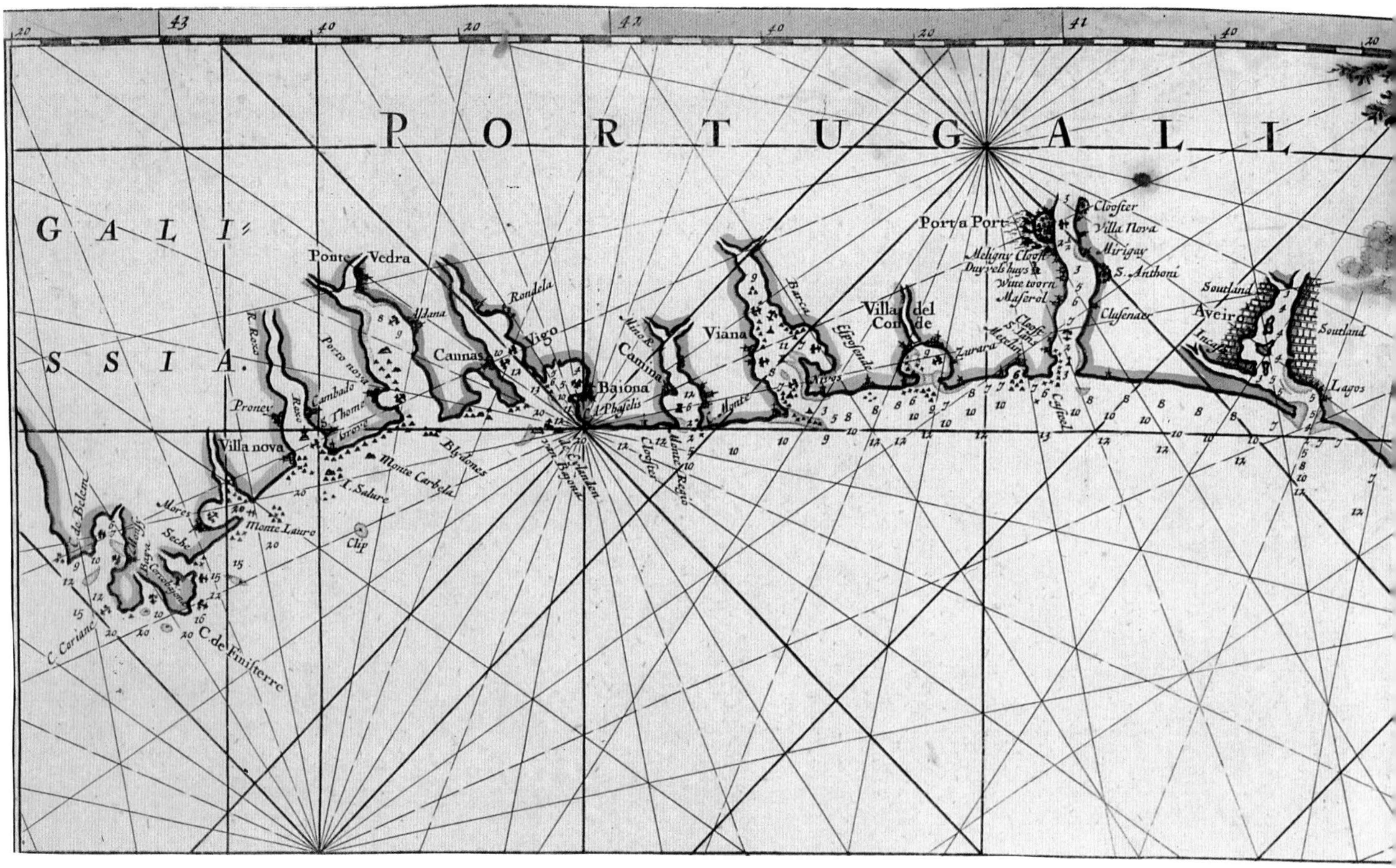

THE ATLANTIC COAST OF PORTUGAL from Van Keulen's 1682 Atlas.

The British Library, Maps 7 TAB 126.

DUTCH SHIPS OF ABOUT 1660, by Van der Velde.

National Maritime Museum, Greenwich.

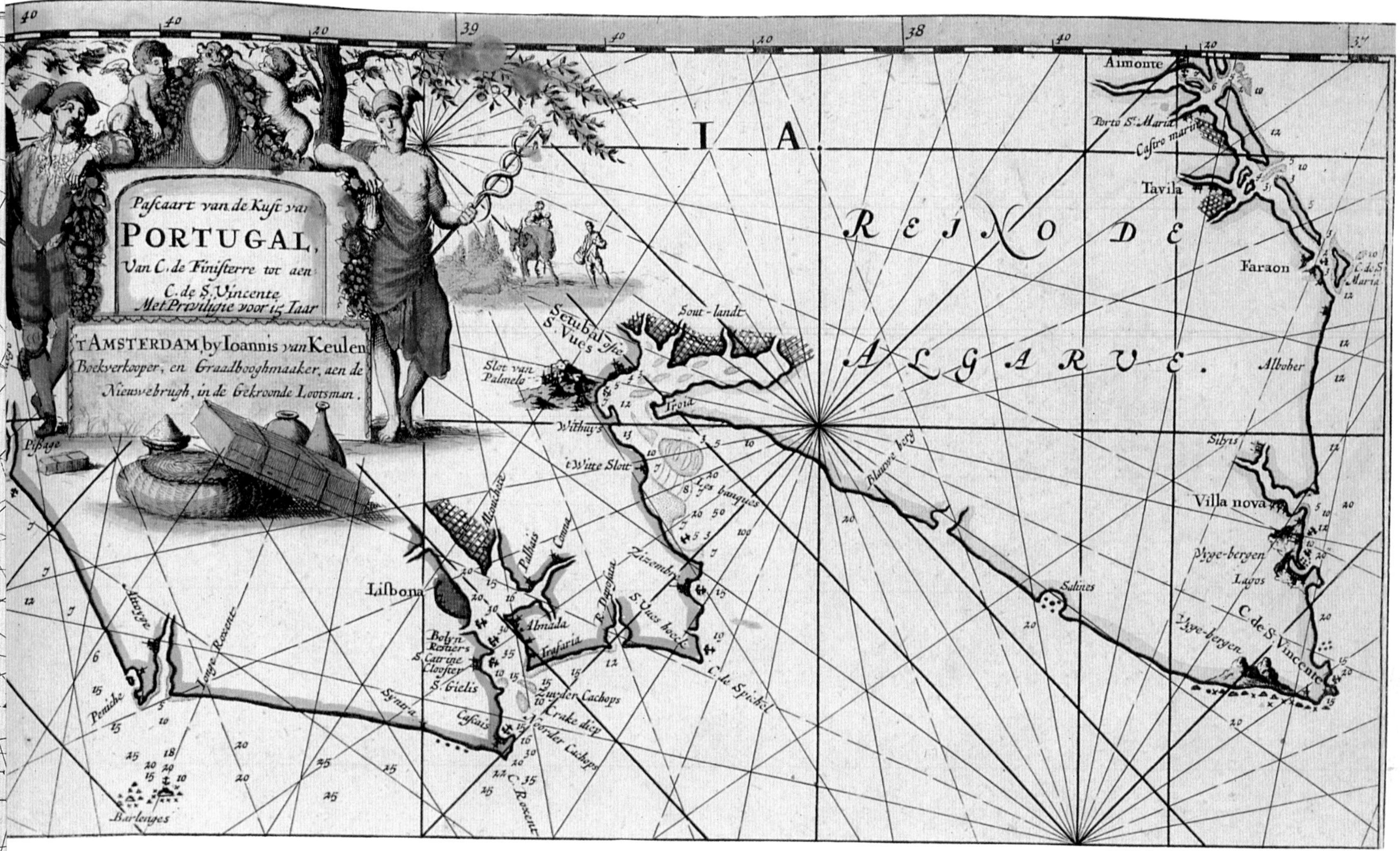

The union of the Spanish and Portuguese crowns in 1580 made Portugal's seaborne empire a tempting target. 1595 was a pivotal year in maritime history, for it saw the first Dutch fleet sail for the East Indies via the Cape under Cornelius Houtman. His trading voyage to Java was eminently successful and a few years later, in 1602, the Dutch East India Company was formed, which was to act as the vehicle of Dutch dominance in the East Indies trade for the rest of the century, a trade they ruthlessly seized from the weakened Portuguese. Incidentally, it was on this voyage that the navigator Pieter Diercx Keyser systematically surveyed the southern heavens and designated twelve new constellations in order to chart the southern sky, constellations designed after exotic animals – the toucan, peacock, flying fish, and so on.

By 1600 the power of the Dutch fleet was such that they were able to loot Spanish settlements in the Canaries and the Caribbean, and defeated the Spanish in a full naval action off the coast of Spain itself. Over the next half century the Dutch strengthened their grip on the eastern trade, taking Portuguese bases or establishing new ones in Java, Timor, the Moluccas, Mauritius, Bengal, and Japan. In these voyages, the Dutch discovered the strong westerly winds between 40 and 50 degrees south, which later became known as the Roaring Forties, and having passed the Cape they would sail some two thousand miles before these winds before turning north to Java. It was on these voyages that the first landfalls in Australia were made, and maps from 1620 onwards begin to show sections of the western and northern coasts, fading into uncharted sea. Dutch success in Brazil and the West Indies was limited, and their frequent attempts to oust the Spanish from Manila were all defeated. The expeditions of Mendaña, Quiros and Torres in the south-western Pacific between 1595 and 1605 represented the last Spanish attempts

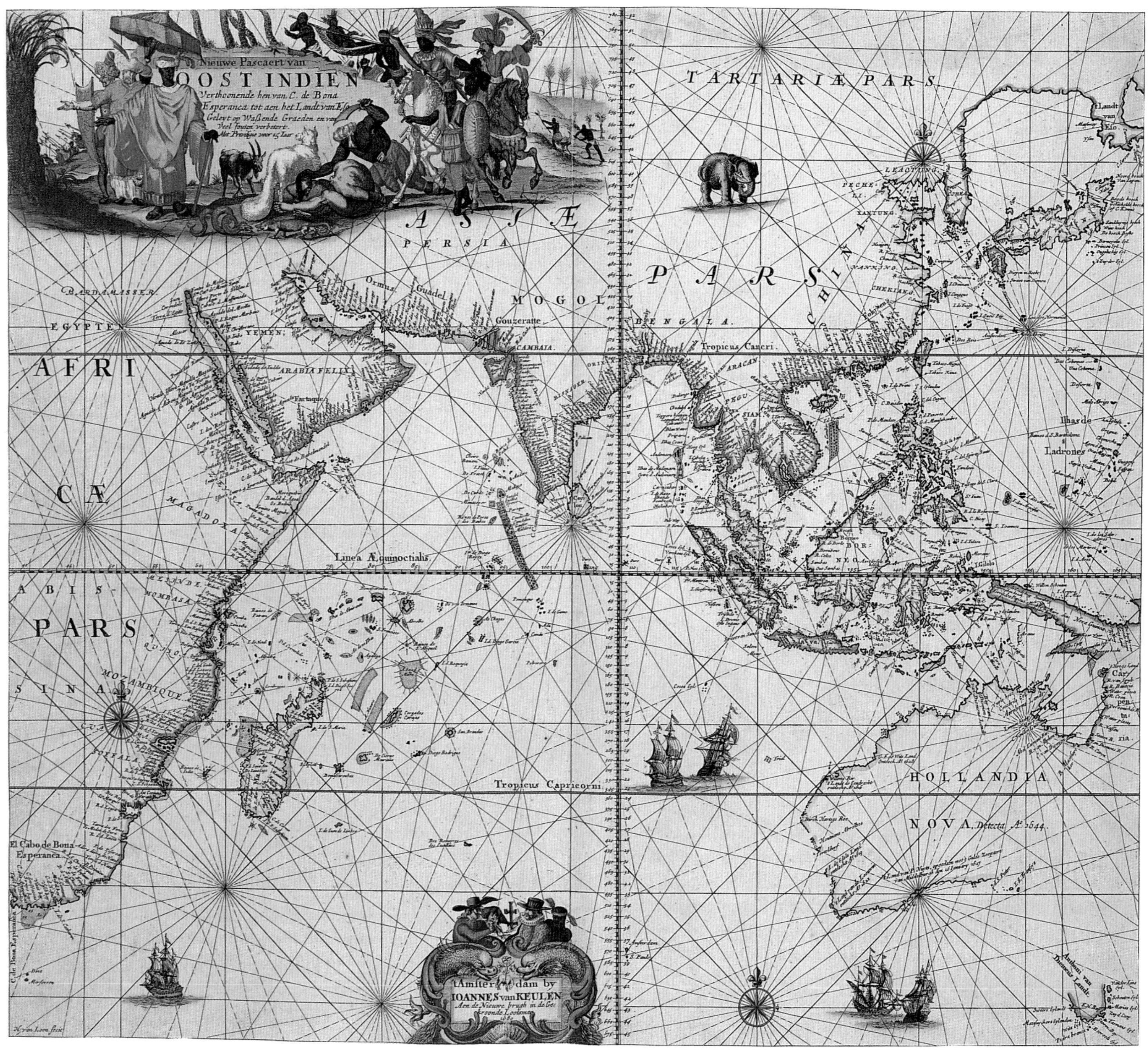

THE INDIAN OCEAN, 1682, by van Keulen. When the Dutch sailed east from the Cape to the spice islands they discovered the 'Roaring Forties', and they learned to run before them for some 2,000 miles before turning north to Java. In this way they sighted and mapped the western coasts of Australia, which had eluded the Portuguese through nearly a century of sailing in the East Indies. The continent's eastern and southern coasts remained unexplored until Cook in the 1770s.

The British Library, Maps 7 TAB 126.

FORT WILLIAM, CALCUTTA, by Lambert and Scott, 1731, with a number of East Indiamen in the foreground, firing salutes.

The British Library, 010C.

And search all corners of the new-found world
For pleasant fruits and princely delicates . . .
From Venice they shall drag huge Argosies,
And from America the golden fleece
That yearly stuffs old Philip's treasury . . .

The clearest expression of this ruthless sense of European superiority was of course the slave trade, which formed a large part of merchant shipping from 1500 to 1800. The encounter with the peoples of America and Africa produced a strange ambiguity in the European mind which polarized between slavers and missionaries – the callous brutality of the one and the religious compassion of the other. It would take three centuries or more to settle the irreconcilable tension between these two.

After the initial phase of overseas adventure, Europeans, especially the English, turned to the more permanent aim of settled colonies, although it is true much of England's overseas empire was taken from her European rivals. England's confrontations with Holland throughout the seventeenth century, and more especially with France in the eighteenth, resulted in the first global wars, where the battlefield was not primarily in Europe but in the Atlantic and Indian Oceans. England was often humiliated – most famously in 1667 when de Ruyter sailed up the Thames to within a dozen miles of London and captured royal ships. But England succeeded in most of the major encounters, so that the three Anglo-Dutch wars between 1650 and 1675 fatally weakened the Dutch navy, leaving England dominant to face her new maritime rival, France. The most famous prize which the English and Dutch fought over was of course New York. Settled by Dutch as early as 1614, the town developed steadily as New Amsterdam until it became a casualty of the second Anglo-Dutch war, and was captured by the English in 1664 and renamed New York. In 1673 during the third Dutch war, a surprise invasion restored Dutch rule

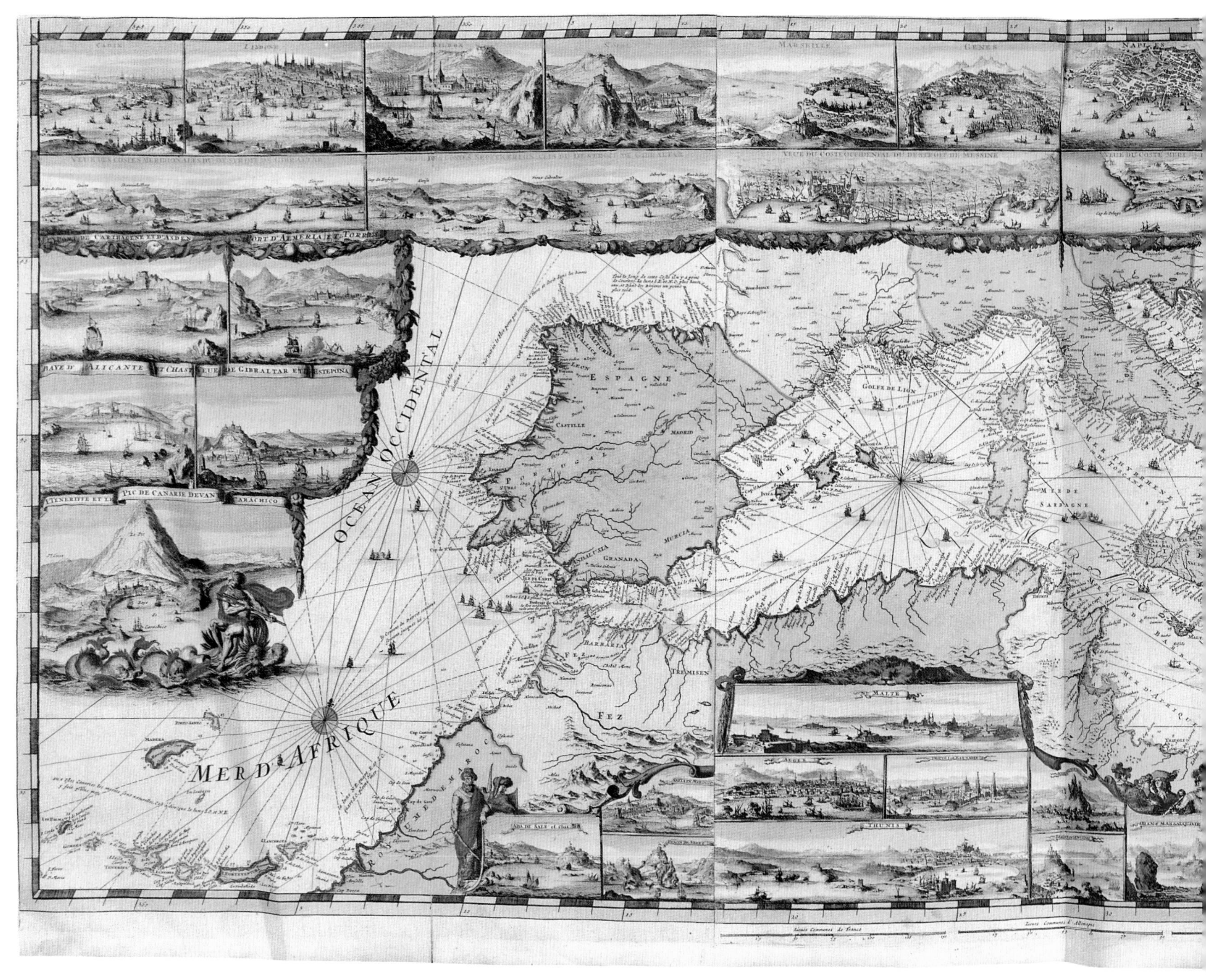
CADIX
LISBONE
MARSEILLE
GENES
OCEAN OCCIDENTAL
MER D'AFRIQUE
ESPAGNE
CASTILLE
MADRID
ANDALUZIA
GRANADA
MURCIA
BARBARIA
FEZ
TREMISEN
GOLFE DE LION
MER DE SARDAGNE
MALTE
THUNIS
ALGER
MADERA
PIC DE CANARIE DEVANT
BAYE D' ALICANTE

THE MEDITERRANEAN, 1694, by Romein de Hooghe. A spectacular display of de Hooghe's outstanding artistry, this chart is surrounded by views of 38 Mediterranean ports and harbours, from Tenerife to Constantinople. Such maps were clearly designed for the library or the salon, rather than for use at sea.

The British Library, Maps 146.d.26.

To THE Right Honᵇˡᵉ IAMES EARLE of PERTH Lord Chancellor of the KINGDOM of SCOTLAND. This Chart is humbly dedicated by Capᵗ Greenvile Collins HYDROGRAPHER to the KING.
A Scale of 5 English Miles.
I. Collins sc.
Latitude
EDINBURGH
Aden
S. Andrews
Largo Law
Johnson
Largo
Leuins Mouth
Methule Haven
Buck Haven
East Wemis
Castle Wemis
West Wemis
Disert
Kirkaldy
Links
Seafeild
Kinghorne
Kinghornnesse
Kincraig
Ely
Ely Castle
Kingcraig Nesse
Vows
Sachar
Dumfermling
Inverkithing
Rosaith
Dunibrisall
Dalgaty
Abirdoor
Bin
Burnt Island
Colum
Ocksters
Muckeriestone
Muckrie
Keith
Brigs
Craig Wasse
St. Margrets Hope
Nᵒ Ferry
Garuic
Hound
Barnbughall
Cramond I.
Grantoun
Becon
Queens Ferry
Munch-hill
Cramond
Royston
Lieth
Castle
Abby
Park
EDINBURGH
Mallinton
Fysherraw
Newhaven
Mussilbrugh
Preston
Cokeny
Seaton
Fyrynesse
Goosford
Abirlady
Lovennesse
Rain
Gullennesse
Gullen-hill
Dirlentoun
Old Battle
North Berwickla
Ibris
Fidra
Lam
St. Tabs He

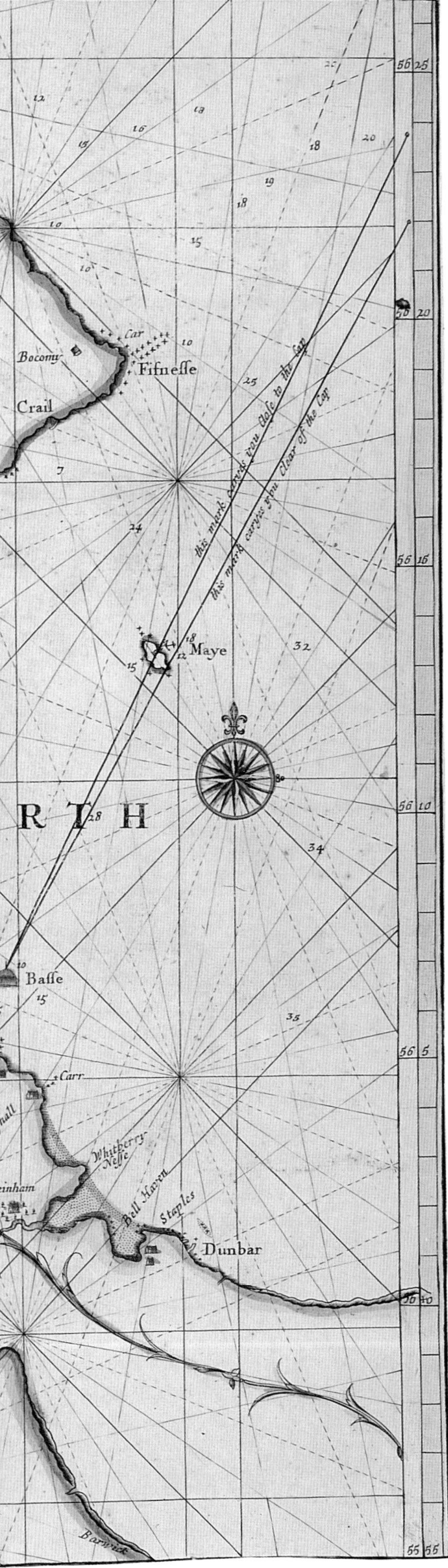

THE FIRTH OF FORTH, 1689, by Greenvile Collins. The first British charts of British waters were published only towards the end of the 17th century, drawn from original surveys commissioned by the Admiralty. Before this date the British Navy and the merchant fleet were dependent on Dutch charts. Collins' charts were a major advance, but they lacked a clear scientific basis: they show no latitude or longitude, and were not tied to any true topographic survey. The 47 charts covered all but the western coasts of Scotland and Ireland. Despite their shortcomings they remained in use until the late 18th century.

The British Library, Maps C.8.d.7.

AN EIGHTEENTH-CENTURY East Indiaman by Peter Monamy, date 1720.

National Maritime Museum, Greenwich.

and the new name 'New Orange' (after the Prince of Orange). Finally in the following year it was returned to the English as part of the peace settlement, and became irrevocably New York. We are fortunate in possessing the diary of Samuel Pepys, a unique and vivid account of these years which were of crucial importance in the development of the British navy. As Clerk of the Navy Board, Pepys recorded the frustrations and disasters that attended the creation of professional navy. Through Pepys we learn that the Dutch humiliation of the English in 1667 was caused by the premature laying up of the fleet while peace negotiations were still in progress, and that the *Royal Charles* was lying quite unguarded when she was taken by a single Dutch boat. When the Navy Board was blamed for the catastrophe, Pepys addressed an eloquent defence to Parliament. It was due largely to Pepys's work after the conclusion of hostilities with the Dutch that the navy was rebuilt and that the office of Lord High Admiral was turned into a successful department of government. Unnoticed by England, another overseas power was developing its maritime strength in this period, namely the American colonies themselves. The shipbuilders of Massachusetts had built and launched around one thousand ships by the end of the seventeenth century, and the colonists' trading activities were sowing the seeds of future conflict with the mother country.

It was during these years that the Dutch found a visual language in which to express their vital relationship to the sea – in the art of maritime painting. Reaching its height in the works of the two Van de Veldes, father and son, this art form took as its subject not the sea itself, which would be a later Romantic development, but the ships which sailed it, ships fighting each other and fighting the elements. Ironically much of their best work was executed in England as court painters to Charles II, and the sea-picture became the province of a school of English imitators: Monamy, Brooking and Scott. The work of this school has preserved for us both a technical record of the ships of this era, and a poetic statement of the seafaring tradition that linked the two North European maritime nations.

Holland was pre-eminent in shaping the other great seafaring record of the seventeenth century, the published sea-chart. The Waghenaer-Blaeu tradition of European coastal charts was overtaken by events, and the need for worldwide charting became evident by the 1620s. The Dutch East India Company maintained a hydrographer whose

A General Map of this following Spanish Manuscript described by William Hack Anno Dni 1685
Acapulco
Nicoya
Popayan
Cocoa Island
Æqui noc ti alis
Isles of Gillappagos
Mar del Zur
Peru
Puño
Potosy
Plata
Tro pi cus capri corni
Sharpes track
Coquimbo
Chili
The Straights of Magellan
Terra del Fogo
This Scale Containeth four hundred English Leagues

SOUTH AMERICA, 1685, by William Hack. In 1682 a Spanish book of sailing directions for the Pacific coast of South America was captured by an English pirate, Bartholomew Sharpe, and brought to England. Its importance was quickly recognized, for only the Spanish possessed detailed charts of this huge area. The production of sea-charts in England was still in the hands of manuscript artists, and William Hack was charged with making multiple copies of the original. This was one of the final chapters in the history of manuscript charts, for a few years later England's chartmakers belatedly made the transition to printing.
National Maritime Museum, Greenwich.

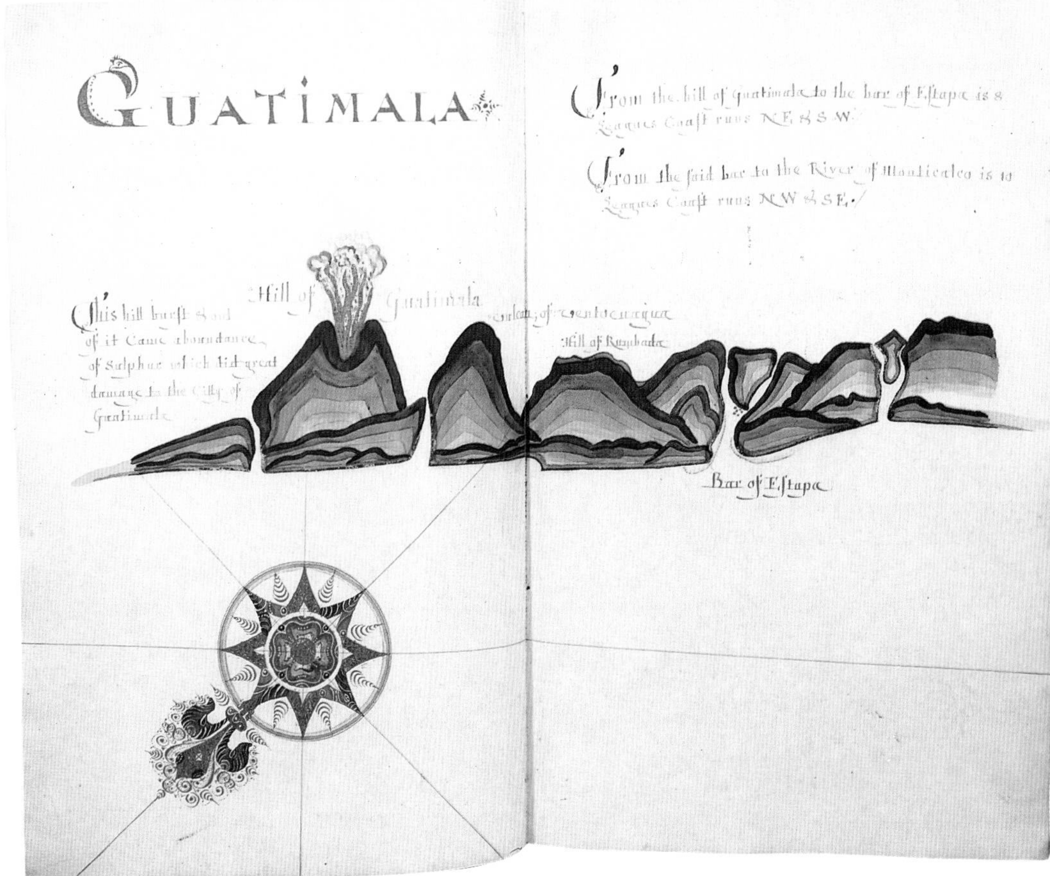

GUATEMALA, 1685, by William Hack.
National Maritime Museum, Greenwich.

function was to collate all incoming information from Dutch mariners and update the chart record. From this archive of manuscript surveys and sketches, the hydrographer edited and published charts for commercial sale. No comparable arrangement existed in any other country. The manuscript archive was at first held to be a secret and valuable asset, but the demands of navigation steadily narrowed the gap between what was secret and what was published, and by 1750 all available hydrographic data was being published. In addition to this official hydrographer, there was vigorous competition among the many commercial map publishers to secure the market by publishing the most comprehensive and accurate chart-atlases. This process reached its culmination in the charts of the van Keulen dynasty, whose atlas *Zee-Fakkel* ('Sea Torch') first appeared in 1681 and grew in edition after edition to comprise almost 400 charts covering all the oceans and seas of the known world. Almost all the van Keulen charts employed the Mercator projection, whose value was now being recognized by enlightened mariners. By the mid-eighteenth century even the makers of Spanish manuscript charts active in Mexico and the Caribbean were drawing their charts correctly plotted on the Mercator principle. Publishing practice in the seventeenth century meant that map publishers copied each other's work ruthlessly, and of the large number of chart collections, relatively few were drawn from original surveys. In each era there was generally one authoritative chart-maker who created the models which others copied, and from 1680 to 1750 van Keulen was that one, his atlases containing a preponderance of detailed, large-scale charts of bays and harbour approaches. The clearest example of slavish copying is the famous myth that California was an island. California had been correctly drawn on sixteenth-century charts, but in 1625 Henry Briggs produced a map to accompany Purchas's book of voyages showing the region with the

THE VENETIAN DOGE'S STATE GALLEY – *Bucentaur*. From Mortier's sea atlas of 1693.
The British Library, Maps 147.d.26.

comment 'California sometymes supposed to be a part of ye westerne continent, but since . . . found to be a goodly Ilande.' The mythical island appeared in virtually all maps until the early eighteenth century.

The situation of chartmaking in England at this time was curious. There was no official chartmaking sponsored by the Admiralty, and the leading map publishers such as John Seller were content to make direct reprints from Dutch charts, so that the charts of English waters used by English mariners in the Dutch wars were Dutch. At the same time a school of manuscript chartmakers grew up and flourished in London's dockland for almost a century from around 1600 to the 1690s. This school sprang up in response to English colonial activities, and their work embodied the geographical reports of mariners returning to the capital. The vellum charts produced by this school were undoubtedly more durable than paper ones, and English mariners and merchants still felt apparently that a chart must be a personal, hand-made artefact produced with professional skill and knowledge. However many of these chartmakers were really trained copyists who had no personal experience of navigation, and who merely reproduced the data with which mariners supplied them. These are latitude charts in the traditional style, colourfully if rather crudely drawn, and included both small-scale ocean charts and large-scale coastal charts copied from original surveys. The London chartmakers known to us by name include John Burston, Nicholas Comberford and Joel Gascoyne, and their work has a strong mutual resemblance and house style. All three are mentioned by Samuel Pepys in his diary, who tells us that Comberford's 'manner of working is very fine and laborious', but he was speaking purely of his graphic skill as a copyist. In 1680 an important collection of Spanish sailing directions for the Pacific coast of South America was taken at sea and

NEW YORK, 1664. This anonymous plan is entitled 'A description of the town of Mannados or New Amsterdam as it was in September 1661'. We may conjecture therefore that it is an English copy of a Dutch map, made soon after the English took the town in September 1664. This would explain the enigmatic title and the presence of the English ships. Not technically a sea-chart, it is a lively picture of a newly-captured, strategic harbour. This map was presented to the Duke of York, the future King James II, for whom the town was renamed.
The British Library, K.Top.121.f.35.

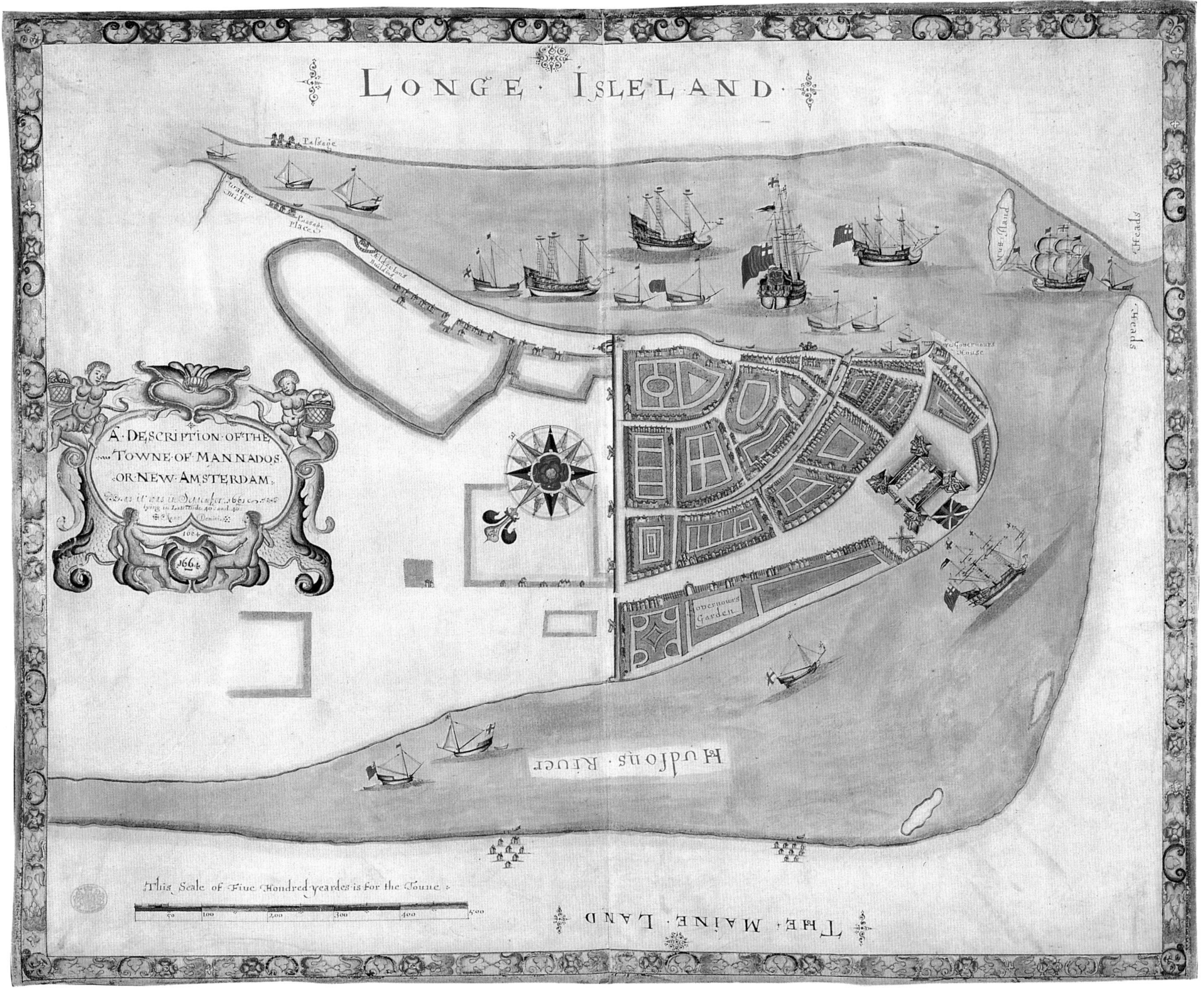

brought to London, and even at that late date it was decided to make this information available by hand-copying. William Hack produced probably several dozen copies of the 'South Sea Waggoner' – at least fourteen surviving copies are known. The transition to printing came very late and very suddenly: in 1685 John Thornton, who had been an apprentice chartmaker to Comberford, published an *Atlas Maritimus* consisting of 58 printed charts, and virtually killed the English hand-drawn chart tradition. By this date it was becoming clear to those involved in English seafaring that British charting was hopelessly anachronistic, relying on copied Dutch charts and on hand-copying; indeed Pepys wrote that 'Our sea coasts were better laid down by Speed (*i.e.* John Speed, whose maps were made eighty years earlier) than in our Waggoners'. In 1681 the Admiralty

AMERICÆ SEPTENTRIONALIS PARS
Gedruckt t'AMSTERDAM Bij PIETER GOOS Op 't Water inde Vergulde Zee Spiegel
NOVA FRANCIA
TERRA NEUF
VIRGINIA
FLORIDA
Tropicus Cancri
HONDURAS
NICARAGUA
PARIA
NUEVA ANDALUZIA
GUAIANA
AMERICÆ MERIDIONALIS
PERU
CHILI
BRASILIA
CAP DE ST AUGUSTIN
C. S. SPIRITU SANTO
PATAGONUM REGIO
STRAET VAN MAGALAEN
Tierra del Fuego
TERRA DOS PATOS
Tropicus Capricorni
Linea Equin

THE ATLANTIC, 1635, by Pieter Goos, printed on vellum. One of the technical problems in the development of sea-charts was that maps printed on paper were ill-suited to withstand use on board ship. This partly explains the persistence of the manuscript chart drawn on vellum, which is far stronger than paper. Some Dutch publishers in the 17th century experimented with the practice of printing on vellum, but it was a much more troublesome and expensive medium than paper, and it was gradually discontinued.

The British Library, Maps STA 3.

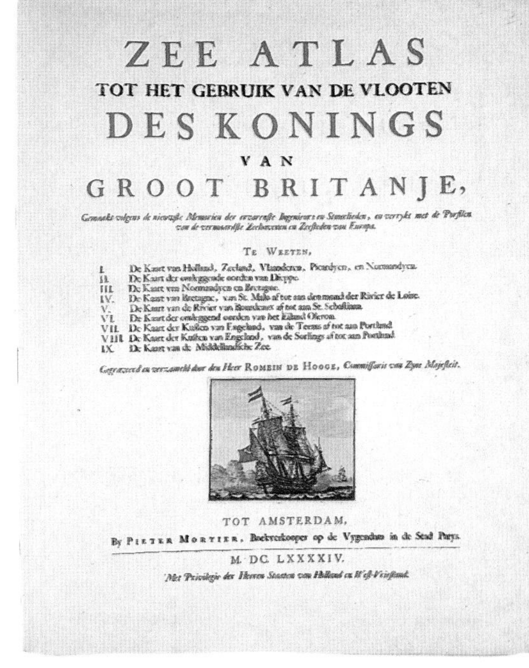

ZEE ATLAS
TOT HET GEBRUIK VAN DE VLOOTEN
DES KONINGS
VAN
GROOT BRITANJE,

Gemaakt volgens de nieuwste Memorien der ervarenste Ingenieurs en Stuurlieden, en verrykt met de Porfilen van de vermaardste Zeehavenen en Zeesteden van Europa.

TE WEETEN,

I. De Kaart van Holland, Zeeland, Vlaanderen, Picardyen, en Normandyen.
II. De Kaart der omleggende oorden van Dieppe.
III. De Kaart van Normandyen en Bretagne.
IV. De Kaart van Bretagne, van St. Malo af tot aan den mond der Rivier de Loire.
V. De Kaart van de Rivier van Bourdeaux af tot aan St. Sebastiaan.
VI. De Kaart der omleggend oorden van het Eiland Oleron.
VII. De Kaart der Kusten van Engeland, van de Teems af tot aan Portland.
VIII. De Kaart der Kusten van Engeland, van de Sorlings af tot aan Portland.
IX. De Kaart van de Middellandsche Zee.

Getekend en verzameld door den Heer ROMEIN DE HOOGE, *Commissaris van Zyne Majesteit.*

TOT AMSTERDAM,
By PIETER MORTIER, Boekverkooper op de Vygendam in de Stad Parys.
M. DC. LXXXXIV.
Met Privilegie der Heeren Staaten van Holland en West-Vriesland.

TITLE PAGE from Romien de Hooghe's Chart Atlas of the English Channel and the North Sea published by Mortier, Amsterdam 1494.

The British Library, Maps 147.d.26(2).

commissioned Captain Greenvile Collins to make the first original survey of the British coasts. More than a decade of work followed before the 48 charts of *Great Britain's Coasting Pilot* were published in 1693, a landmark in British hydrography. Eminently practical though they were, Collins's charts had little scientific basis: they are still plane charts, showing neither latitude nor longitude, and they were not tied to any system of land triangulation. There was still no British charting of international waters, for which they relied on Dutch publications.

Towards the end of the seventeenth century the political balance in Europe shifted once again and this time the ascendant power was France. Under the Sun King Louis XIV, France had experienced a renaissance that was cultural, economic and military. She had developed her overseas territories, principally in North America where she formed the grandiose aim of linking the St Lawrence Great Lakes region with the huge reaches of the Ohio-Mississippi; she rebuilt her navy until, under Duquesne, it was able to sweep the Dutch and the Spanish from the Mediterranean; she extended and secured her European frontiers; and she established a royal academy of sciences and a royal observatory in order to put science to work for political ends. All these activities set alarm-bells ringing throughout Europe and caused a re-alignment in which England, Holland, Spain and Austria now perceived France as the great threat. Throughout the eighteenth century, conflict among these nations was the signal for naval warfare in the Mediterranean and in the seas beyond Europe, as colonies and trade routes were disputed. The most momentous colonial changes occured in the Seven Years War of 1756–63, in which there were no direct hostilities between Britain and France, yet in which Britain annexed France's Canadian and Indian possessions, laying the foundations of her own empire. Britain's triumph was short-lived as she found herself unable to defend these vast territories, and the French alliance with America forced her to yield her American colonies. The story of British-French rivalry at sea would not be properly settled until the post-revolutionary period.

France had developed far more sophisticated methods of mapping and charting than her English rival. The French academy and French royal observatory had pioneered a new, theoretical approach to determining the figure of the earth, measuring an arc of

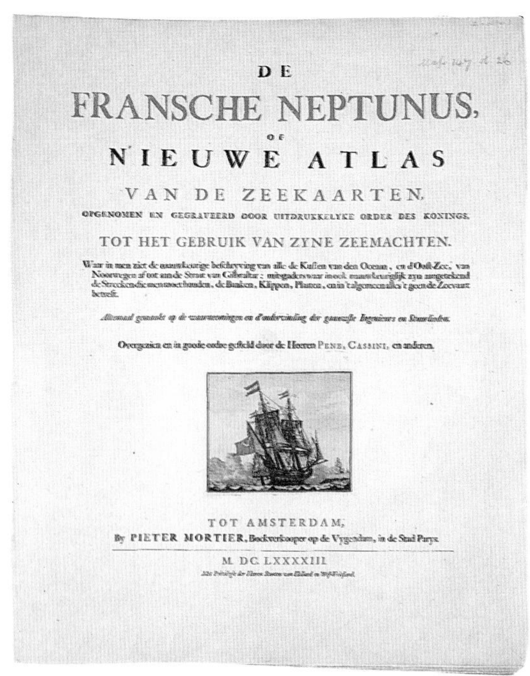

DE

FRANSCHE NEPTUNUS,

OF

NIEUWE ATLAS

VAN DE ZEEKAARTEN,

OPGENOMEN EN GEGRAVEERD DOOR UITDRUKKELYKE ORDER DES KONINGS.

TOT HET GEBRUIK VAN ZYNE ZEEMACHTEN.

Waar in men ziet de naauwkeurige beschryving van alle de Kusten van den Oceaan, en d'Oost-Zee, van Noorwegen af tot aan de Straat van Gibraltar; mitsgaders waar in ook naauwkeuriglijk zyn aangetekend de Streeken die men moet houden, de Banken, Klippen, Platen, en in 't algemeen alles 't geen de Zeevaart betreft.

Overgezien en in goede ordre gesteld door de Heeren PENE, CASSINI, en anderen.

TOT AMSTERDAM,

By PIETER MORTIER, Boekverkooper op de Vygendam, in de Stad Parys.

M. DC. LXXXXIII

PIETER MORTIER's New Chart Atlas, Amsterdam, 1593.

The British Library, Maps 147.d.26.

GREECE AND THE AEGEAN, 1668, by Frederik de Wit. De Wit's sea-charts are instantly recognizable in their contrast of the severe, functional sea area and the elaborate title cartouches. These were composed of elements relating to the region in the map; this one illustrates the conflict between Christian and Turk, while the statues lying shattered on the ground gesture towards the classical past. The index table naming small islands and capes became a common feature on charts showing complex coastlines.

The British Library, Maps C.45.f.2.(2).

longitude, planning the triangulation of the entire country, and determining longitude from the observation of Jupiter's moons. Thanks to this institutionalized science, France acquired official topographic maps and sea-charts before England. In 1693 *Le Neptune François* was published, comprising 29 accurate charts of European waters, the results of two decades of original surveys sponsored by Louis XIV's minister Jean Baptiste Colbert. The superiority of these charts to any earlier ones of western Europe was immediately recognized and the Amsterdam publisher Pierre Mortier audaciously placed on sale a complete pirated edition. In 1720 a French Hydrographic Office, the Depôt des Cartes et Plans de la Marine, was established. The *Neptune Françoise* was revised and extended under the exemplary direction of Jacques Nicholas Bellin, and a series of worldwide charts was published entitled *Hydrographie Françoise.* It is noticeable that many sea-charts of this period, especially the French charts, show a great deal of topographic detail, indeed they may be seen as dual-purpose maps.

The sea-charts of the seventeenth and eighteenth centuries, like their topographic counterparts, became both more detailed and more comprehensive in their coverage: by 1700 it was possible to consult specific charts of the Bay of Bengal, of the Caribbean Islands, of the South China Sea, and of New Guinea and Western Australia. But in order to achieve greater precision, charts needed to be tied to an objective framework of terrestrial and celestial geometry. Position could be gauged objectively by observation of the heavens, but the great difficulty was that the celestial sphere is (apparently) in constant motion about the earth. By a fortunate accident, the Pole Star provided an almost fixed point for seafarers in the northern hemisphere, so that to calculate latitude by observing this star was fairly simple. But in the southern hemisphere, and again in the vital problem of determining longitude, there were no such fixed points. The navigator must use other celestial bodies, all in motion. He therefore had recourse to tables of pre-calculated astronomical positions in order to solve problems in spherical geometry before he could translate what he saw in the sky into a position on a chart. Moreover he must have a chart that was mathematically constructed, that is the places on the chart are related to each other in a known and systematic way. Mercator had provided such a chart, and astronomical science could offer solutions to all the positioning problems which faced the

Orientalior districtus
MARIS MEDITERRANEI
Apud Fred. de Wit
t' Ooster gedeelte van de
MIDDELANDSE
ZEE
PONTUS EUXINUS
Hodie MARE NIGRUM
ROMANIA.
MACEDONIA
MARE DI MARMORA
ARCHIPELAGO
NATOLIA.
ASIÆ PARS
CARAMANIA.
MARE IONIUM
Sive GRÆCUM
Golfo di Taranto
Morea
Negroponte
Smyrne
Rhodus
MARE DI CANDIA
Candia
Cyprus
Alexandrette
Tripoli
PARS
GOLFO DI SIDRA
BARCA REGNUM
BARBARIA.
ÆGIPTEN.
ICÆ PARS
Geometrische of Duytsche Mylen van 15 in een Graadt
Miliaria Geometrica 15 in uno Gradu
France Mylen van 25 in een Graadt
Miliaria Gallica 25 in uno Gradu

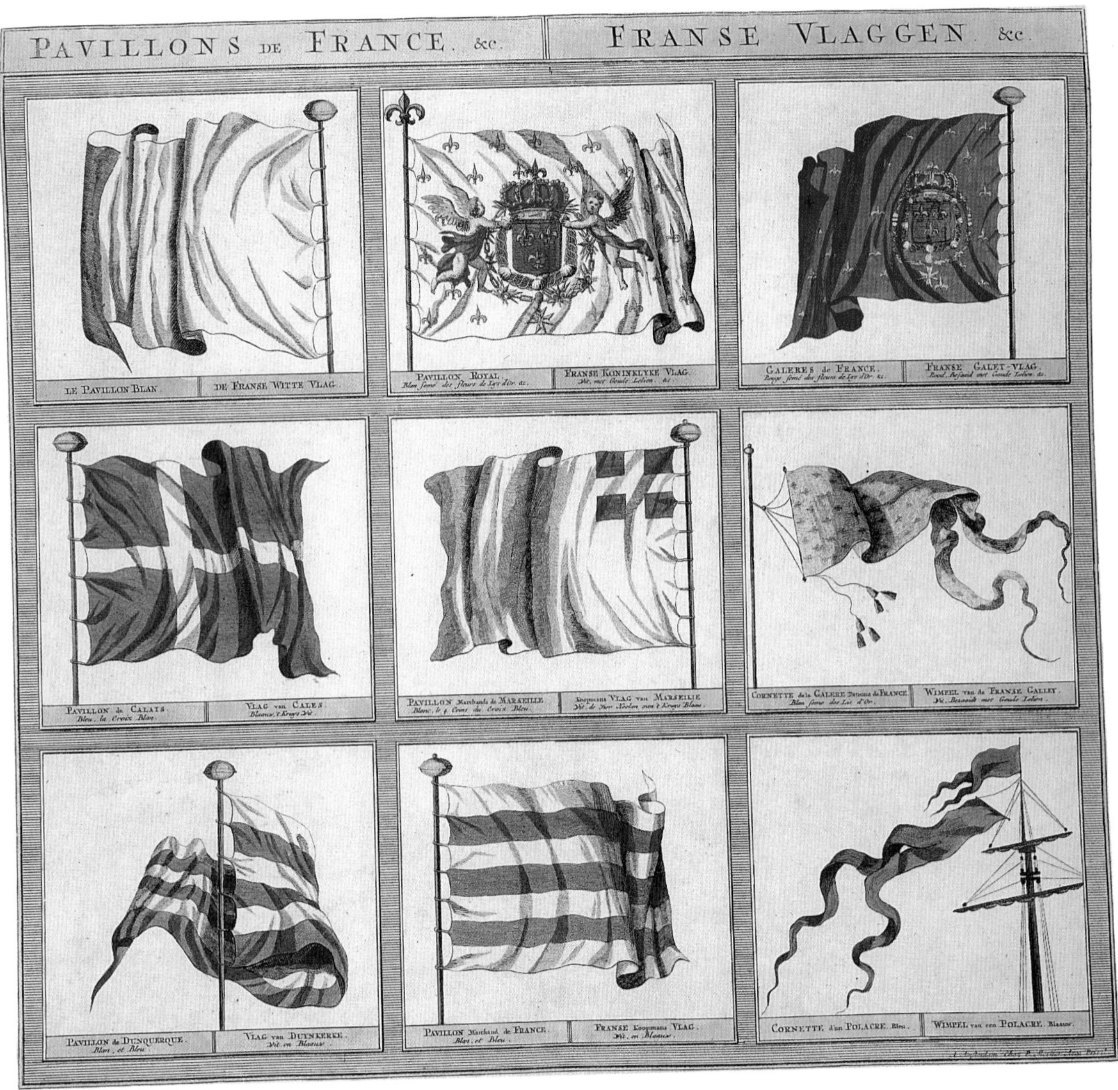

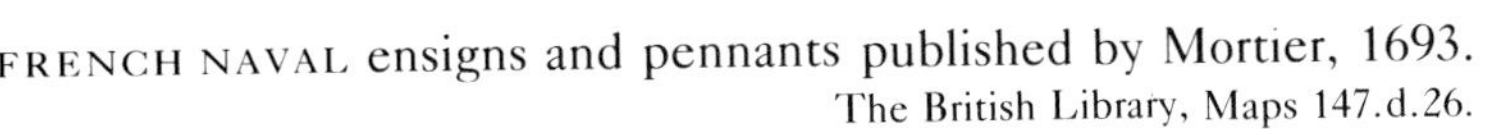
FRENCH NAVAL ensigns and pennants published by Mortier, 1693.
The British Library, Maps 147.d.26.

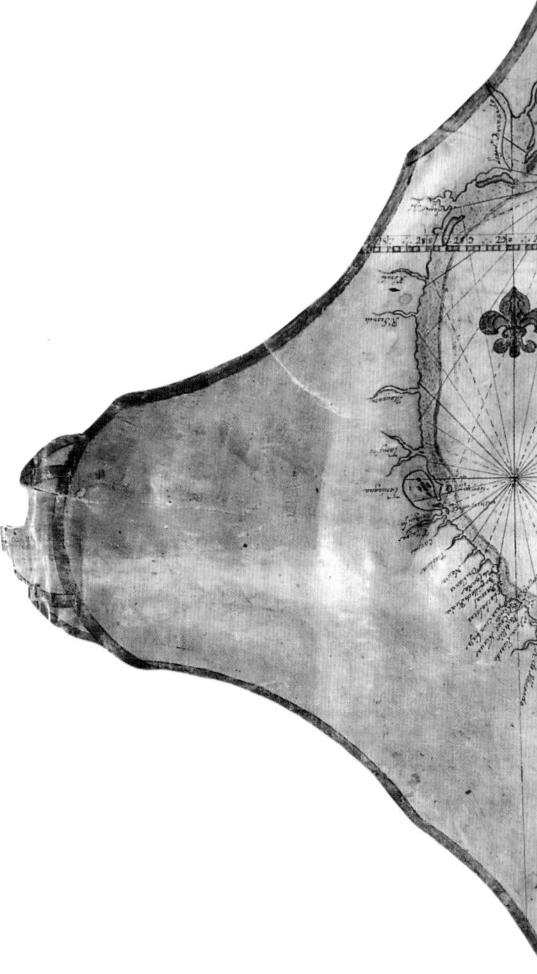

navigator; but to make that science accessible in a form that mariners could use occupied almost two centuries of technical experiment.

As early as 1612 Galileo had proposed that his discovery of the moons of Jupiter could be used to determine longitude. Their orbits and positions might be tabulated for a given longitude, and observers on other meridians could compare what they saw with this tabulated data. The time-difference between them would then translate into differences of longitude, each hour's difference being equal to fifteen degrees of longitude. The moons of Jupiter were thus to be used as a universal clock. This was sound in theory, but the practical problems, first in tabulating the positions and then in observing them on board ship, made it quite impractical to apply at sea. The same objection applied to using lunar distances for finding longitude. The moon has a relatively rapid motion in relation to the fixed stars, so that the angular distance between the moon and a selected star could be used as a clock in the same way as the moons of Jupiter in Galileo's method. Another approach to the problem of universal clocks was of course to carry objective time on board ship. The practical obstacle here was that no existing chronometer was suitable for use at

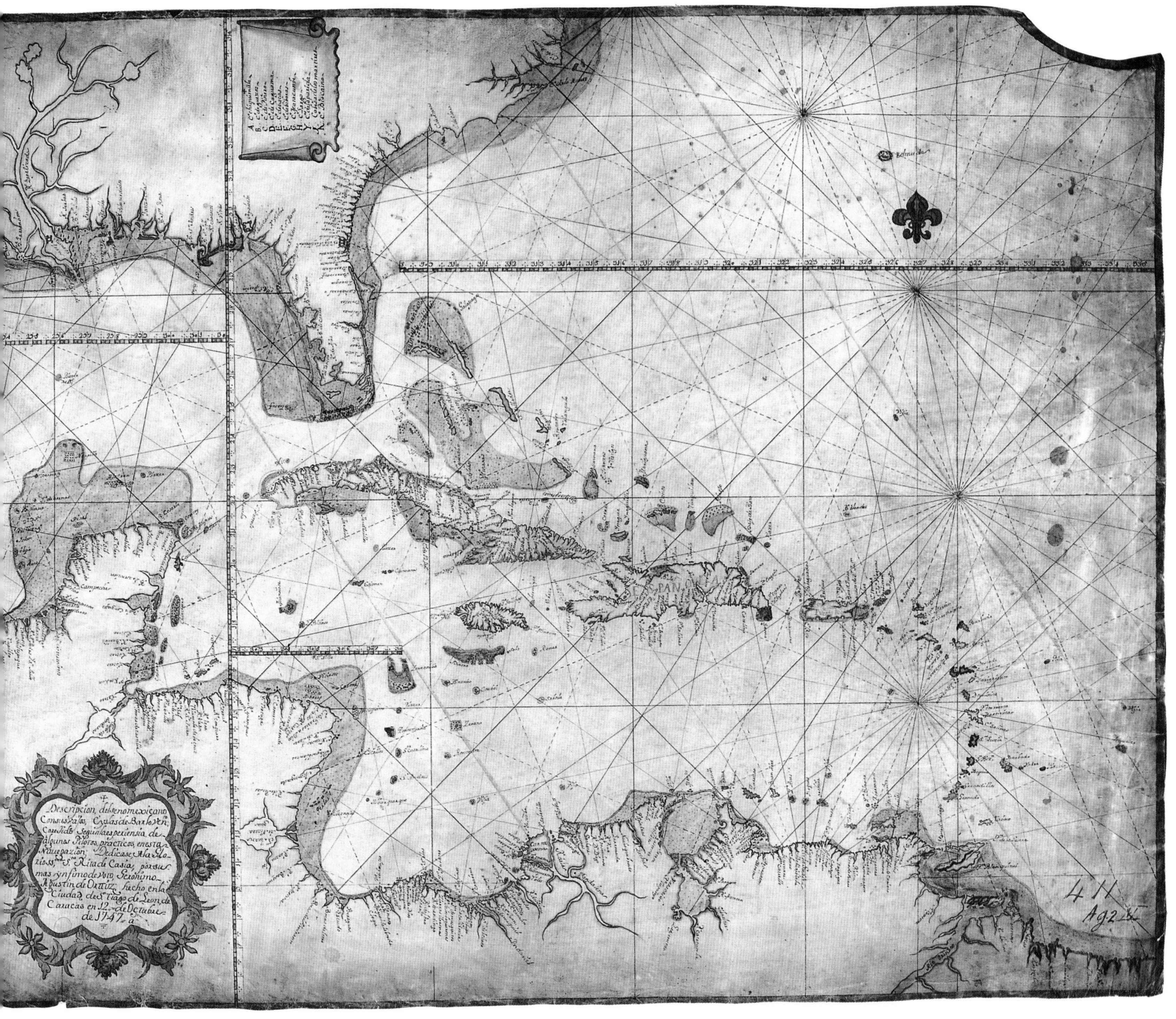

THE CARIBBEAN, 1747, by Agustin de Ortiz. As late as the mid-18th century, sea-charts were being drawn by hand on vellum. This one was made in Caracas for the merchants who traded in the Caribbean. The intriguing thing about this chart is that although it has a very traditional appearance, it is in fact constructed on the Mercator projection. By this date an understanding of the mathematics of navigation and mapmaking had clearly penetrated to chartmakers far distant from Europe.

Hydrographic Office, Taunton.

ESPAÑOLA
Caiman
Plazes
Sola
Ranas
Bibora
Combei
Zexana
Zexanilla
S.ta Catalina

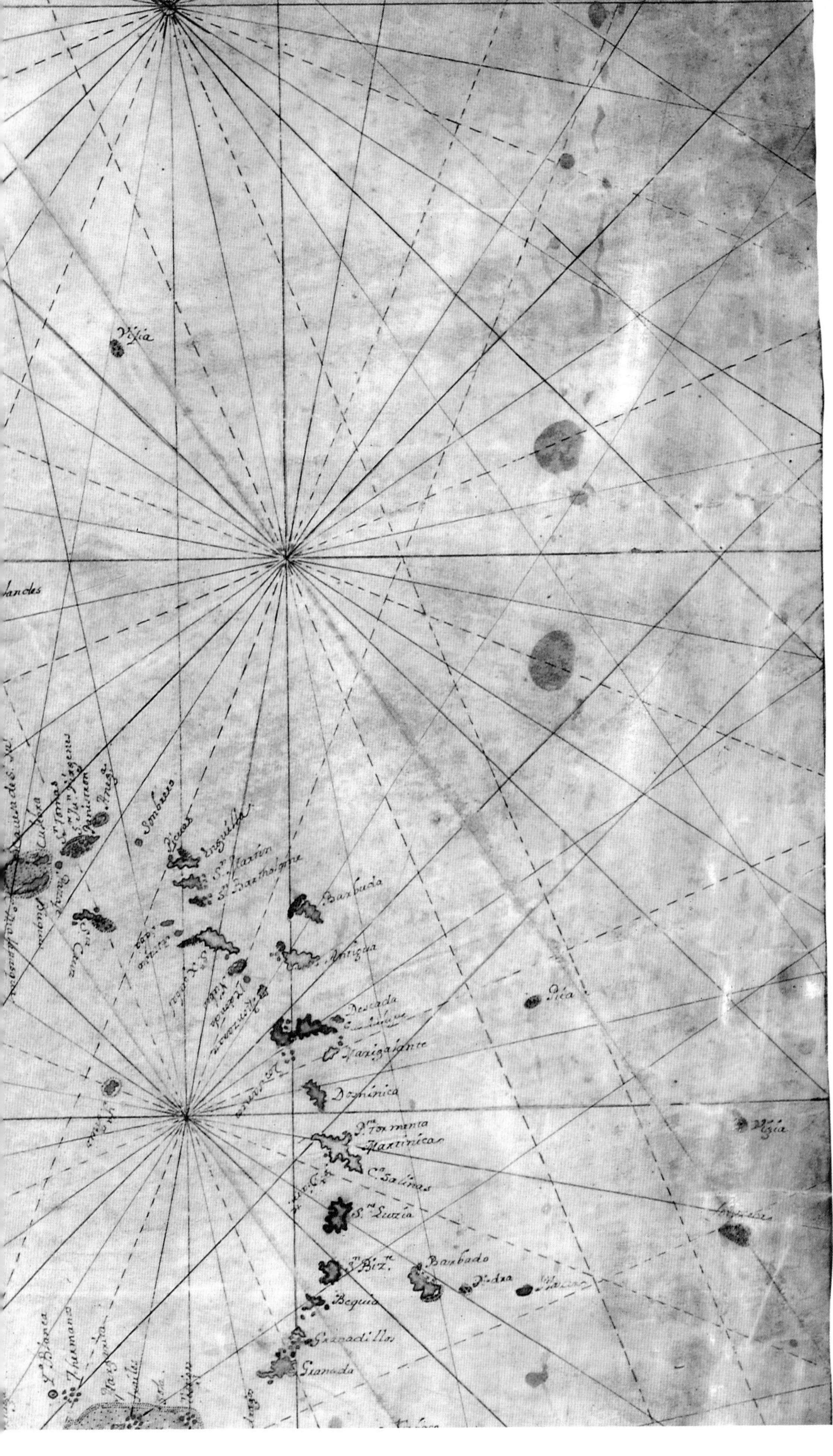

DETAIL FROM Augustin de Ortiz' chart of the Caribbean, 1747. See page 99.

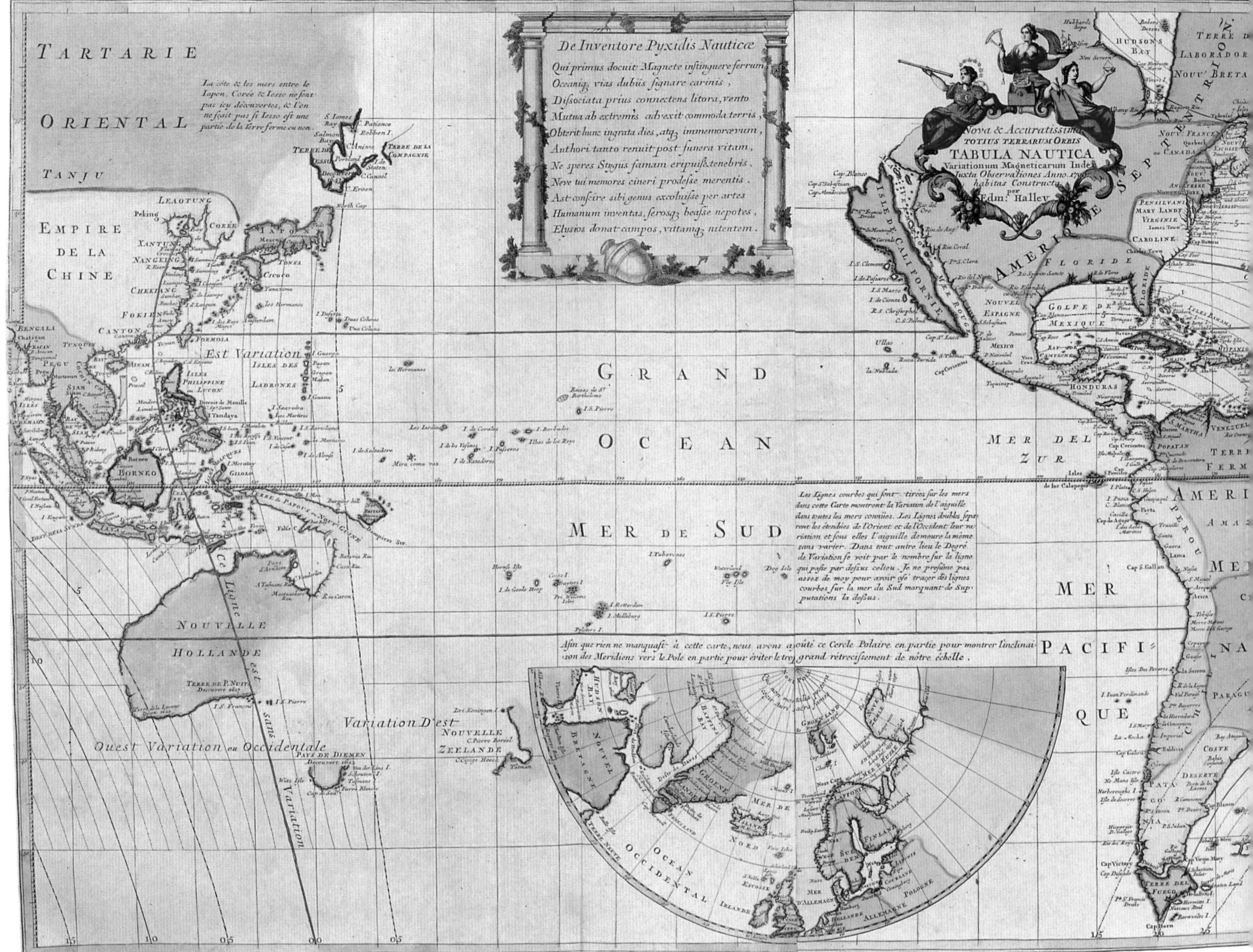

sea or was accurate enough. In the eighteenth century both approaches were pursued: astronomers in England, France and Germany worked at the problem of lunar tables, while instrument-makers sought new designs of chronometers without weights and pendulums which might be used at sea.

Both problems were solved within a few years of each other. In 1765 the Astronomer Royal, Nevil Maskelyne, published a set of lunar tables for mariners, while by 1760 John Harrison had built the last of his four chronometers which fulfilled the highest demands of accuracy. Both methods still had difficulties however: the calculation of time from the lunar distances was laborious, even with the aid of the tables; while the chronometer was a highly expensive instrument which was out of the reach of many mariners. Nevertheless a new era of precision in navigation began in the 1760s. Some fifty years earlier, science had solved another long-standing nautical problem – the variation of the magnetic

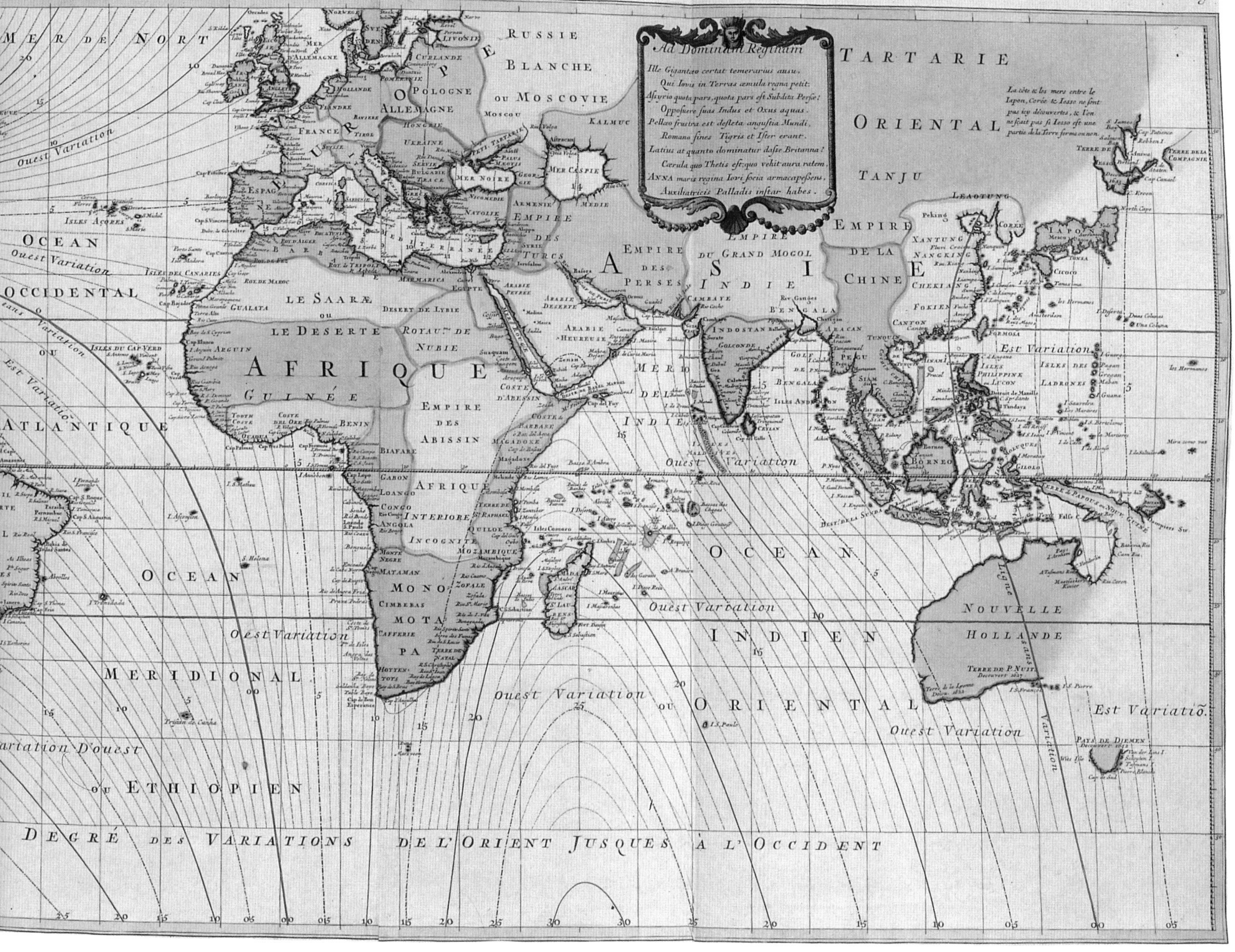

WORLD CHART OF MAGNETIC VARIATION, *c.*1701, by Mortier. The phenomenon of magnetic variation was noticed during the first ocean voyages in the 1490s, but it was not understood. it was Edmond Halley who from 1698–1700 undertook an Atlantic voyage to measure the variations and plot them systematically. After 1700, a version of this chart was part of the navigator's essential equipment.

The British Library, Maps 147.d.26.

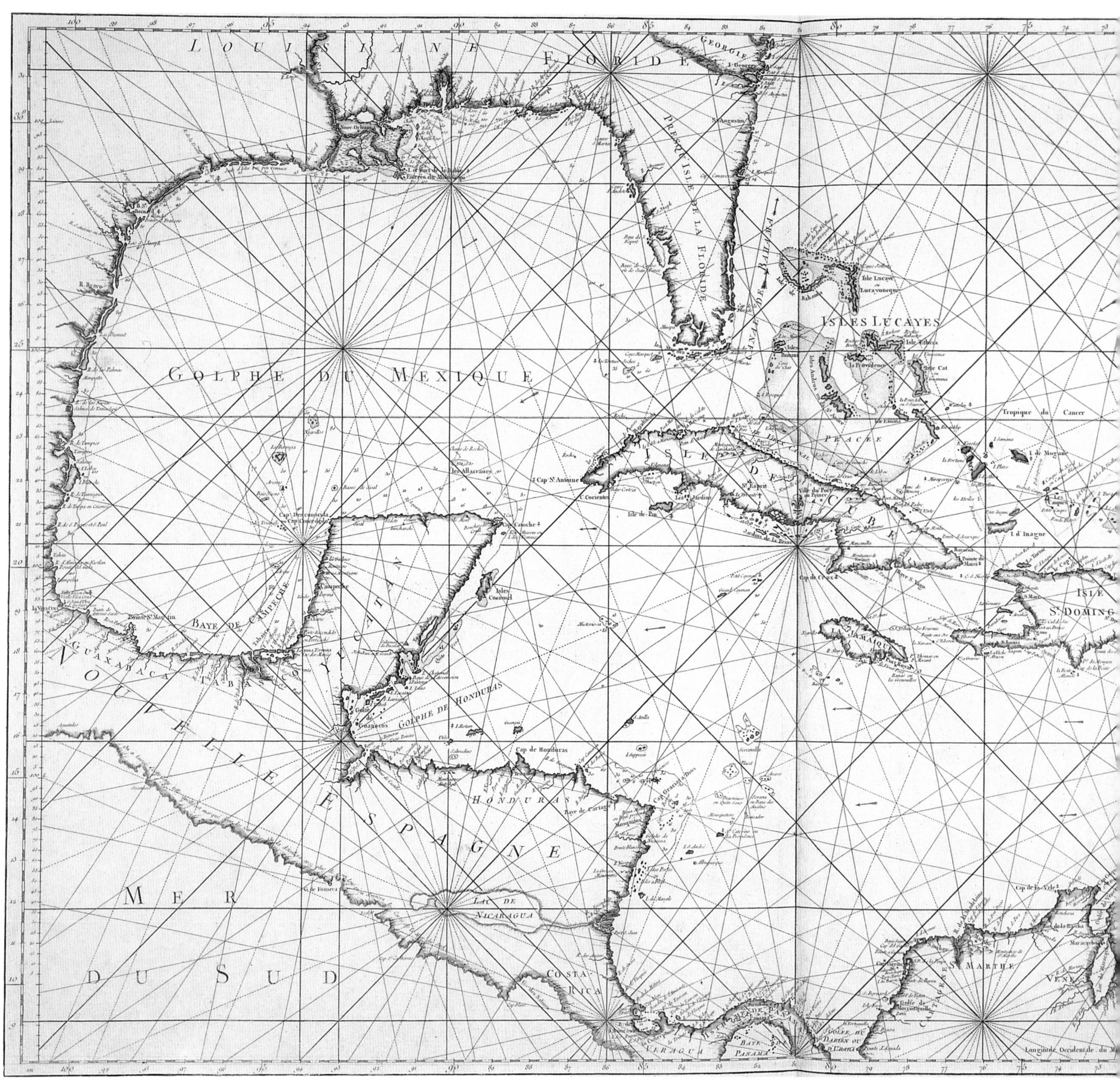
LOUISIANE
FLORIDE
GEORGIE
Nouv. Orleans
S. Augustin
PRESQU'ISLE DE LA FLORIDE
CANAL DE BAHAMA
ISLES LUCAYES
Isle Lucaye ou Lucayoneque
Isle Cat
Tropique du Cancer
GOLPHE DU MEXIQUE
Les Allacranes
Cap St. Antoine
ISLE DE CUBE
Isle de Pin
Cap de Croix
I. d'Inague
ISLE S.T DOMINGUE
JAMAIQUE
Isles Cozumel
BAYE DE CAMPECHE
YUCATAN
Campeche
GUAXACA
TABASCO
GOLPHE DE HONDURAS
Cap de Honduras
HONDURAS
Bayo de Cartago
NOUVELLE ESPAGNE
LAC DE NICARAGUA
MER DU SUD
COSTA RICA
VERAGUA
BAYE DE PANAMA
GOLFE DE DARIEN
S.T MARTHE
Cap de la Vela
Longitude Occidentale du M

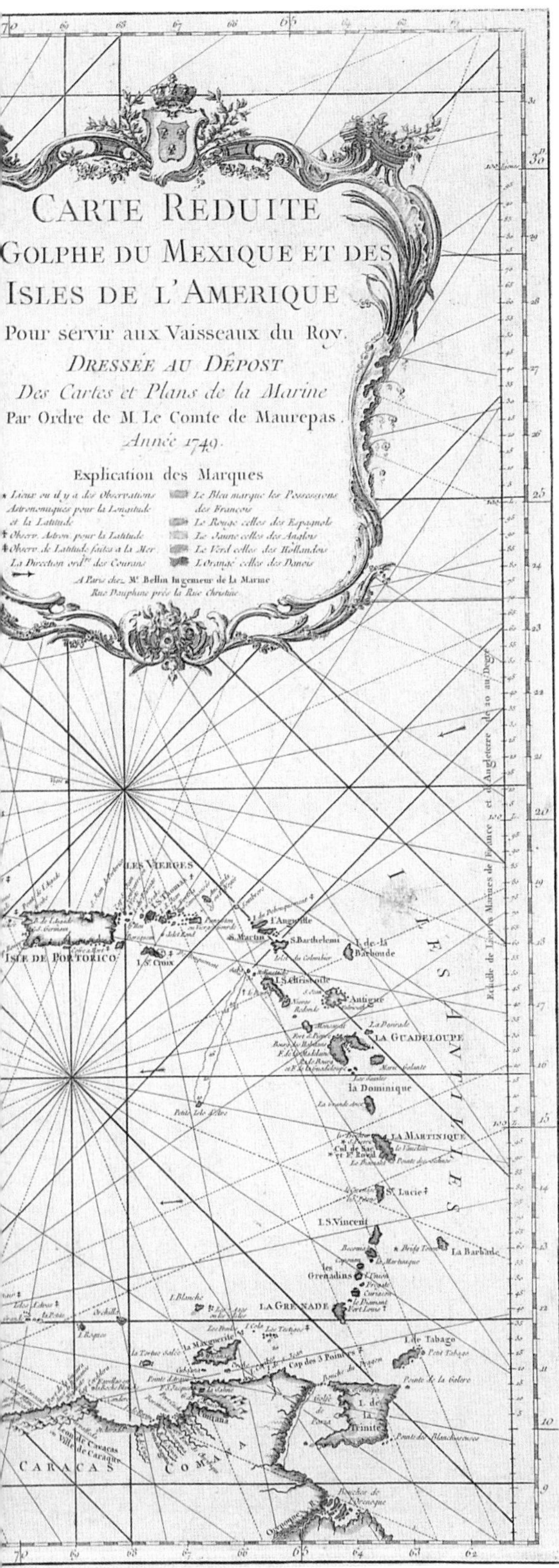

compass. Between 1698 and 1700 Edmond Halley undertook a two-year voyage to study the question, and in 1701 he published the first chart of worldwide magnetic variation, which became a basic reference tool for navigators. The invention of the modern quadrant in 1731 prepared the way for the sextant of 1757, which made possible the quick and accurate sighting of any celestial object against the horizon. The sextant, the astronomical tables, the magnetic variation chart and the chronometer completed the equipment of the serious navigator in this age of science. This period saw the publication of the first English books on maritime surveying, including those by Alexander Dalrymple and Murdoch Mackenzie. Mackenzie is credited with developing the instrument which became fundamental to coastal surveying – the station pointer – which quickly fixed a ship's position on a chart at the intersection of two horizontal sextant angles. These scientific advances were to bear fruit in a new era of marine surveying and chartmaking inaugurated by the work of James Cook.

The years 1600–1800 saw the evolution of the sea-chart from a very traditional, empirically-based picture of the world's seas and coasts, into an objective model of part of the earth's surface. To achieve this, an objective framework was needed, consisting of two parts: the figure of the earth transferred mathematically to paper, and a positioning system derived from astronomical data. To this extent the development of the chart paralleled that of the topographical map. But the modern sea-chart then began to diverge from the topographical map, for the representation on the chart of the earth's surface was not to be an end in itself. The fundamental geography of the chart enabled bearings to be taken and positions to be established. But the geographic mapping, essential though it was, became merely a framework upon which was superimposed layer upon layer of further information necessary to the navigator. During the nineteenth and twentieth centuries this information steadily increased in volume and complexity as ships became larger, sea-traffic heavier and a mariner's training more specialized. This information was expressed in symbolic or coded form, so that the development of the chart has taken it in the direction of the working or technical diagram, and away from the topographical map.

GULF OF MEXICO, 1772, from Bellin's *Hydrographie Françoise.* The French had established an official charting programme in the 1680s, a century ahead of the British. Jacques Nicolas Bellin was *Ingénieur Hydrographe de la Marine* from 1741–1772 and he brought French charting to its peak. There are few depth-soundings on this small-scale chart, but the Mexican continental shelf is shown in contour-fashion. The Caribbean islands are colour-coded to show their possession by the French, British or Spanish.

The British Library, Maps 143.e.14.

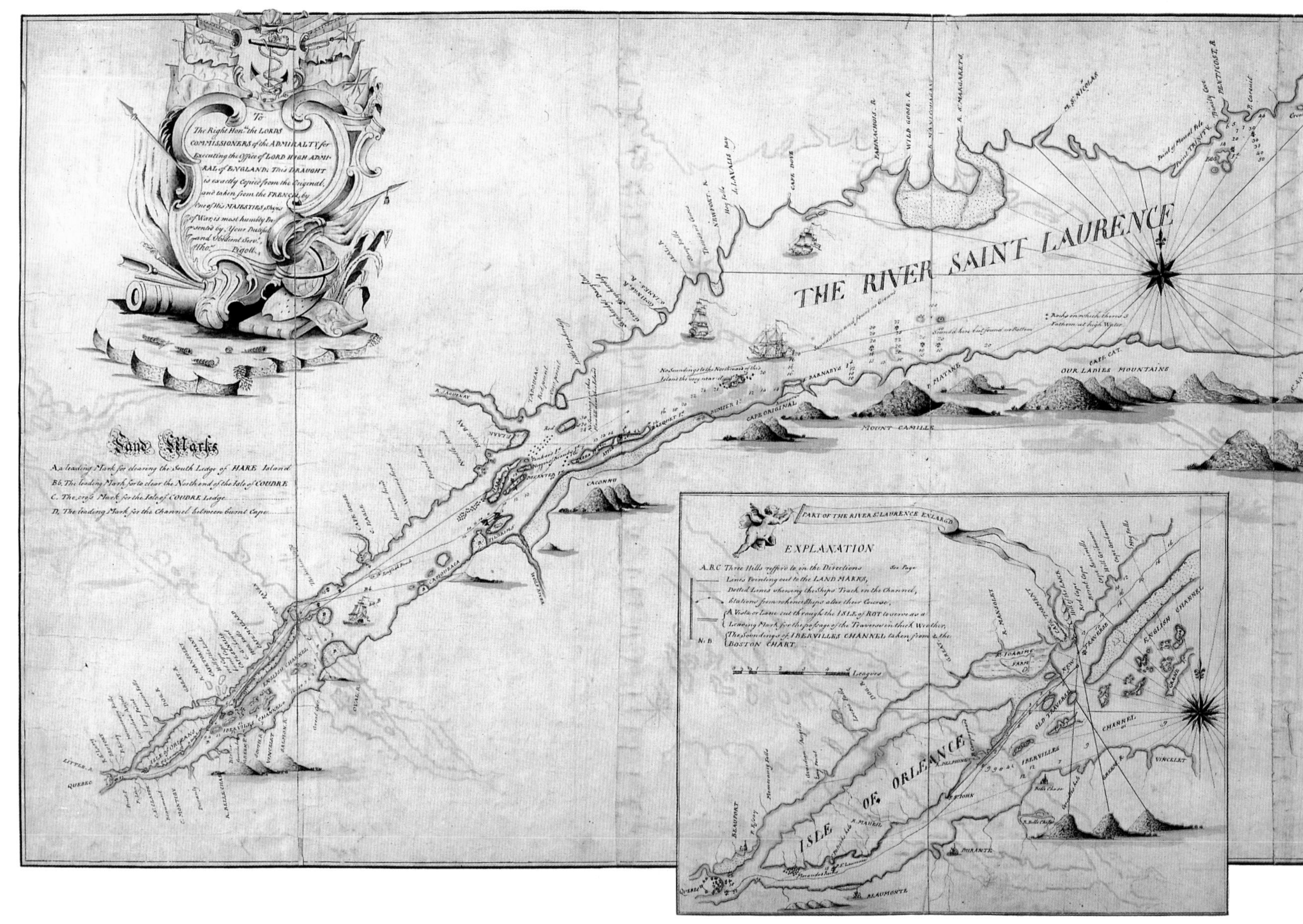

ST LAWRENCE RIVER, *c*.1750 by Thomas Piggot. 'This draft is exactly copied from the original and taken from the French by one of His Majesty's ships of war' explains Piggott. The capture of charts from enemy ships was an important source of information for waters not open to international survey. Charts like this were dispatched to the Admiralty in London, and in this case used in planning the attack on French Canada.

Hydrographic Office, Taunton.

War, Empire and Technology: the last two hundred years

In 1758, midway through the Seven Years War, a British squadron sailed for Canada to reinforce the attack on the French dominions. Among the ships was the 60-gun *Pembroke*, whose master, James Cook, was to make a vital contribution to the campaign through his survey of the St Lawrence. A river-borne assault on Quebec had been considered impossible by the French because of the dangerous shallows in the St Lawrence, yet Cook sounded the channels and charted the eastern approach to Quebec to such effect that the British fleet was able to move upstream and land the troops which took the city. Cook's genius for navigation and surveying were recognized, and he was launched on a career in which he was to explore more of the earth's surface than any other single man in history. His work was the culmination of the maritime enterprise begun by the Portuguese three centuries earlier, but at the same time it inaugurated a new era of deliberate reconnaissance and charting that was sponsored by governments not simply in pursuit of trade or military supremacy, but in pursuit of geographical knowledge, to chart the still-unexplored oceans of the world. The first phase of this reconnaissance, which lasted perhaps from 1760 to 1860, had two primary aims: the accurate delineation of the world's coasts, and their precise location on the earth's surface, especially their longitude, which could now be determined by chronometer. The volume of hydrographic information on charts of this period might often be fairly sparse, but an accurate chart base was created. Later in the nineteenth century, the advent of larger and larger steam vessels would require closer surveys and a greater range of information.

After the Quebec campaign, Cook spent much of the next eight years in Canada, charting Nova Scotia and Newfoundland. His great opportunity came in 1768 when he was chosen to command a scientific expedition to Tahiti to observe the transit of Venus across the sun. When the observations had been made in June 1769 Cook opened the Admiralty's sealed orders, which were to sail the Pacific in search of 'a continent or land of great extent . . . to the southward . . . of the tract of any former navigators'. Even at this late date, the possibility of a great southern continent was still enticing to the maritime powers of Europe eager to expand their overseas empires. Despite several landfalls on the western coast of Australia, its extent had not been resolved, nor its relation to New Zealand and New Guinea.

Cook's expedition was not the first of its kind, for the eighteenth century had seen continuous speculation about the Pacific, but little real achievement. Gulliver's Lilliput and Robinson Crusoe's islands could easily be placed there without challenge, and the South Sea Company floated a merchant enterprise to exploit it while scarcely sending a single ship there. In 1764 the Admiralty had sent John Byron in HMS *Dolphin* on an earlier mission to find 'lands and islands of great extent hitherto unvisited by any European power in the Atlantic Ocean between the Cape of Good Hope and the Magellanic Strait'. Byron charted and claimed possession of the Falkland Islands, without knowing that a French colony was already living there, but found no other land before passing the Strait of

ENGLISH SHIPS set afire at Quebec by the French, 1760. By Samuel Scott.

National Maritime Museum, Greenwich.

Magellan into the Pacific, where he failed to secure any further territory. He was followed almost immediately by Samuel Wallis in the *Dolphin* and Philip Carteret in the *Swallow*. The success of these expeditions was limited to some minor discoveries: in 1767 Wallis's was the first European ship to land on Tahiti, which rapidly acquired the reputation in Europe of being an earthly paradise. Wallis named it King George III Island – it was Cook who reverted to the native name. In July of the same year, one of the *Dolphin's* crew, Pitcairn, sighted the tiny island which bears his name and which later became famous as the refuge of mutinous crew of the *Bounty*. (It was the fact that Wallis located the island incorrectly on his chart that led the mutineers to believe that they could hide there securely, and in fact their community remained undiscovered until 1808.) For the French, Antoine de Bougainville sailed the waters between Tahiti and New Guinea, also seeking the great southern continent and claiming many smaller islands.

In his first voyage, Cook coasted and charted New Zealand, the east coast of Australia and the strait between Australia and New Guinea, whose existence had apparently been forgotten since Torres's passage through it in 1605. Despite this geographical breakthrough vast tracts of water still remained, and a territorial race was now on between the British and the French. Between 1772 and 1775, Cook's second voyage finally dispelled any possibility of an undiscovered continent in temperate latitudes – Antarctica of course still remained hidden. From the Cape of Good Hope he sailed south-east and became the first man to cross the Antarctic Circle. Forced north by ice, he turned east keeping to an average of 60 degrees south. After revisiting New Zealand and Tahiti he plunged south-east again, reaching a latitude of 71 degrees south, where he was halted by walls of ice, probably just a few miles from the coast of Antarctica, which he never sighted. After charting the Marquesas, the Society Islands, the Friendly Islands and other groups, Cook finally turned for home, and once again the South Atlantic was traversed, charting South Georgia and the South Sandwich Islands. His third voyage of 1776–79 had a new objective: after yet another Pacific traverse he was to turn his attention to the west coast of North America, and search for the Pacific end of that explorer's dream, the North-West Passage. In 1778 Cook discovered Hawaii, which he named the Sandwich Islands, from where he sailed north-east to chart the coasts of Canada and Alaska. Through the Bering

NEWFOUNDLAND, 1763, by James Cook. The War of the Austrian Succession gave England a pretext to attack the French possessions in North America. The young James Cook played a material part in the action by surveying the St Lawrence River in preparation for the attack on Montreal. When hostilities were over, he spent three years surveying Newfoundland, a task which displayed his skill and character and led directly to his commissions in the Pacific.

Hydrographic Office, Taunton.

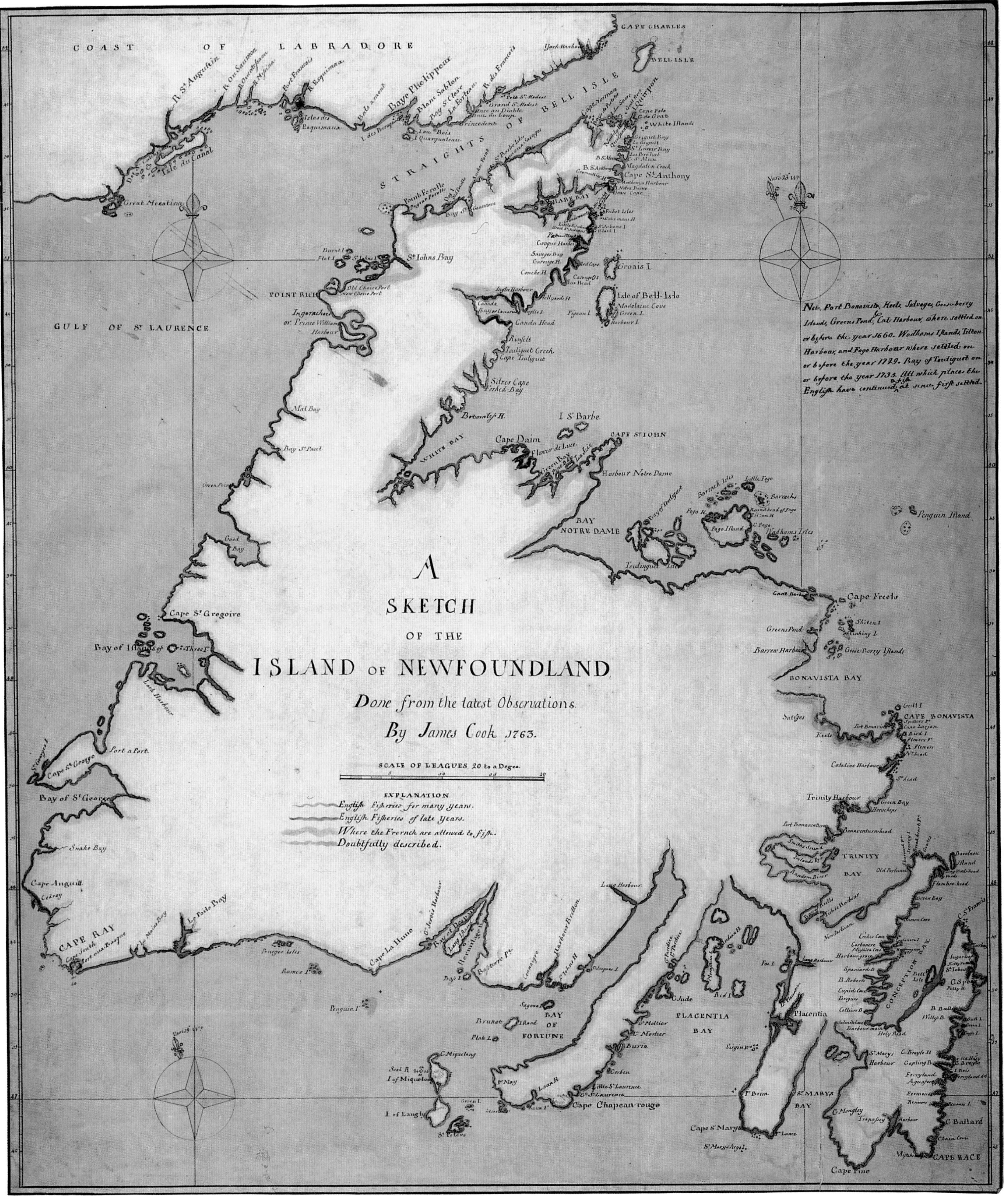

A SKETCH OF THE ISLAND OF NEWFOUNDLAND
Done from the latest Observations
By James Cook 1763.
SCALE OF LEAGUES 20 to a Degee.
EXPLANATION
English Fisheries for many years.
English Fisheries of late years.
Where the Frernch are allowed to fish.
Doubtfully described.
New, Port Bonavista, Keels, Salvages, Goose-berry Islands, Greens Pond, & Cat Harbour, where settled on or before the year 1660. Wadhams Islands, Tilton Harbour, and Fogo Harbour where settled on or before the year 1729. Bay of Toulinguet on or before the year 1735. All which places the English have continued to fish at, since first settled.
COAST OF LABRADORE
STRAIGHTS OF BELL ISLE
GULF OF ST. LAURENCE
CAPE CHARLES
BELL ISLE
Cape St. Anthony
Groais I.
Isle of Bell Isle
St. Johns Bay
POINT RICH
WHITE BAY
I. St. Barbe
CAPE ST. JOHN
Harbour Notre Dame
BAY NOTRE DAME
Fogo Island
Wadhams Isles
Penguin Island
Cape Freels
BONAVISTA BAY
CAPE BONAVISTA
Trinity Harbour
TRINITY BAY
CONCEPTION BAY
PLACENTIA BAY
Placentia
ST. MARYS BAY
Cape St. Marys
CAPE RACE
Cape Pine
BAY OF FORTUNE
Cape Chapeau rouge
Burin
I. of Miquelon
I. of Langly
St. Peters
Cape La Hune
CAPE RAY
Cape Anguille
Bay of St. George
Cape St. George
Port a Port
Bay of Islands
Cape St. Gregoire
Good Bay
Bay St. Paul

THE DESTRUCTION OF *L'Orient* at the Battle of the Nile, 1798. The explosion was so tremendous that the opposing warships were shaken into silence for fifteen minutes. By George Arnald.

National Maritime Museum, Greenwich.

Strait he reached 70 degrees north before impenetrable ice stopped him, and he turned back to Hawaii and to his tragic, unnecessary death at the hands of the islanders. His crew followed their instructions and returned to the Bering Strait but were again defeated by ice, returning south-west via Kamchatka, Japan, Macao and the Straits of Malacca.

Cook's chart legacy, and the painstaking method by which he achieved it, placed maritime exploration and surveying on a new footing. Cook built up his coastal outlines from running surveys (see above page 74) but his base line was now established by astronomical observation. Multiple intersecting sightings were taken of the coastal features, and distances were measured by timing gunshots between two vessels. On his first voyage Cook carried no chronometer, and longitudes were determined by lunar distances. On the second voyage his longitudes were improved by the chronometer method. Cook was assiduous in studying tides and currents wherever he sailed, both by noting visual drift and by testing the discrepancy between dead reckoning and astronomical fixes. Cook was a seminal figure in British hydrography, and the men he trained, such as George Vancouver and William Bligh (notorious for his command of the *Bounty*, but an outstanding navigator and surveyor), shaped a tradition which developed during the nineteenth century through men like William Owen, Frederick Evans and William Wharton. The immediate material result of Cook's exploration was to demonstrate the potential of Australia's east coast, green and hospitable in contrast to the barren west coast. Cook was only distantly aware of events in North America in the 1770s which would lose one section of the British Empire, just as he was laying the foundation for another.

The British had long been aware of the inadequacy of the charts of the American coast, and it fell to Joseph des Barres, another great surveyor who had worked with Cook in Canada, to produce a new generation of American charts. Des Barres (1721–1824 – he lived to be the oldest mapmaker known to history) was of Swiss birth, but settled in

NEW ZEALAND, 1778, by James Cook. In the course of the first of his three great Pacific voyages, Cook circumnavigated both islands of New Zealand. He retained the Maori names omitted on most later charts. A number of mistakes are detectable – *e.g.* 'Banks Island' is a peninsula, a reminder that one reconnaissance even by a skilled surveyor is rarely definitive. After his return, mapmakers throughout Europe publicized his discoveries and his name became forever linked with the mapping of New Zealand.

The British Library, Maps C.21.c.3.(4).

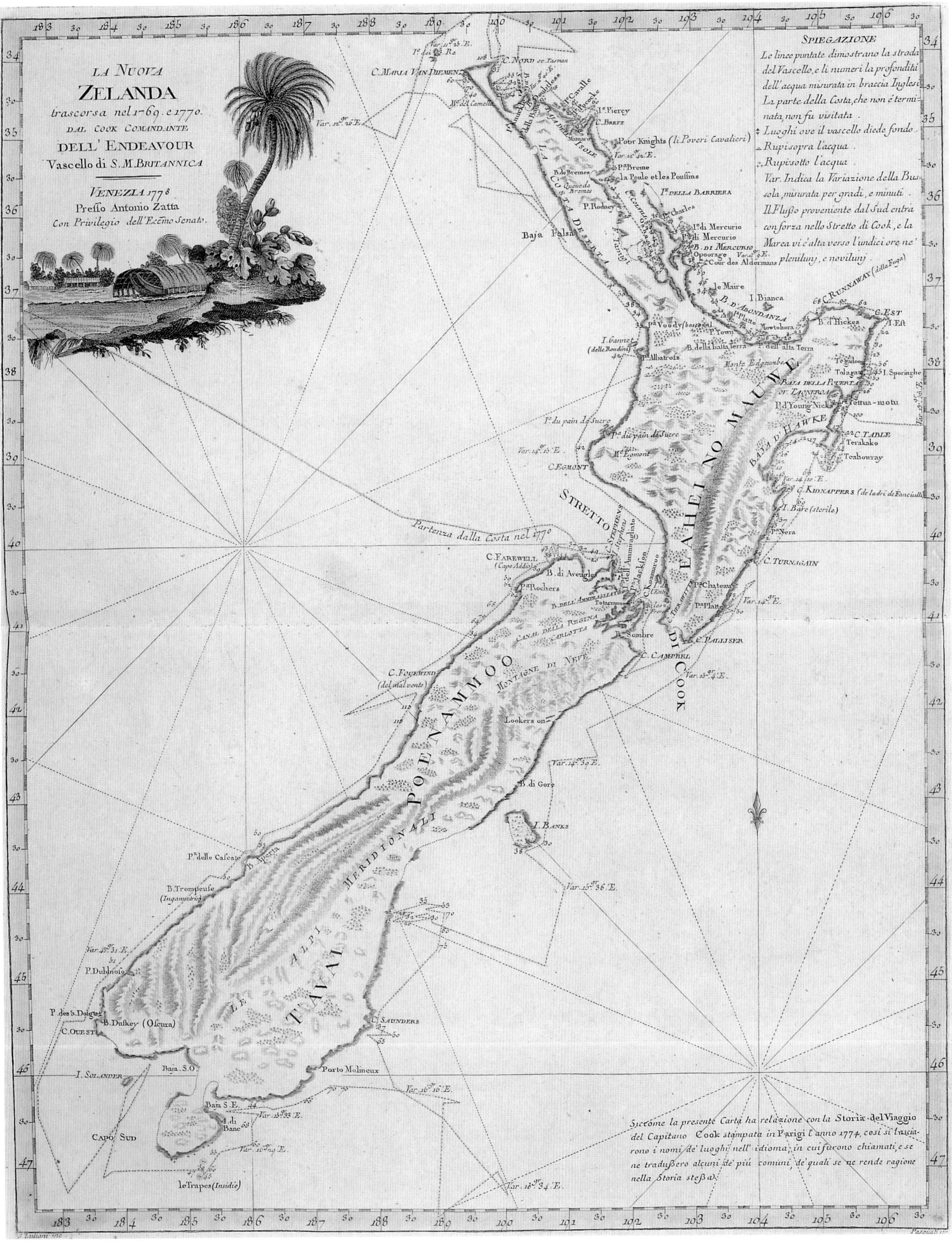

LA NUOVA
ZELANDA
trascorsa nel 1769. e 1770.
DAL COOK COMANDANTE
DELL' ENDEAVOUR
Vascello di S. M. BRITANNICA
VENEZIA 1778
Presso Antonio Zatta
Con Privilegio dell' Ecc.mo Senato.
SPIEGAZIONE
Le linee puntate dimostrano la strada del Vascello, e li numeri la profondità dell'acqua misurata in braccia Inglesi
La parte della Costa, che non è terminata, non fu visitata
Luoghi ove il vascello diede fondo
Rupi sopra l'acqua
Rupi sotto l'acqua
Var. Indica la Variazione della Bussola misurata per gradi, e minuti
Il Flusso proveniente dal Sud entra con forza nello Stretto di Cook, e la Marea vi è alta verso l'undici ore ne' pleniluny, e noviluny
C. Maria Van Diemen
C. Nord ou Tasman
C. Brett
Poor Knights (li Poveri Cavalieri)
La Costa Deserta
Baja Falsa
I.e della Barriera
I.e di Mercurio
C. Runnaway (della Fuga)
B. d'Abondanza
C. Est
Monte Edgcumbe
Eahei no Mauwe
Baja della Poverta
Baja d'Hawke
C. Table
C. Kidnappers
C. Egmont
Stretto di Cook
Partenza dalla Costa nel 1770
C. Farewell (Capo Addio)
B. di Aveugles
C. Turnagain
C. Palliser
C. Campbel
C. Foulwind (del mal vento)
Montagne di Neve
Lookers on
B. di Gore
I. Banks
Poenammoo
Tavai
Le Alpi Meridionali
P.ta delle Cascate
B. Trompeuse (Ingannatrice)
P. Dubbioso
B. Duskey (Oscura)
C. Ouest
I. Solander
Baja S.O.
C. Saunders
Porto Molineux
Baja S.E.
Capo Sud
le Trapes (Insidie)
Sicome la presente Carta ha relazione con la Storia del Viaggio del Capitano Cook stampata in Parigi l'anno 1774, così si lasciarono i nomi de' luoghi nell' idioma, in cui furono chiamati, e se ne tradussero alcuni de' più comuni, de' quali se ne rende ragione nella Storia stessa.

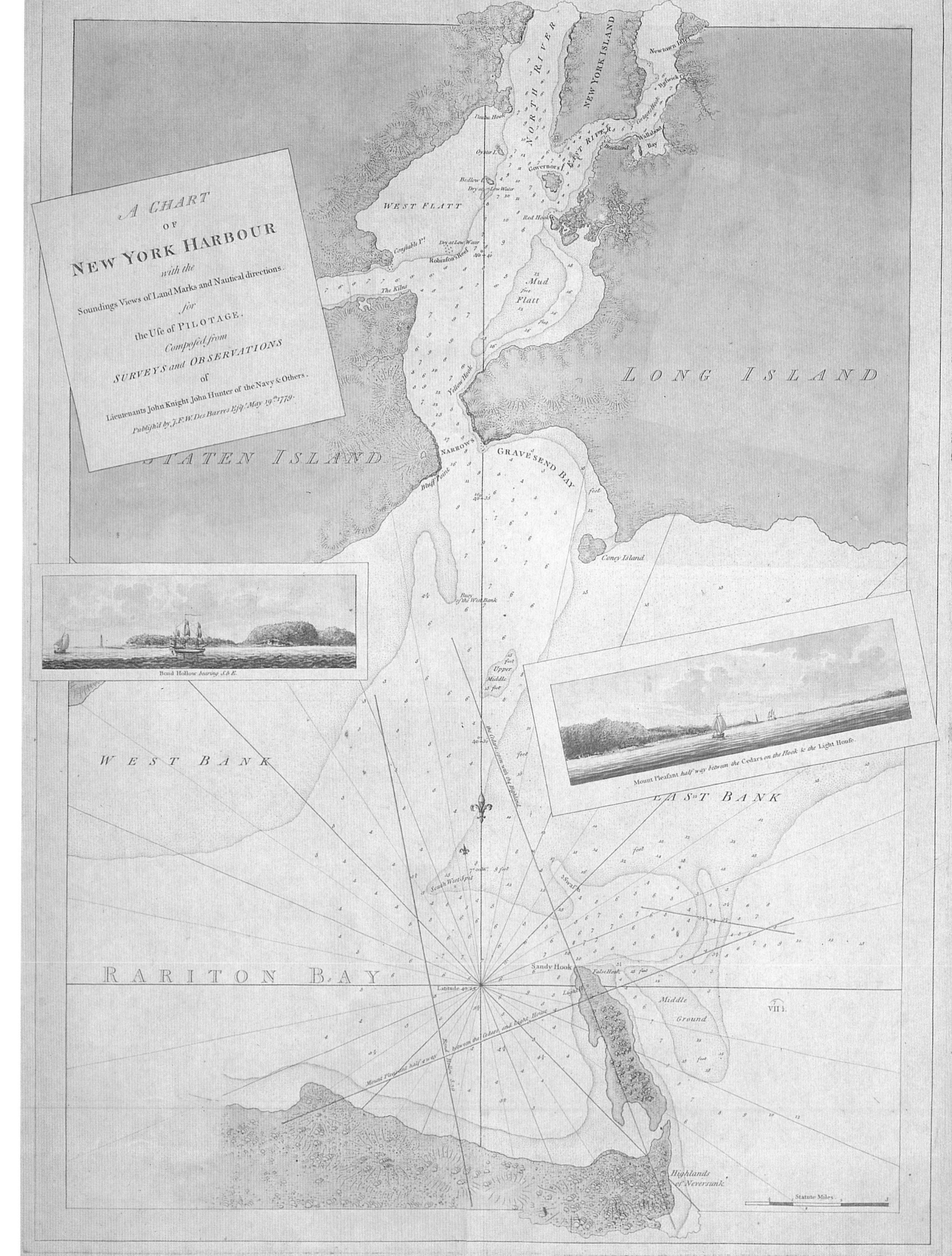
A CHART
OF
NEW YORK HARBOUR
with the
Soundings Views of Land Marks and Nautical directions.
for
the Use of PILOTAGE.
Composed from
SURVEYS and OBSERVATIONS
of
Lieutenants John Knight John Hunter of the Navy & Others.
Publish'd by J.F.W. Des Barres Esq.r May 19th 1779.
NORTH RIVER
NEW YORK ISLAND
EAST RIVER
Governors I.
Red Hook
WEST FLATT
Mud Flatt
The Kilns
Yellow Hook
NARROWS
STATEN ISLAND
LONG ISLAND
GRAVESEND BAY
Coney Island
Bond Hollow bearing S.b.E.
Upper Middle
WEST BANK
EAST BANK
Mount Pleasant half way between the Cedars on the Hook & the Light House.
RARITON BAY
Sandy Hook
Middle Ground
Highlands of Neversunk
Statute Miles

NAUTICAL DIRECTIONS

to *Sail* into the *Harbour* of *New-York*, &c.

WHEN off *Sandy Hook* in ten Fathoms Water, do not ſhoal your Soundings by approaching the Bar until you have brought *Mount Pleaſant* half Way between the *Light-Houſe* and the *Cedar-Trees*; (the Light-Houſe will bear about Weſt half South) then ſteer acroſs the Bar Weſt by North, if Flood-tide; and Veſt-North-Weſt, if Ebb Tide; (*Quarter-leſs-four* is the leaſt Water on the Bar at half Flood).

When you have deepened to ſix Fathoms, and Mount-Pleaſant is well to the Northward of the North Point of ᵉ Hook, ſhape your Courſe Weſt, and paſs within two Cables Length of the Point, which is bold to, when a-breaſt, ᵃt ſhoals in an Eaſterly Direction towards the North-Weſtern Extremity of the Middle Ground, where the Chanᵉl between it and the Shore of the Hook is reduced to a very narrow and intricate Paſs of three Fathoms and a half Vater. The outſide of the Middle Ground deepens gradually, and you may, ſtanding to it, ſafely truſt to your Lead.

If you mean to ſtop at the Hook: bring the Light-Houſe to bear Eaſt-South-Eaſt to Eaſt by North, and anchor ſix Fathoms good Ground; but if bound to New-York, continue your Courſe Weſtwards, obſerving not to approach ᵉ Eaſt-Bank nearer than five Fathoms, at which Depth you will be cloſe to its Edge. When you have brought *and's Hollow* (the Weſt Fall of Never Sink) to bear *South half Eaſt or South by Eaſt, you are paſt the South Weſt ᵖit*, and may ſhape your Way Northwards to the Narrows, being cautious, for avoiding the Upper Middle, not to ᵒrrow to the Eaſt-Bank ſo much as to ſhut the Cedars on the Hook with the High-Land of Never Sink. (Here it proper to remark, that the Flood ſets ſtrong to the Weſtward, from the South-Weſt Spit until you are ᵒove the Upper Middle, whence it runs up Channel-Courſe to the Narrows). When a-breaſt the Upper Middle ᵈ above the Draught of the Amboy-Tide, haul over to the North-Eaſt until you open Snake-Hill with the Bluff ᵒint of Staten-Iſland, and ſteer for the Narrows. Being to the Eaſtwards of the Weſt-Bank, you may ſail cloſe to is Part of Staten-Iſland, which is ſteep to. There is a Reef extending about a Cable's Length from the Eaſt-Shore the Narrows. Keep Mid-Channel until you open the Paſſage between Staten-Iſland and the Main (commonly ˡled the Kills). In order to avoid the Edge of the Weſt Flat, which is ſteep to, keep the High-Bluff on the ᵉſt Shore of Hudſon River well open to the Eaſtward of Bedlow-Iſland; and to ſail clear of Mud-Flat, on the Eaſtᵈe of the Channel, have the Points of Hudſon River open with each other. Mud-Flat deepens regularly and may avoided by the Lead. There is good Anchorage in eight Fathoms a-breaſt of the Old Church; but in ſix ᵃthoms the Ground in this Part of the River is bad.

N. B. The above Bearings are by Compaſs; the Variation being 7° Weſterly.

The Light-Houſe on Sandy-Hook lies in 40° 27′ Latitude North, and in 74° 03′ Longitude Weſt from the ᵒyal Obſervatory of Greenwich.

		H	M
It is High Water on the Days of the Full and Change *at the Hook* at	-	7	30
ᴺote, That the Stream of the Tide continues to ſet in till Nine o'Clock at the Rate of two Knots.			
At New-York *in the Eaſt-River*	-	9	00
in the North-River	-	11	00

ᵀdes riſe perpendicularly about ſeven Feet, but are ſometimes checked to ſuch a Degree by the Weſterly or North ᵉſterly Winds as to lower the Water on the Bar to three Fathoms and a quarter; and Eaſterly or North-Eaſterly ᵂinds have frequently riſen it to five Fathoms.

The EAST-RIVER.

The Tide, during the laſt quarter Ebb, ſets from the North-River, around Fort-Point, and flows up the Eaſt-ᵛer at the Rate of three Knots; whence, with a like Velocity, it returns two Hours before the North-River High-ᵃter Time. This affords great Convenience to Ships in ſhifting their Birth from one River to the other. The ᵏng's Ships, during the Summer Seaſons, ride in either River in the Stream; in the Winter they haul to, or moor ᵗween the Wharfs. The *Twelve Feet Ledge* off the Town, and the ſunken Wrecks and Chevaux-de-frize, ſhew by ᵉ Ripple of the Tide. The beſt Paſſage up the Eaſt-River is to the Northward of Governor's-Iſle, keeping Mid-ᶜannel until you are paſt the rocky Flats off Long-Iſland (oppoſite the Careening Yard) and the South-Eaſt ᵉef of New-York-Iſland, (which runs out 150 Fathoms in a Southerly Direction from Red Bank) from this ᵒng-Iſland Shore is bold to Brunſwick Creek, where it ſhoals a little Way off Pat-Point. In Order to clear the ᵒrk-Iſland Shore Flat oppoſite Brunſwick Creek, borrow towards the Creek, keeping the Water-Mill in Wallabout ʸ on, or open, Weſtward of Bruckland Church Spire, (on a Hill to the Weſtward.) You may ſail cloſe under the ᵈ rocky Cliffs on the Weſtern Shore. Blind Rock and Governor Table Rock extend, South-Weſt, 600 Fathoms, a Range from Blackwell Iſland. The Channel on the Weſt Side of the Iſland is clear, and throughout deep, a ᵃt's Length from the Shores. There is a ſunken Rock, two-thirds of the Way, up the Eaſtern Channel, and ᵃut 30 Fathoms from the Starboard Shore. Before you enter into either of the Blackwell Iſland Channels, if ᵒod, let the Tide be nearly ſpent; if Ebb Tide, endeavour, by ſtemming the Stream which continues ſwift until a ᵃarter of an Hour before the Turn of the Tide, to reach Hell Gate at Low Water Slack, the moſt deſirable Time ᵍet through. As you run up between Flood Rock, which is ſteep to, and the Point of Long-Iſland, bear up more ᵉerly, keeping Mid Channel. The leaſt Drain of Tide will ſhew the *Hogsback-dangers* on your Larboard, and *Pot-Rock* on your Starboard, by the uncommon Ripple and boiling Appearance of the Water. There is ſuffiᵉnt Depth for large Ships until you come up with Marſh Iſle, where it ſhoals and forms a Bar acroſs the Channel, ʰ only four Fathoms at the Top of High Water; and about a third of the Way over from the Iſle, there is ᵃngle Rock with no more than ten Feet Water.

ᵀo return through Hell Gate, High Water Slack is the moſt convenient Time, as the Tide is favourable down to ᴺw-York; there is however ſufficient Depth at Low Water for any Ship in the Gate. Should the Pilot have miſᶜulated the Tide, and the Ship, with a ſtrong favourable Tide and a leading Breeze, is advanced near the Gate, you ᵘſt attend the true Set of the Stream, in which you may eaſily keep the Ship with lofty Sails, low Sails being liable be becalmed by the Land. The principal Ebb-ſtream leads around Mill Rock, which is very bold, whence it ᵘns ſhort to the Southwards by Flagſtaff Point in the Weſtern Blackwell Iſland Channel. The Paſſage between ᴹl Rock and Scot-Cap is deep, but very narrow. The Southermoſt Paſſage, between Flood Rock and Long-Iſland, ᵘſed, on the Flood only, when the Stream leads fair through.

LONG-ISLAND SOUND.

ᶠrom Marſh Iſland Eaſtwards the Sound is navigable for the largeſt Ships. The Stream continues moderate for ᵃut three Leagues to Frog Point, where the New-York Tide meeting the Sound Tide in contrary Directions, ᶜſe a perfect Stagnation. The Ship Channel is to the Northward of the Two Brethren Iſles and Hulet Iſland, ᵒerving to keep near the Main until paſt Lawrance Reef, (which extends third Channel over from the Eaſt Point Fluſhing Bay) and thence keeping clear of the North Shore, until you have doubled Frog Point Peninſula. Your ᶜurſe to New City Iſland is about N. N. E. You muſt obſerve not to borrow towards the Eaſt-ſide of the Peninᵃ, on Account of the Mud Flat extending from it towards New City Iſland Anchorage. The Stepping Stones ᵖrtly dry at low Water) leave a ſufficient Channel to the Northwards to work up or down. The Executioners ᴿocks dry at half Tide) lie North-Eaſt two Miles from Heart-Iſland, and North about one Mile from Sands's Point; Channel to the Southwards of them is the moſt frequented. Here the Sound widens, and affords ſecure Anchorin Oyſter Bay, Huntington Bay, and Hamſtead Bay for Ships, and in the Ponds above for ſmall Craft; and ᵉcepting the outer Points of Oyſter and Huntington Bay) the Soundings are regular: and as you approach towards Extremity of the Iſland the Sound becomes narrower, and you will feel the Strength of the Tide encreaſing.

ᴵn the Entrance into Gardener's Bay, between Long-Iſland and Plumb Iſland, and between Plumb Iſland and ᶠhers Iſland, the Tide ſtreams with vaſt Rapidity; and in calm Weather the Ripple (or Race) is heard at a great ᵈtance: it has the Appearance of Shoal Ground, although there is no leſs than twenty Fathoms Water. The ᶜannel between Fiſhers Iſle and the Gull Rocks (which are ſmall low Graſs Iſlands, diſtant about two Miles from ᴾmb Iſland) is five Miles wide, and there is a Shoal with ſeventeen Feet of Water, which lies South-Eaſt about a ᴸague from the Body of Fiſhers Iſland, and may be eaſily avoided by keeping the North Shore on Board.

England and trained as a military engineer. Following the British success in Canada, Des Barres began twelve years of surveying from 1762–1774, and a further ten years elapsed before all the mass of detailed work had been published. Des Barres himself carried out the northern sections while other surveyors continued the work as far south as the Gulf of Mexico. The collection entitled *Atlantic Neptune* began to appear in 1777, in the urgent atmosphere of the American War of Independence. In all, the *Atlantic Neptune* consisted of some 250 charts of unparalleled detail and accuracy, but from the British point of view their publication came a vital few years too late, since the older and less accurate charts are known to have had a material influence on some of the actions in the war. The *Atlantic Neptune* became an unintentional gift to the new American republic, and the charts were standard equipment on all American ships well into the nineteenth century. Des Barres's example of accurate charting was as important as Cook's, but he lacked Cook's exploring spirit, and his selfish, uncompromising character limited his career.

Cook's last voyage had left unsettled the geography of the northern Pacific, and the French sent François La Pérouse in yet another attempt to penetrate the North-West Passage in reverse. Alexander Mackenzie's historic river journeys of 1789–93 from the Great Slave Lake to the Beaufort Sea and to the Pacific created a determination to clarify the geography of this coast. George Vancouver was dispatched to explore the strait at 48 degrees north which the Spaniard Juan de la Fuca was said to have discovered in 1595, and which was believed to lead to the North-West Passage. Cook had missed this strait in 1778 in bad weather. Vancouver spent three years from 1792–4 surveying from California to the Bering Strait. In charting the island that bears his name and the Fuca strait, he finally proved that there was no waterway linking inland Canada with the Pacific coast. Just a few years later in 1801–3 Matthew Flinders finally completed the circumnavigation and charting of all Australia that had eluded so many navigators for two centuries.

The surveying work of Cook, Des Barres and Vancouver was sponsored throughout by the Admiralty, yet all the resulting charts were published by commercial map publishers, and officers of the Royal Navy or the merchant marine had to acquire them on their own initiative through commercial channels. The experiences of exploration and warfare between 1760 and 1790 convinced the Admiralty of the need for an official programme of surveying and chart publication, and the Hydrographic Office was established in 1795. These thirty years had seen the rise to pre-eminence of British chartmakers, in response to the political forces that shaped British naval policy. The growing sophistication of navigation during these years had produced a new type of chart: functional, scientific, adapted to a serious technical purpose in a demanding political context. It is no accident that this same period also saw the maturity of naval architecture with the publication of Frederik Chapman's *Architectura Navalis Mercatoria* in 1768 and John Charnock's *History of Marine Architecture* on 1801. These years saw the entire maritime world mapped, with the exception of the two polar regions, in the deliberate pursuit of geographical knowledge, made possible by the application of science to shipbuilding, navigation and charting.

Yet the Hydrographic Office began modestly enough, with the first Hydrographer,

NEW YORK, 1779, by Des Barres. In the late 18th century the British Navy still had no orginal charts of the colonies in North America, but were dependent on small-scale French charts. J. F. W. des Barres (a British surveyor of Swiss extraction) had worked with Cook in Canada, and was chosen to oversee the production of a new generation of American charts, published as the *Atlantic Neptune*. They extended from Nova Scotia to the Gulf of Mexico. The loss of the British colonies in America meant that these charts became inadvertently a parting gift to the navy of the newly-independent United States.

National Maritime Museum, Greenwich.

Alexander Dalrymple, and two assistants, who spent six years collating the accumulated chart archive of the Admiralty, before the first official Admiralty chart of Quiberon Bay was published in 1800, to be followed in the next year by ten others. Dalrymple had published in 1771 his *Essay on Nautical Surveying*, the first mature work of its kind in English. The new approach to charting had no impact on the Napoleonic Wars. The Hydrographic Office was too small, and the waters recently surveyed by Cook, Des Barres and Vancouver played no part in the war. The British navy still had no charts of its own of European waters, and it is the height of irony that Nelson and his fleet were reliant on French charts for their navigation in the Mediterranean and the Bay of Biscay. We know that the *Victory* was actually carrying French charts of the Mediterranean in 1803–1805. It was during the Napoleonic wars that the British Navy acquired its distinct place in the national consciousness. Revolutionary France was perceived not merely as a rival power but as a malignant force threatening to overthrow civilization. As an island nation with an overseas empire, the only defence against this threat was the Royal Navy. Nor were these fears of Napoleonic ambitions entirely misplaced: Napoleon continually planned for an empire beyond Europe. His expedition to Egypt was the first stage of a planned eastward expansion, thwarted by defeat at the Battle of the Nile. The French seizure of Haiti in 1802 opened the possibility of a campaign against the British Caribbean islands and Mexico itself, while the dream of repossessing Canada reached full planning stage in 1803. Still more ambitious was the idea of an overland invasion of India from a subdued Russia, to be followed by a Pacific campaign. All these grandiose dreams were frustratd by the British containment of the French fleet, as was the actual invasion of Britain planned in 1805. In this context, national fervour was directed towards the navy and became focused on the heroic personality of Nelson. Even in our prosaic age, it is impossible to remain unmoved by this frail, maimed but indomitable man, who had chosen the sea as his element since boyhood, meeting death at the crowning moment of his life, knowing that his courage had turned the course of European history. There is a grim irony in Napoleon's exile to St Helena, a remote fragment of the British empire, surrounded by the waters he had been unable to conquer. Yet only two decades after Trafalgar, British and French ships were fighting side by side in the last battle of the age of sail, the Battle of Navarino, in which they destroyed a Turkish fleet that was threatening Greece.

During the Napoleonic period the publication of Admiralty charts had proceeded slowly, the hydrographer Dalrymple being over-meticulous in his methods. In 1808 he was replaced by Captain Thomas Hurd, under whose direction there was a swift increase in chart production, so that by 1825 the first Admiralty catalogue listed 736 charts. There now began a programme of deliberate reconnaissance and charting with the aim of providing the Royal Navy with a worldwide chart resource to support its activities. The decision was taken in 1823 to place admiralty charts on general sale, and the number of complementary publications gradually increased alongside the charts: tide tables, lists of lights and, most important, Sailing Directions. Commonly known as Pilots, these are the modern descendants of the *periploi* and *portolani*. They are comprehensive descriptions of coastal regions which explain the currents, weather conditions, rocks, shoals, landmarks, seamarks and any other features which may aid navigation. They were illustrated with coastal views which were refined versions of the roughly-drawn profiles that appeared in the Waghenaer sea-atlases of the sixteenth century. The technique of drawing these coastal views was learned by navigation officers as part of their training. They adorned numerous charts and Pilots, and in the hands of certain practitioners such as Mansell they became a delightful minor art-form. The first Sailing Directions were published in 1828, and in the course of the nineteenth century they were expanded to cover the entire world; they formed an immense repository of nautical information, written in a lucid, engaging prose style.

BAY OF NAPLES, 1794, by Rizzi-Zannoni. This is not strictly a sea-chart, for it lacks any hydrographic data; but its detailed mapping of this coast at about 1:100,000 scale would have made it invaluable to mariners. The inclusion of topographic and antiquarian detail was typical of Italian charts of this period, and exercized a great influence on William Smyth's charts of the Mediterranean.

Hydrographic Office, Taunton.

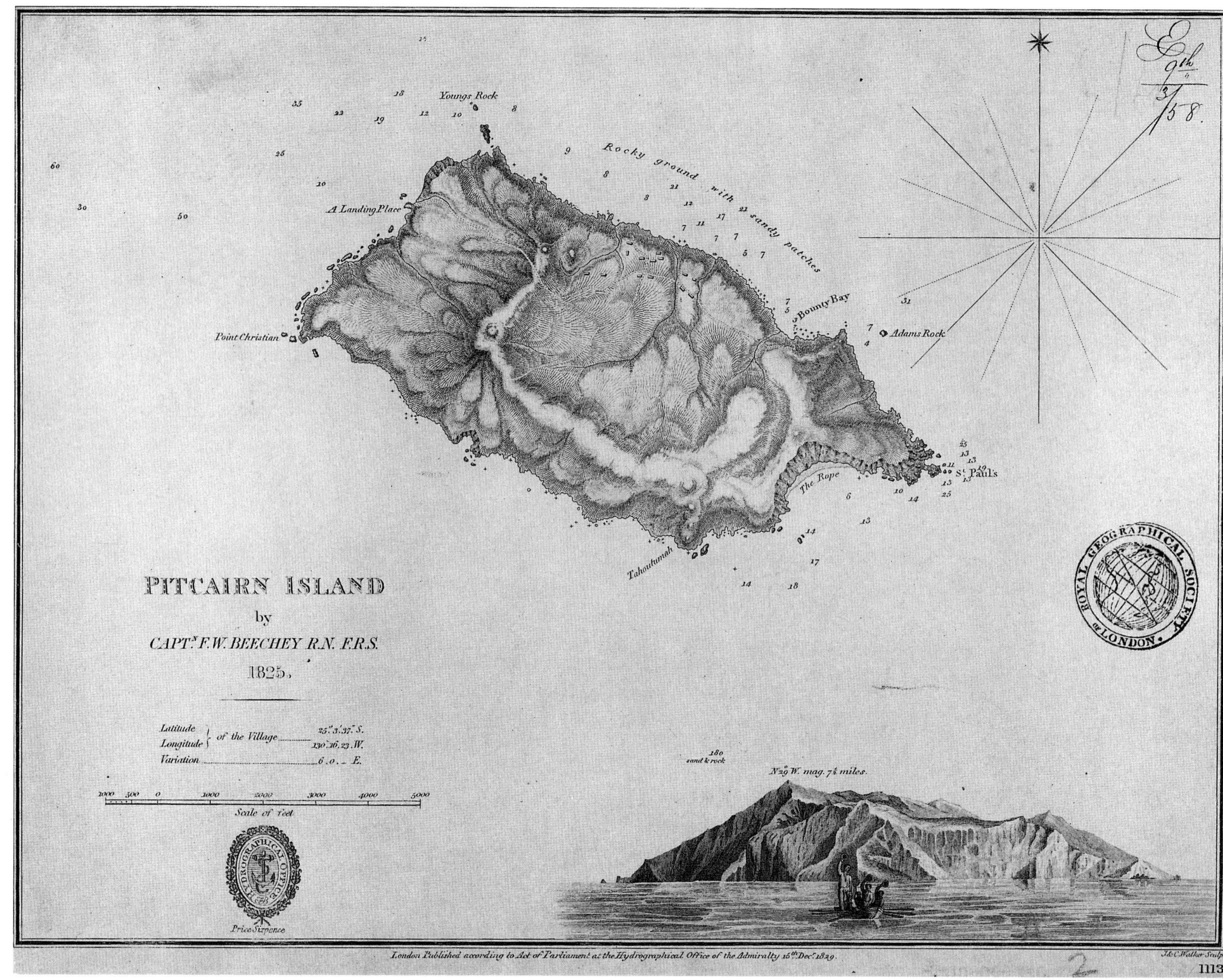

PITCAIRN ISLAND, 1829. First sighted and named in the course of a British reconnaissance voyage under Captain Samuel Wallis, this remote and tiny island achieved fame as the haven of the *Bounty* mutineers in 1789. The fact that the island was wrongly placed on the charts convinced the mutineers that they could remain there in safety, and they were not in fact discovered until 1808. This survey was carried out by Captain Bechey whose ship the *Blossom* touched Pitcairn in 1829, when the last surviving mutineer, Seaman Adams, was still living.

Photograph: Hydrographic Office, Taunton (The British Library: Maps Sec. 15 (1113)).

PALERMO, 1824, by William Smyth. Smyth was a scholar and scientist who carried out the first British surveys in the Mediterranean. His finely engraved charts were embellished with superb views of towns and harbours. After the rigours of the Napoleonic Wars, Smyth had clearly secured for himself an agreeable commission, and he remained ten years in the Mediterranean. He later became president of both the R.G.S. and the R.A.S.

Photograph: Hydrographic Office, Taunton (The British Library: Maps Sec. V (169)).

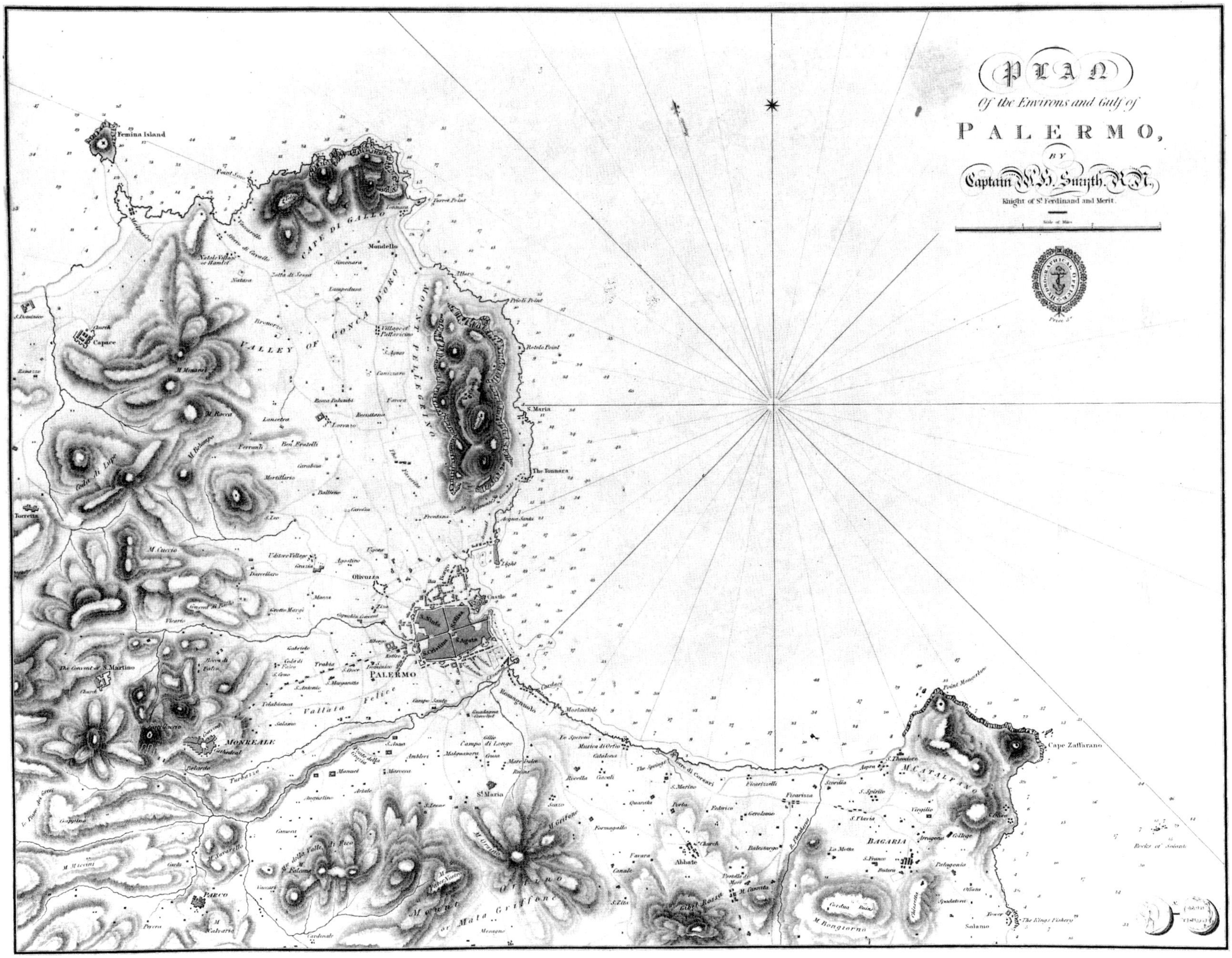

PLAN
Of the Environs and Gulf of
PALERMO,
BY
Captain W.H. Smyth, R.N.
Knight of St. Ferdinand and Merit.

Scale of Miles

HYDROGRAPHICAL OFFICE

Price 5s.

Femina Island
CAPE DI GALLO
Mondello
VALLEY OF CONCA D'ORO
MOUNT PELLEGRINO
S. Maria
The Tonnara
Capace
M. Rocca
PALERMO
MONREALE
Vallata Felice
The Convent of S. Martino
Olivuzza
Cape Zaffarano
M. CATALFANO
BAGARIA
S. Maria
M. Griffone
PARCO
M. Bongiorno
The Kings Fishery

Britain had become the world's pre-eminent maritime nation, but she was far from alone in developing an official charting policy. Denmark had set up a naval hydrographic department in 1784, Spain in 1800 and Russia in 1827. The position in America was curious for in 1816 the U.S. Coast and Geodetic Survey had been organized, but this was not under direct naval control, and a naval Hydrographic Office was established separately in 1830. It was many decades before their functions became defined, the former undertaking coastal surveys of U.S. waters, the latter carrying out charting worldwide. It is evident that a nation's overseas possessions and trade would determine both the need to make charts and the ability to gather information. Britain's position in the nineteenth century with a worldwide empire clearly required a worldwide chart base, and by 1850 almost 2,000 charts had been published. Their open sale to mariners of all kinds made them an invaluable resource to the whole maritime community. Beginning in the years after Trafalgar British hydrographers spread their activities across the globe. Sir Francis Beaufort surveyed the River Plate in 1806–7, and the Eastern Mediterranean in 1810–12. His intense interest in meteorology led him to evolve the gauge of wind-strength which bears his name. His period as Hydrographer to the Royal Navy from 1829–1855 was full of innovations in both chart publications and in the technical basis that underpinned them. The first British survey of the Mediterranean occupied William Henry Smyth during the years 1813–1824, and his charts are among the most elegant ever published, enriched with splendid harbour and coastal views. William Owen surveyed the coasts of Africa on a naval expedition which had the additional aim of surpressing the now-illegal slave trade. Fever on the west African coast wrought such havoc among Owen's crew that these surveys were later said, in a famous report, to have been drawn in blood.

In addition to strict surveying, the Admiralty was taking an increasing interest in earth science and was prepared to sponsor expeditions which combined surveying with scientific research. The most momentous such voyage was that of Captain Robert Fitzroy's HMS *Beagle* in 1831–36, which carried one of the most famous passengers in nautical history – Charles Darwin. While Fitzroy surveyed the Falklands, Patagonia, Chile and the Galapagos, Darwin was amassing the observations of plants, animals, rocks and landforms which would form the basis of his epoch-making theories. It is certain that without the fieldwork carried out on this voyage, his theory of evolution would not have taken shape as it did. From the months the *Beagle* spent in the Pacific, Darwin formulated a theory of the origin of coral reefs which is still broadly accepted.

By the early nineteenth century the only areas of the earth's oceans still unexplored were the two polar regions. It was clear by now that no commercial or imperial prizes awaited the explorers of these desolate territories, but the drive to complete the map had now become an end in itself. National prestige was allied with scientific curiosity in a renewed attempt to penetrate the icy perimeters of the Arctic and Antarctic. The North-West Passage was the most enduring goal. The outlets, if any existed, from Baffin Bay and Hudson's Bay clearly held the key to any passage to the north of Canada, but these waters were ice-bound for at least eight months of the year, and navigation was made doubly difficult by the proximity of the north magnetic pole (at this time located on the Boothia Peninsula at approximately 72°N. and 93°W.) which made compasses all but

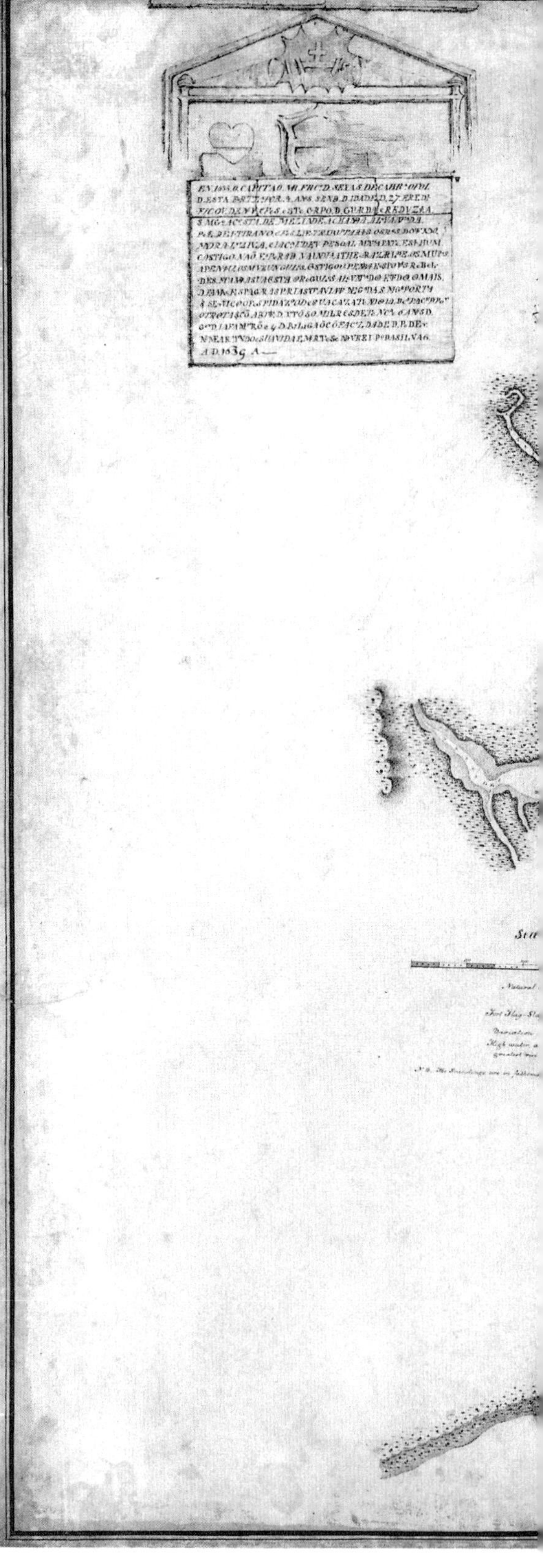

MOMBASA, 1824. The ancient port of Mombasa was founded by Arab traders of the 11th century. It was visited by the great traveller Ibn Battutah, and in 1498 Vasco da Gama found it 'a place of considerable commerce'. As a strategic base, it was fought over by Arabs, Persians, Portuguese and Turks, finally coming under British control in 1895. This chart was made by William Owen in the course of the Admiralty survey of African waters in 1821–26. The vignette shows part of Fort Jesus, the Portuguese stronghold, built in 1595.

Hydrographic Office, Taunton.

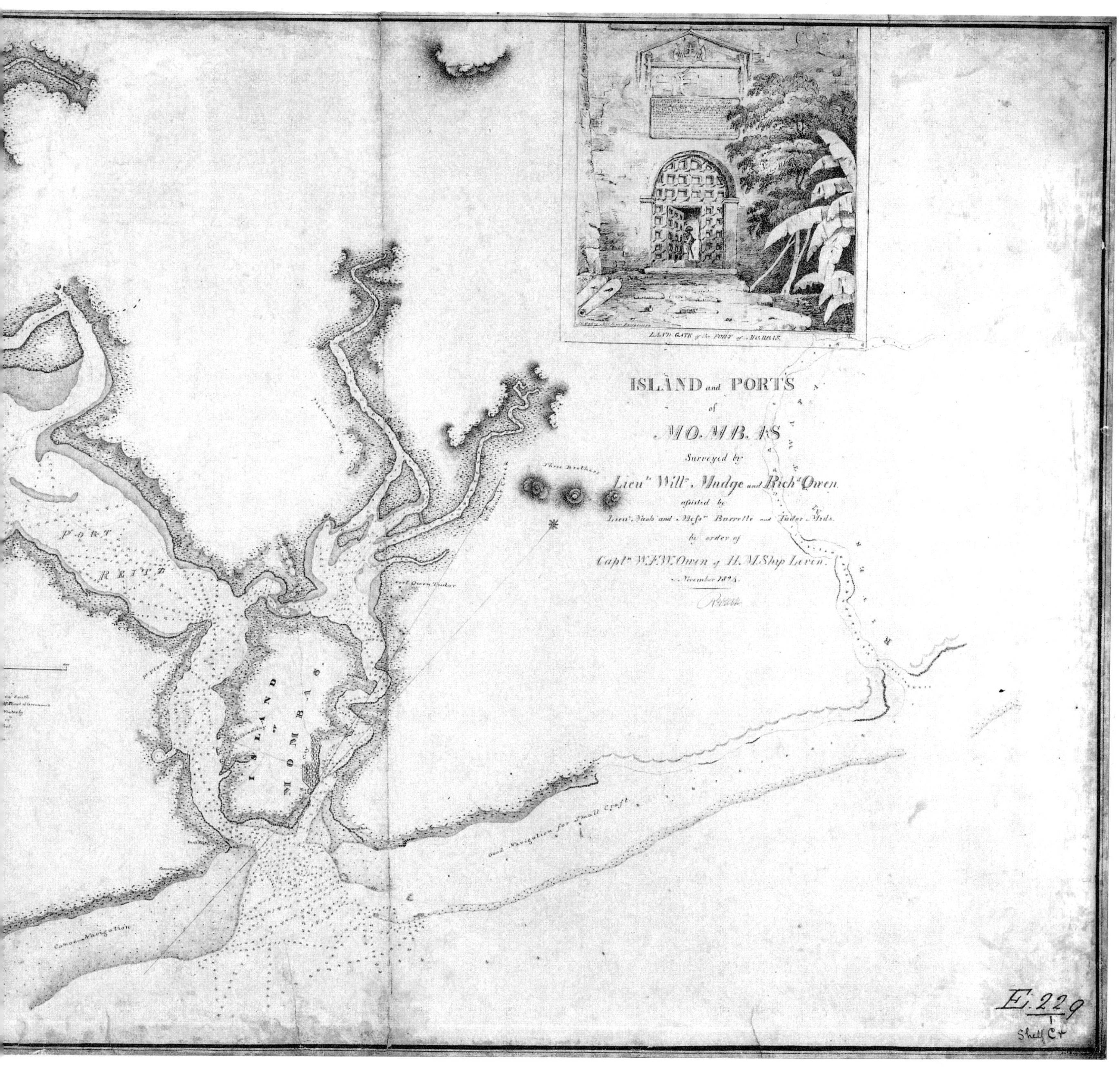
LAND GATE of the PORT of MOMBAS
ISLAND and PORTS
of
MOMBAS
Surveyed by
Lieu^t Willm Mudge and Richd Owen
assisted by
Lieu^t Nash and Messrs Barrette and Tudor Mids.
by order of
Captⁿ W.F.W. Owen of H.M. Ship Leven.
November 1824.
Three Brothers
PORT
REITZ
Port Owen Tudor
ISLAND of MOMBAS
Good Navigation for Small Craft
Canoe Navigation
E.229
Shelf C+

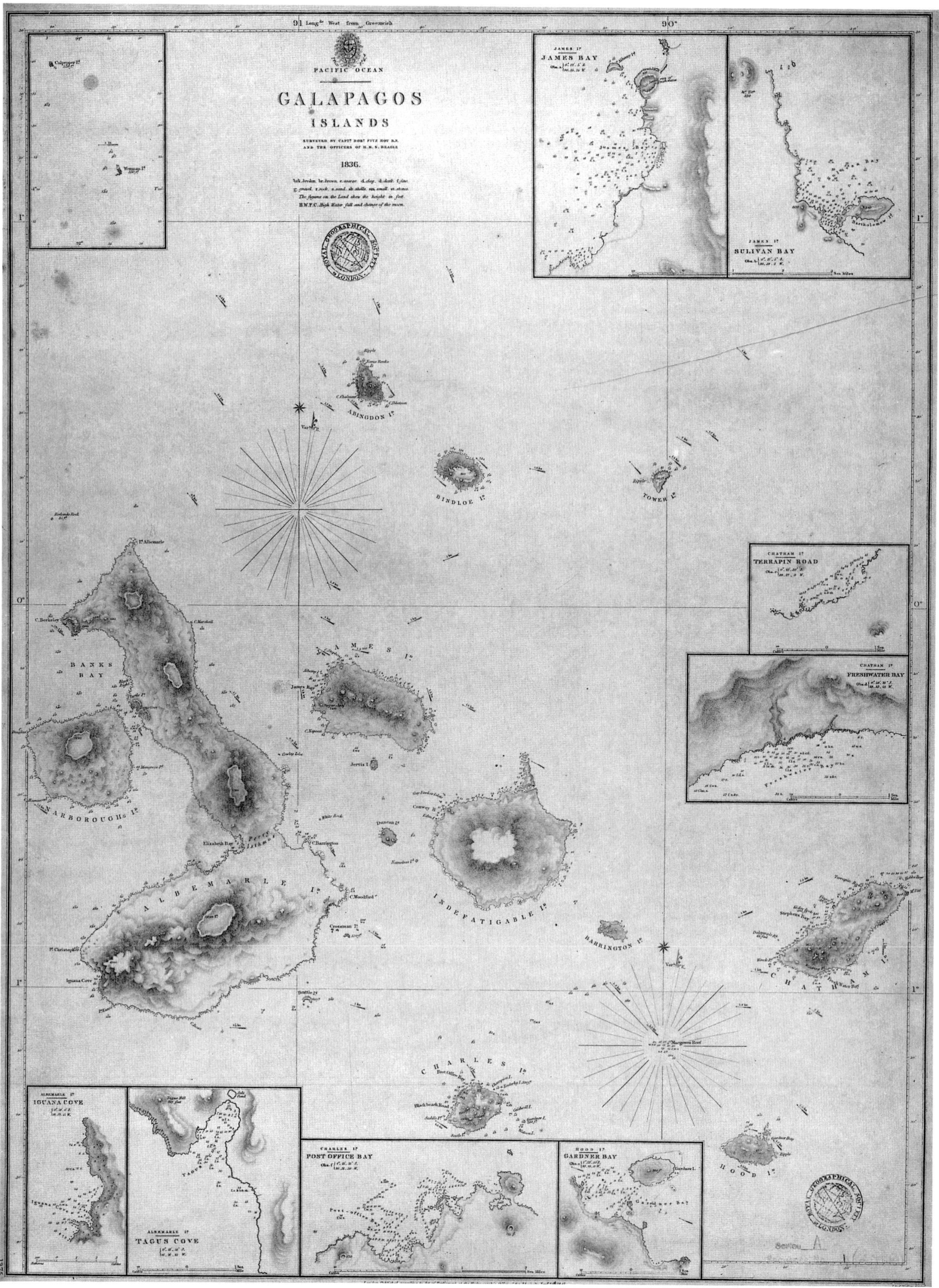

91 Longde West from Greenwich
90°
PACIFIC OCEAN
GALAPAGOS
ISLANDS
SURVEYED BY CAPTN ROBT FITZ ROY R.N.
AND THE OFFICERS OF H.M.S. BEAGLE
1836.
ROYAL GEOGRAPHICAL SOCIETY LONDON
JAMES Id
JAMES BAY
JAMES Id
SULIVAN BAY
ABINGDON Id
BINDLOE Id
TOWER Id
CHATHAM Id
TERRAPIN ROAD
CHATHAM Id
FRESHWATER BAY
BANKS BAY
JAMES Id
NARBOROUGH Id
ALBEMARLE Id
INDEFATIGABLE Id
BARRINGTON Id
CHATHAM Id
CHARLES Id
HOOD Id
ALBEMARLE Id
IGUANA COVE
ALBEMARLE Id
TAGUS COVE
CHARLES Id
POST OFFICE BAY
HOOD Id
GARDNER BAY

HONG KONG, 1847 by L. G. Heath. Coastal views had been printed as navigational aids since at least the 16th century, and the art of drawing them was part of the navigator's training in the British Navy. Some of them reached a high artistic level in their own right.
Hydrographic Office, Taunton.

useless. The early voyages of Ross and Parry between 1818 and 1833 built up considerable knowledge of the region from Lancaster Sound to Melville Island, and in 1831 Ross reached the north magnetic pole – 'The centre of one of nature's great and dark powers'. But it was the mystery surrounding Sir John Franklin which caught the public imagination. Franklin was already aged sixty and a famous figure when he sailed with the *Erebus* and the *Terror* in 1845 in search of the North-West Passage; the darkness which closed over his tracks became a *cause célèbre*. Between 1848 and 1859 no less than forty expeditions were mounted to search for Franklin and his men, before the cairn containing the ship's log was found on King William Island. It showed that the ships had been ice-bound for a year and a half, during which time Franklin himself had died, and that the crew had abandoned their ships in April 1848, and set off to find the nearest habitation – a Hudson's Bay Company base at Fort Resolution 500 miles away. From this journey not one of the 129 men survived. They had taken the ship's boat, hoping to ascend Back's Fish River, but they lacked the strength to drag it across the ice. This boat was found, and nearby in the ice two skeletons, with a watch, handkerchief, comb, a prayer book and a copy of *The Vicar of Wakefield*.

The expeditions searching for Franklin added enormously to knowledge of the Canadian Arctic, and map publishers including the Admiralty issued special charts to illustrate the progress of polar exploration during this period. One of the searchers, Robert McClure, actually became the first man to traverse the North-West Passage in 1850, although this was accomplished partly on sledges after he had abandoned his ship, and it was accomplished in reverse as he had entered the Arctic sea through the Bering Strait. The long-sought passage linking the Atlantic and the Pacific was not finally navigated until 1906 by the Norwegian Roald Amundsen in a three-year adventure, during which he too found skeletons of Franklin's men which had lain sixty years in the Arctic ice.

THE GALAPAGOS ISLANDS, 1836. The nineteen islands forming the Galapagos group were discovered by the Spanish in the 16th century, were known thereafter to pirates and whalers, but remained uninhabited until Ecuador took formal possession of them in the 1830s. They became internationally famous following Darwin's researches in 1835 into the unique animal species that had evolved in isolation there. Darwin was a passenger on board the *Beagle*, and Admiralty survey ship, whose captain, Robert Fitzroy, was responsible for this first detailed survey of the islands.
Hydrographic Office, Taunton.

The other historic passage to the North-East from Europe to the Bering Strait had been achieved in 1879 by the Swede, Adolf Erik Nordenskiöld. It was during the late nineteenth century that the absence of any identifiable polar topography, and the noticeable drift of the ice-mass, led mariners and scientists to suspect that the Arctic was not a true continent but a frozen sea. The concept was conclusively proved by Fridtjof Nansen's ice-bound 'voyage' of 1893–96, in which his ship was carried 1,500 miles through the ice-cap, passing within a few degrees of the pole itself. By contrast, it was clear from the first sightings in the 1820s that Antarctica was a continental land-mass, with mountains and glaciers. It was first circumnavigated by the Russian Thaddeus Bellinghausen in 1819–21, who initiated an eighty-year period during which attempts were made to chart the continental coastline beyond the ice, especially in the Weddell Sea and the Ross Sea. Maritime involvement in the Antarctic was not essentially different from that in the Arctic, despite their fundamental physical differences: it concerned access for overland attempts to reach the poles, scientific research, and assessment of commercial potential in matters such as whaling. The strategic value of these regions, especially the Arctic, emerged only in the twentieth century. Polar exploration became an international race which offered no tangible rewards, but in which science, personal courage and national rivalry became strangely intermingled. Men like Nansen, Amundsen and Shackleton became national heroes, and the accounts of their endurance in this most savage environment form the final chapter in the history of European exploration which began with Marco Polo.

Progressing beyond geographical charting, the maritime powers of the mid-nineteenth century became involved in the beginnings of oceanography. Matthew Maury of the U.S. Hydrographic Office pioneered the collation of data on winds, currents, ocean floors, ice movements and the other topics that form the material of physical oceanography. The U.S. Naval Observatory had been founded in 1833 and it played a fundamental role in supplying scientific data for the U.S. Navy, especially in the determination of time. The laying of ocean floor telegraph cables in the Atlantic in the 1850s was a great stimulant to the investigation of the seabed, in which British and American surveyors cooperated. The voyage of the Royal Navy research ship *Challenger* between 1872 and 1876 produced an enormous volume of new data on the composition of the sea, on marine life, on the ocean floor, and on meteorology. The discovery of continental shelves and of the mid-ocean Atlantic ridge were the first links in the chain of evidence that led to the theory of continental drift proposed by Alfred Wegener in 1915, and ultimately to the modern understanding of plate tectonics. Efforts to analyse tides purely in terms of lunar and solar positions had been frustrated by the complexity of the seabed and shoreline. Oceanographic data enabled William Ferrel to construct in 1884 an analogue tide-predictor that remained in use until the electronic age.

There were few strategic opportunities for the Royal Navy to test its new approach to hydrography, but in the Chinese Opium Wars marine surveyors played an important role in the capture of Canton, and the Crimean War, whatever the disasters of the land campaign, saw successful naval operations. There were no fleet engagements, but swift accurate surveying of the northern Black Sea, an area for which no British charts existed, enabled troops to be landed and bombardments to be put in place. The Crimean War also involved a Baltic campaign in which 10,000 troops were landed to attack the Russian fortress on Aland Island, again made possible by the presence of naval surveyors. As the Admiralty spread its survey net over the world, local reaction to the presence of European surveyors was not always favourable. In 1863 Captain Henry St John was surveying the coasts of Japan when he was drawn into a one-and-a-half hour battle with a shore battery in Kagoshima, in which part of the town was burned; it was the kind of incident that might have led to war in those days of gunboat diplomacy.

Imperial rivalry between the European powers continued to shape naval policy. France had lost most of her empire after 1815, but steadily acquired a new one with conquests in Africa, while taking Tahiti and the Marquesas Islands in the 1840s, and Indo-China in 1859. After the Napoleonic Wars, Britain had retained the Cape Colony, Ceylon, Mauritius, the Seychelles and Malta. British sovereignty over the whole of Australia and

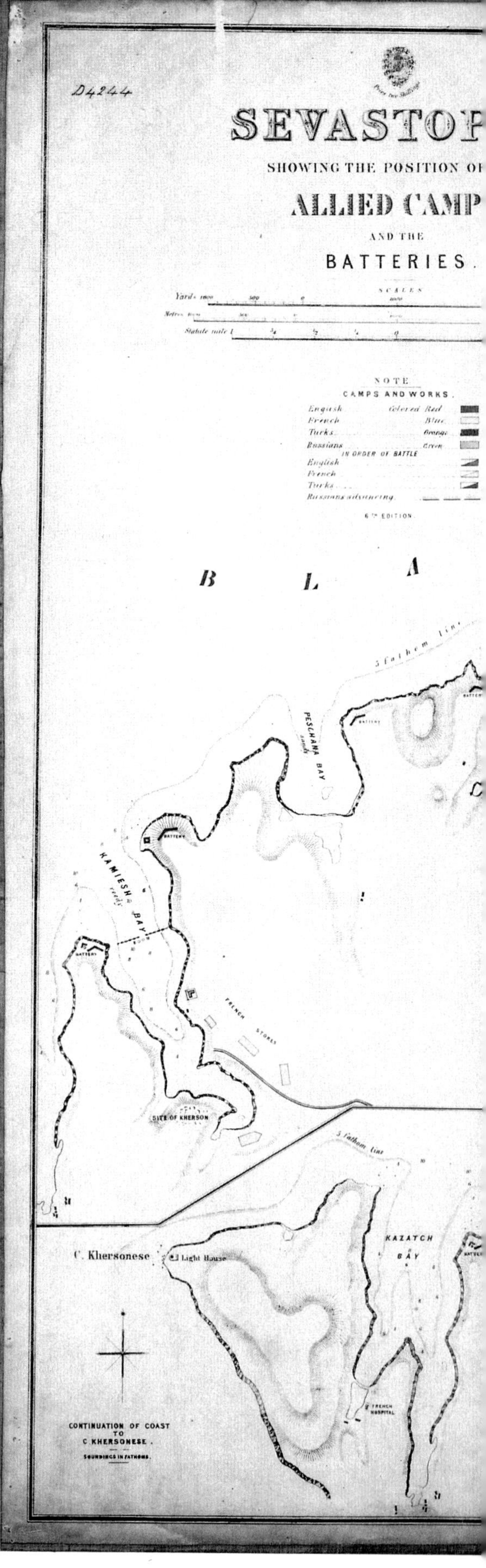

SEVASTOPOL, 1854. In the Crimean War of 1854–56, the first objective of the British and French was to take the city of Sevastopol, which became the object of a year-long siege. This special chart was published to show the allied positions, in particular the English fleet, which was engaged in a sea attack on the town on 17 October. It was produced by George Marsh, master of HMS *Firebrand.*

Hydrographic Office, Taunton.

POSITION OF THE ENGLISH FLEET ENGAGED IN THE SEA ATTACK ON SEVASTOPOL 17TH OCTR 1854.
investigated from the following authorities, by
MR GEORGE MARSH, MASTR H.M.S. FIREBRAND.
SEVASTOPOL HARBOUR
RUSSIAN ENCAMPMENT
BATTLE OF INKERMAN NOVR 5TH
FRENCH WORKS
LORD RAGLAN'S HEAD QUARTERS
English Light Cavalry charge on 25 Novr 1854.
RUSSIAN ATTACK OCTR 25TH
TURKISH WORKS
Maltby & Sons, lith

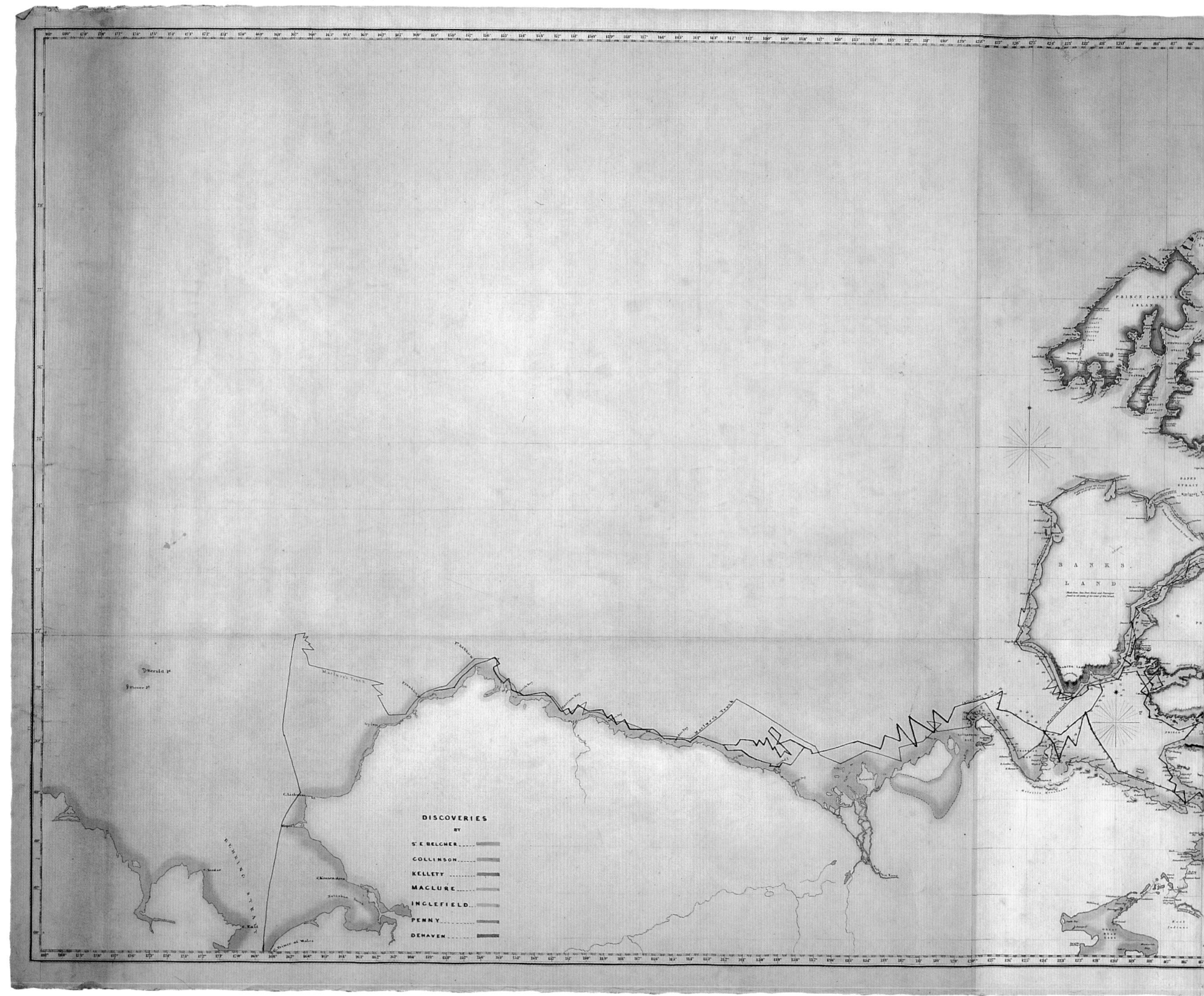

New Zealand was claimed in the 1820s, and she continued to acquire further territories: Singapore in 1819, Gold Coast in 1821, Malacca in 1824, Hong Kong in 1842, Natal in 1843, Burma in 1852, Lagos in 1861 and Sarawak in 1888. Many of these territories were strategic points in a worldwide network of sea routes. Britain was particularly concerned with the sea route to India, her most prized possession, and this entire system plainly depended on naval power to guarantee the merchant fleet that sailed from Europe to these distant waters. By 1890 British investment overseas was greater than that of France, Germany, Holland and the United States combined. More and more of the world was becoming drawn into a single trading network directed by the industrialized powers. The case of China is typical: China had resisted penetration by the western powers and had

SHACKLETON'S SHIP IN THE ICE. Of all Shackleton's Antarctic voyages, that of 1914–16 was the epic. His ship the *Endurance* was crushed by ice in the Weddell Sea, and the men drifted on ice-floes for four months before they could launch their boats. Landing on one of the South Shetland islands, Shackleton sailed with five men through immense dangers to South Georgia, and returned with a rescue expedition which saved the main party. Shackleton and his men knew nothing of the slaughter in Europe as they engaged in their private war for survival against ice and sea.

National Maritime Museum, Greenwich.

THE ARCTIC SEAS, 1854. The disappearance of Sir John Franklin in 1847 while searching for a north-west passage aroused intense public interest. Some forty expeditions were mounted in the following twelve years to search for him, and they added greatly to the knowledge of the Arctic. The Admiralty took the unusual step of issuing this special chart to show the rapidly-changing state of knowledge of the region. There is virtually no hydrographic information, and the chart has here a non-technical, public function.

Hydrographic Office, Taunton.

become a considerable exporter in her own right. The two Opium Wars of 1840–42 and 1856–60 were used a pretext to enforce economic treaties which gave the west, mainly Britain and France, access to China, and these treaties were guaranteed by the naval presence in the China Sea and in the Yangtze River. In 1800 Europe and its possessions, including former colonies, claimed about 55% of the earth's surface. But many of these claims were quite tenuous, and effective control existed over around 35%. Rivalry between the colonial powers during the nineteenth century led to the hardening of many of these claims, so that by 1880 some 65% of the world was dominated by Europe and America, and by 1914 after the last great scramble for territory in Africa, the figure had risen to a staggering 85%.

SHIPS OF THE British Fleet in Portland Roads.
National Maritime Museum, Greenwich.

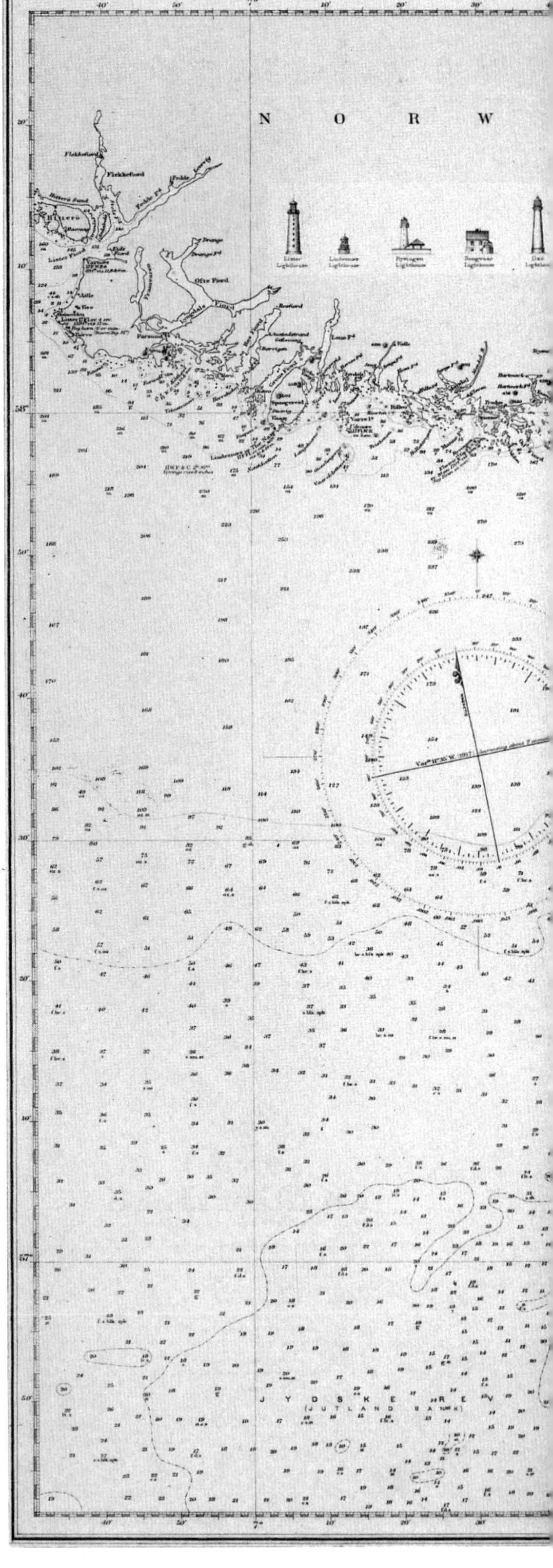

JUTLAND, 1913. The unprecedented fire-power of the great battleships was matched only by their mutual vulnerability. Jellicoe was said to have been haunted by the knowledge that he could 'lose the war in an afternoon'. For this reason almost two years of the Great War passed before the main fleets of Britain an Germany met in full battle. The long-delayed encounter took place in the North Sea at the mouth of the Skaggerak on 31 May 1916. Tactically and numerically the British Fleet was strongly placed, but signalling errors, sea-mist and approaching darkness frustrated their efforts. The two fleets lost contact during the night, and the action ended indecisively. The British fleet sustained greater losses, but the German fleet was thereafter confined to its harbours and played no further part in the war.
Photograph: Hydrographic Office, Taunton
(The British Library: Maps Sec. 3 (2289)).

By the mid-nineteenth century the greatest revolution in maritime history was under way – the advent of powered ships, in the first instance steam-powered. After several decades of experiment and relative failure, it became clear that the future lay with powered ships, which were faster, bigger, more comfortable and more efficient than sail; in time and cost, one steam ton was reckoned the equivalent of four sail tons. The grace and tradition of the great sailing ships could not compensate for speed and economy, especially after the opening of the Suez Canal in 1869 cut the eastbound steamship's fuel problems. The steamship had the effect of shrinking the world, and without this power revolution the vast waves of emigration from Europe would have been impossible. It is estimated that some 50 million people left Europe between 1830 and 1910, most destined for the Americas and Australasia. The warship of the late nineteenth century was steam-powered and steel-built, so that Britain was forced to construct virtually a new navy. But the industrial revolution was international, and it permitted the creation of three new navies – the German, the American and the Japanese – to challenge Britain's dominance.

The United States's rise to world power arguably began with its expedition to penetrate the seclusion in which Japan had cloaked itself for two hundred years. Matthew Perry's two extraordinary naval missions during 1853–54 succeeded in their aim of establishing a trading relationship between the two nations, but also had a profound effect on Japan itself, with incalculable consequences on the entire Asia-Pacific region. The United States acquired Alaska from Russia in 1867, and the brief war with Spain in 1898, which was necessarily an entirely naval war, provided the opportunity to annex Hawaii and the Philippines, as well as Puerto Rico and, temporarily, Cuba. The opening of the

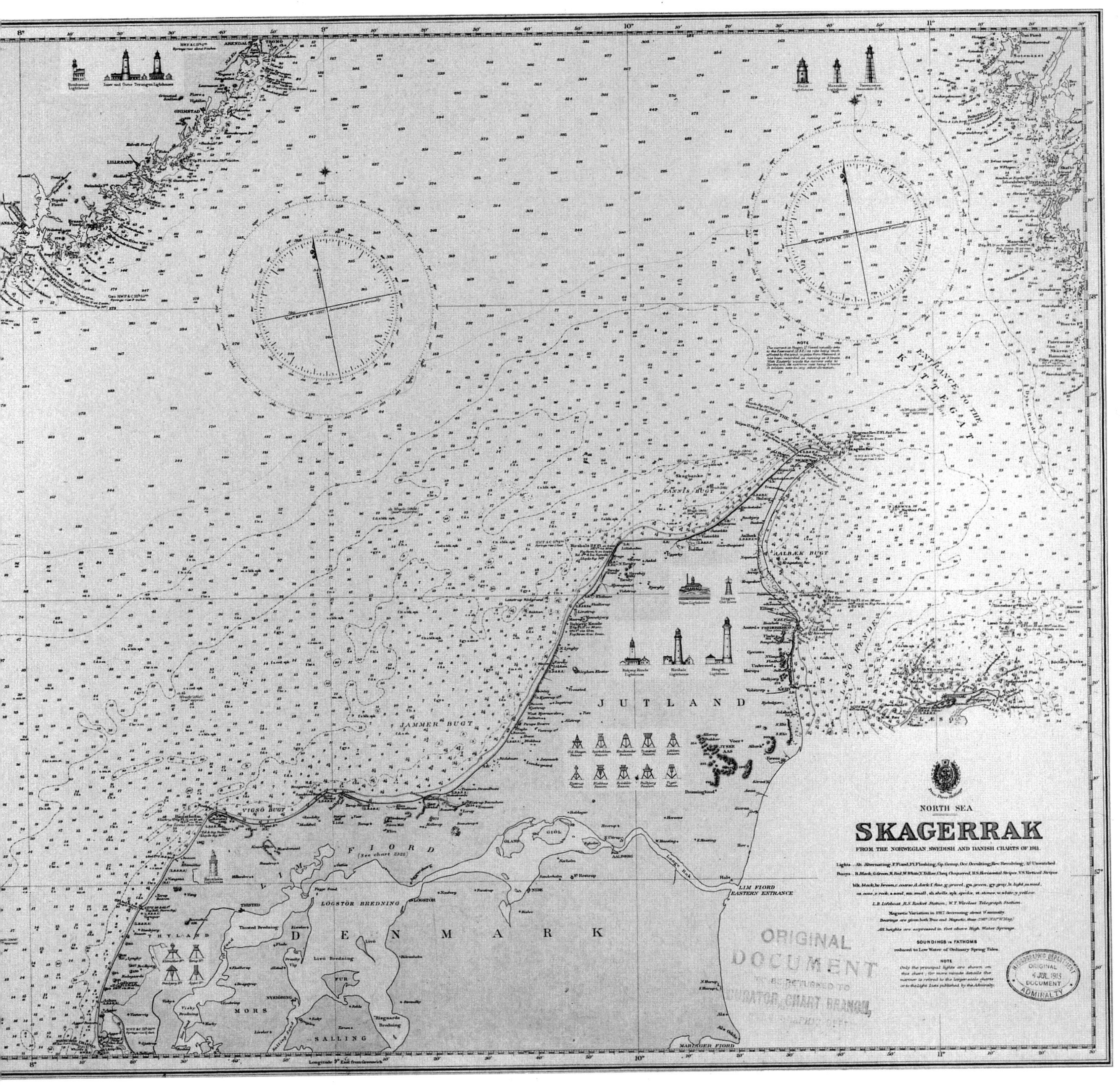
NORTH SEA
SKAGERRAK
FROM THE NORWEGIAN, SWEDISH AND DANISH CHARTS OF 1911.
Lights .. Alt. Alternating, F. Fixed, Fl. Flashing, Gp. Group, Occ. Occulting, Rev. Revolving, (U) Unwatched
Buoys .. B. Black, G. Green, R. Red, W. White, Y. Yellow, Cheq. Chequered, H.S. Horizontal Stripes, V.S. Vertical Stripes
L.B. Lifeboat, R.S. Rocket Station, W.T. Wireless Telegraph Station
All heights are expressed in feet above High Water Springs.
SOUNDINGS IN FATHOMS
reduced to Low Water of Ordinary Spring Tides.
NOTE
Only the principal lights are shown on this chart; for more minute details the mariner is referred to the larger scale charts or to the Light Lists published by the Admiralty.
HYDROGRAPHIC DEPARTMENT
ORIGINAL
4 JUL. 1913
DOCUMENT
ADMIRALTY
ORIGINAL
DOCUMENT
JUTLAND
JAMMER BUGT
TANNIS BUGT
AALBÆK BUGT
VIGSÖ BUGT
LIM FIORD
LIM FIORD EASTERN ENTRANCE
LOGSTÖR BREDNING
D E N M A R K
MORS
SALLING
FUR
ENTRANCE TO THE KATTEGAT
LÆSO
ARENDAL
LILLESAND
THISTED
AALBORG
MARIAGER FIORD
NOTE
Longitude 9° East from Greenwich

THE SINKING of the *Scharnhorst*, 1943.
National Maritime Museum, Greenwich.

Panama Canal in 1914 placed a powerful economic and strategic weapon in American hands. Japan's new-found industrial strength expressed itself in an awakened militarism and in the building of a modern war fleet, which went on to annihilate the Russian fleet in 1905 at the Battle of Tsushima Strait. At the same time another historically non-maritime nation, Germany, directed her industrial skills and her political ambitions into the deliberate construction of a modern navy, to compete with and perhaps supplant her European rivals. Imperial opportunities were limited by this time, but in the 1880s Germany acquired large African territories (Cameroon, South-West Africa, and East Africa) and in the Pacific the Bismarck Archipelago. The tensions set up in this great imperial game led to World War One, in which, as has often been pointed out, the participant fleets were so precious as strategic weapons that neither side was willing to risk them in action – a deeply ironic conclusion to half a century of naval innovation and rivalry. The 1914 action off the Falkland Islands, in which the first *Scharnhorst* and *Gneisenau* were sunk, demonstrated that years of naval planning and investment might be destroyed in hours, and it was nearly two years before the two fleets met again at the indecisive Battle of Jutland. The German colonies were left exposed and were swiftly removed from the map – ironically with the aid of the Japanese navy. The more secretive and deadly weapon of submarine warfare emerged to threaten the enormously powerful but vulnerable battleship, as well as wreaking havoc with commercial shipping. Ultimately however, it was largely the economic naval blockade of Germany which ended the western stalemate which had resisted all military solutions.

It is evident that this international rivalry produced an enormous increase in charting. The number of British Admiralty charts published reached 2,000 by 1914, and the American, German and Japanese navies were rapidly building up their chart base for their areas of geographic interest. By 1914 the United States Hydrographic Office had published more than a thousand charts, naturally with the emphasis on the Atlantic and Pacific. At the same time the U.S. Coast and Geodetic Survey had also passed the thousand mark in chart publication, although more than 75% of these were of American coastal waters. The historical accident of having two official chartmaking bodies led to some anomalies,

NORTH CAPE, 1944. The Arctic convoys during World War Two were of vital importance in conveying supplies to Russia via the port of Archangel. They were highly vulnerable, and suffered heavy losses. Off the North Cape of Norway on 26 December 1943 in ferocious weather, the British cruisers escorting a large convoy encountered the powerful German battle-cruiser *Scharnhorst*. In a night battle illuminated by starshells, the *Scharnhorst* was pounded by torpedoes and guns from the *Duke of York* and the *Jamaica*, and sank. In the Arctic darkness, only 36 of her crew of more than 2,000 were pulled from the icy seas.
Hydrographic Office, Taunton.

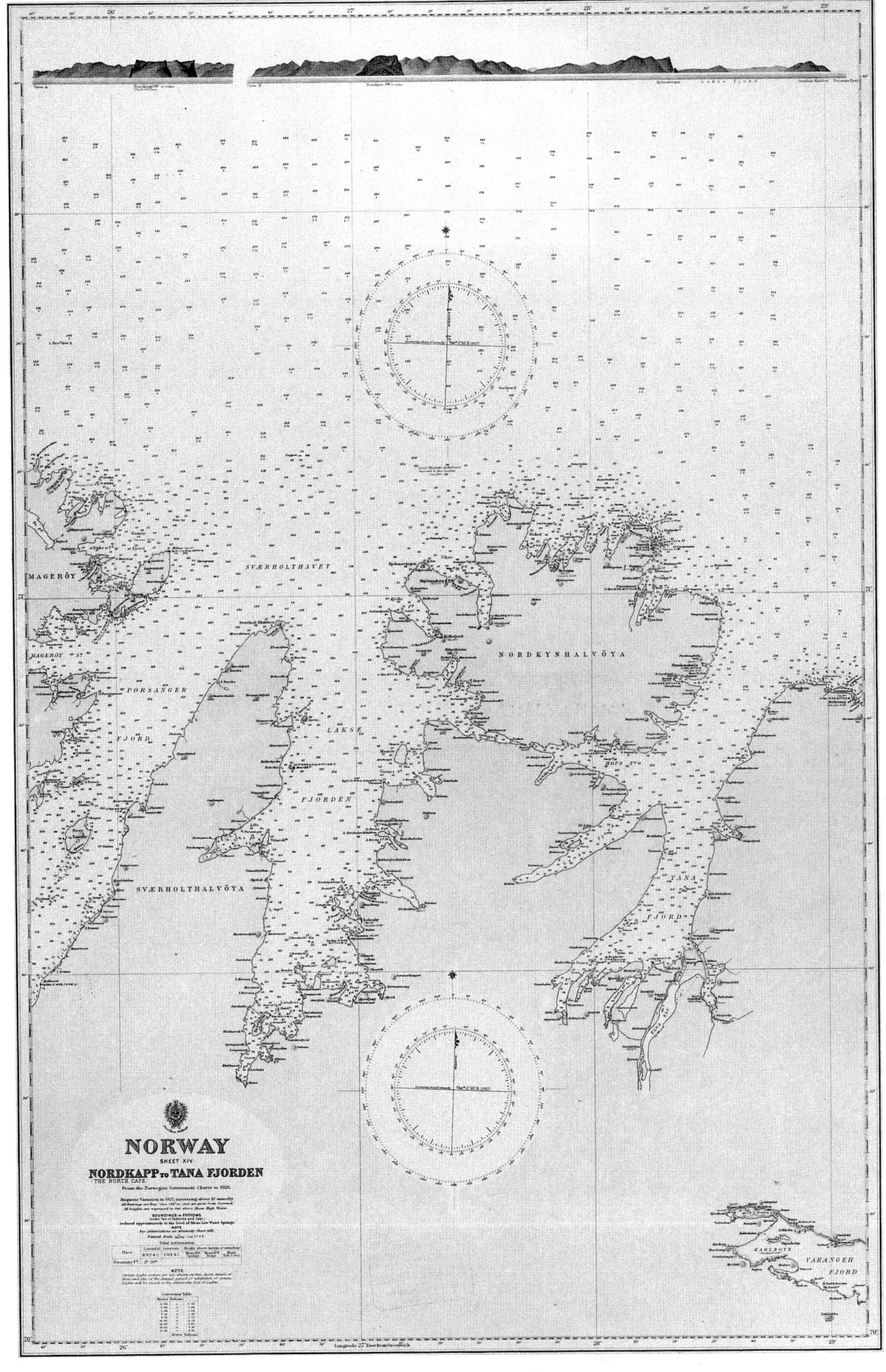
MAGERÖY
SVÆRHOLTHAVET
MAGERÖY ST
PORSANGER
FJORD
LAKSE
FJORDEN
NORDKYNHALVÖYA
SVÆRHOLTHALVÖYA
TANA
FJORD
VARANGER
FJORD
NORWAY
SHEET XIV
NORDKAPP TO TANA FJORDEN
(THE NORTH CAPE)
From the Norwegian Government Charts to 1926.
SOUNDINGS IN FATHOMS
NOTE
Tidal Information
NOTE
Conversion Table

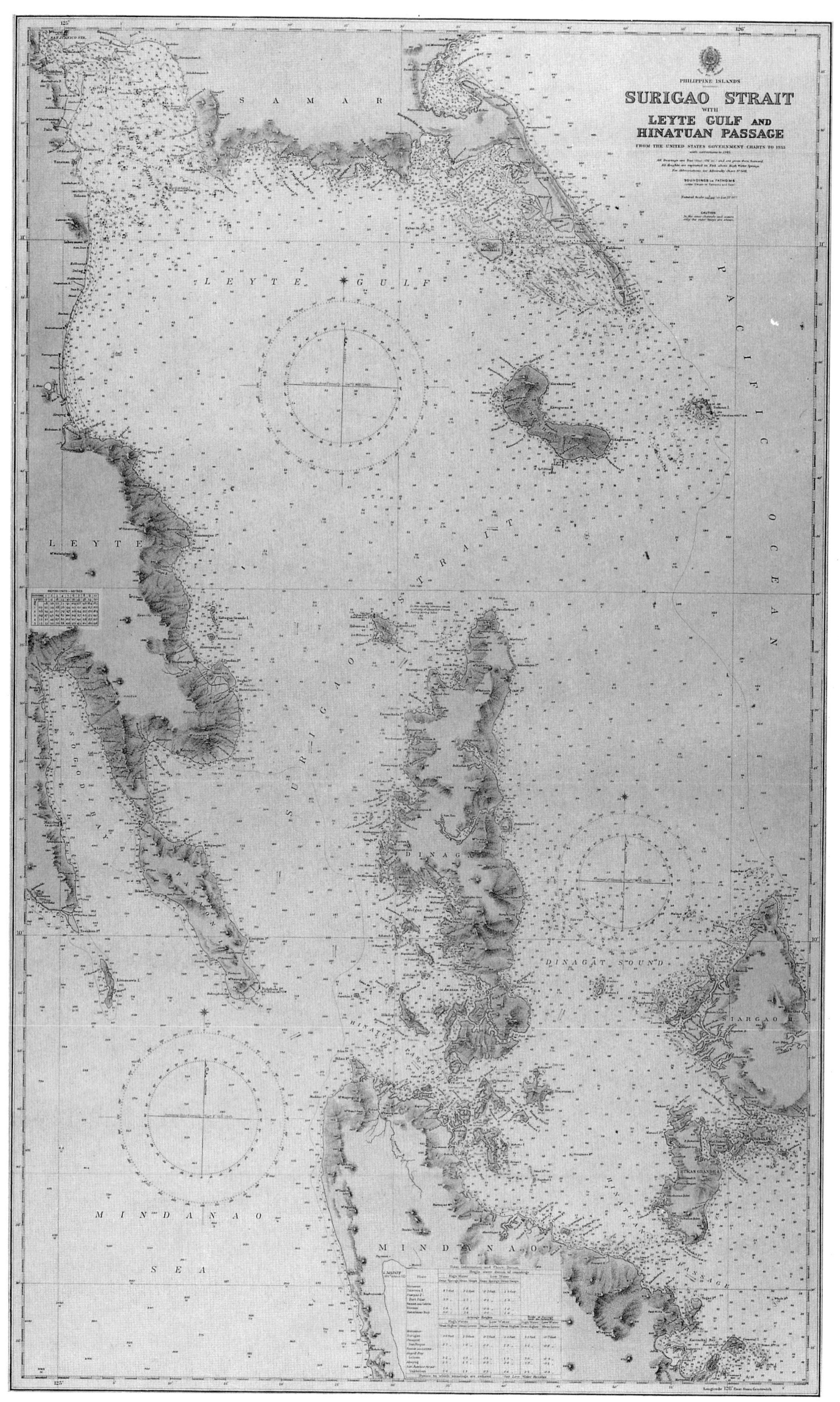
PHILIPPINE ISLANDS
SURIGAO STRAIT
WITH
LEYTE GULF AND
HINATUAN PASSAGE
FROM THE UNITED STATES GOVERNMENT CHARTS TO 1933
SOUNDINGS IN FATHOMS
CAUTION
SAMAR
LEYTE GULF
PACIFIC OCEAN
LEYTE
SURIGAO STRAIT
SOGOD BAY
DINAGAT SOUND
SIARGAO I.
HINATUAN PASSAGE
MINDANAO
MINDANAO SEA
Kalicoan I.
125°
126°
11°
10°

LEYTE GULF, 1944. In terms of the size of the opposing forces, Leyte Gulf was the biggest battle in naval history. In October 1944 the Americans were assembling a vast landing-force off the coast of Leyte Island to recapture the Philippines. The Japanese fleet planned a massive counter-attack, and the ensuing battle lasted four days and spread 500 miles from Leyte itself. The Japanese lost three battleships, four aircraft-carriers, ten cruisers and nine destroyers, while the Americans lost only six vessels. The Japanese navy was irreparably damaged in this immense battle.

Hydrographic Office, Taunton.

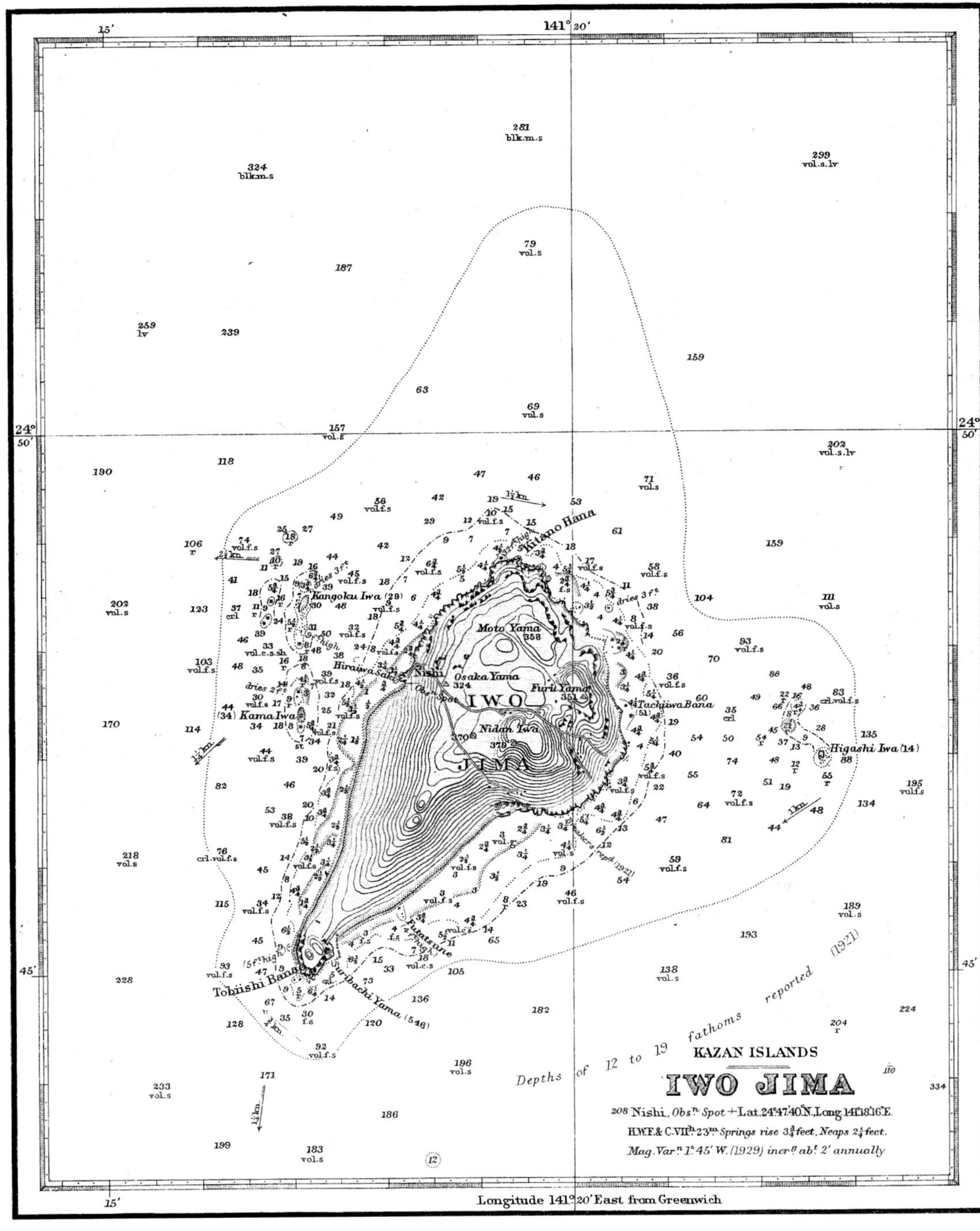

IWO JIMA, The tiny volcanic island of Iwo Jima is barely eight miles square, but has the bloodiest history of any island in the world. The Japanese base there was an essential strategic target in the planned U.S. invasion of Japan. On 19 February 1945 some 70,000 U.S. marines began landing on the island, which was defended by 21,000 Japanese. After 25 days of the most savage fighting seen in the entire war, 20,000 U.S. troops had been killed or wounded, while the Japanese garrison had died almost to a man.

Hydrographic Office, Taunton.

for example the Coast and Geodetic Survey charted the Philippines at this time, while the Hydrographic Office did not. The volume of data carried by these charts became ever larger and more complex, and with the ever-increasing size of naval and merchant ships, precision of detail became more and more vital. To the fundamental requirement for accurate depth soundings were added data on currents and tidal streams, marker buoys, navigational lights, radio beacons, wrecks and seabed features. The chart became increasingly technical and the cost of navigational failure became ever higher.

World War Two was fought on a global scale far exceeding that of World War One, covering every sea and ocean of the world. In an age of total war, merchant shipping was as involved as naval, and the volume of special charts produced in the war was enormous

THE INDIAN OCEAN. A false-colour image showing variations in the height of the sea surface during the monsoon season. In the red areas the sea surface is actually higher than mean-sea-level. The monsoon, of crucial importance to sailors in the Indian Ocean for centuries, is here visible in an eloquent image.
NASA/SPL.

– charts of minefields, wrecks, troop landing areas, convoy routes and so on. Strategic and tactical demands gave enormous impetus to research and development in navigation, charting and oceanography. It was in this war that electronics revolutionized position-finding, offering for the first time a self-contained system independent of sightings and calculations. Even before World War One, the advent of radio had led to the introduction of radio beacons which overcame the mariner's ancient navigational enemies, darkness and fog. Radio communication had also a decisive impact on the calculation of time and the fixing of longitude. Simultaneously came the electrically-driven gyrocompass which uses gyroscopic inertia to maintain a setting on the true north pole, free of the deviation that besets the magnetic compass. In the 1930s the echo-sounder, sensitive to the return of a sonic pulse from the seabed, had revolutionized that most basic function of the marine surveyor, the measurement of the depth of water.

The years between the two wars saw the infancy of air travel, with its need for fast, accurate position-finding, which in turn had a enormous impact on seaborne navigation. The great novelty of air navigation was that it must be carried out in real time: the airman could not spend several hours reducing astro-sightings to chart positions. Because the

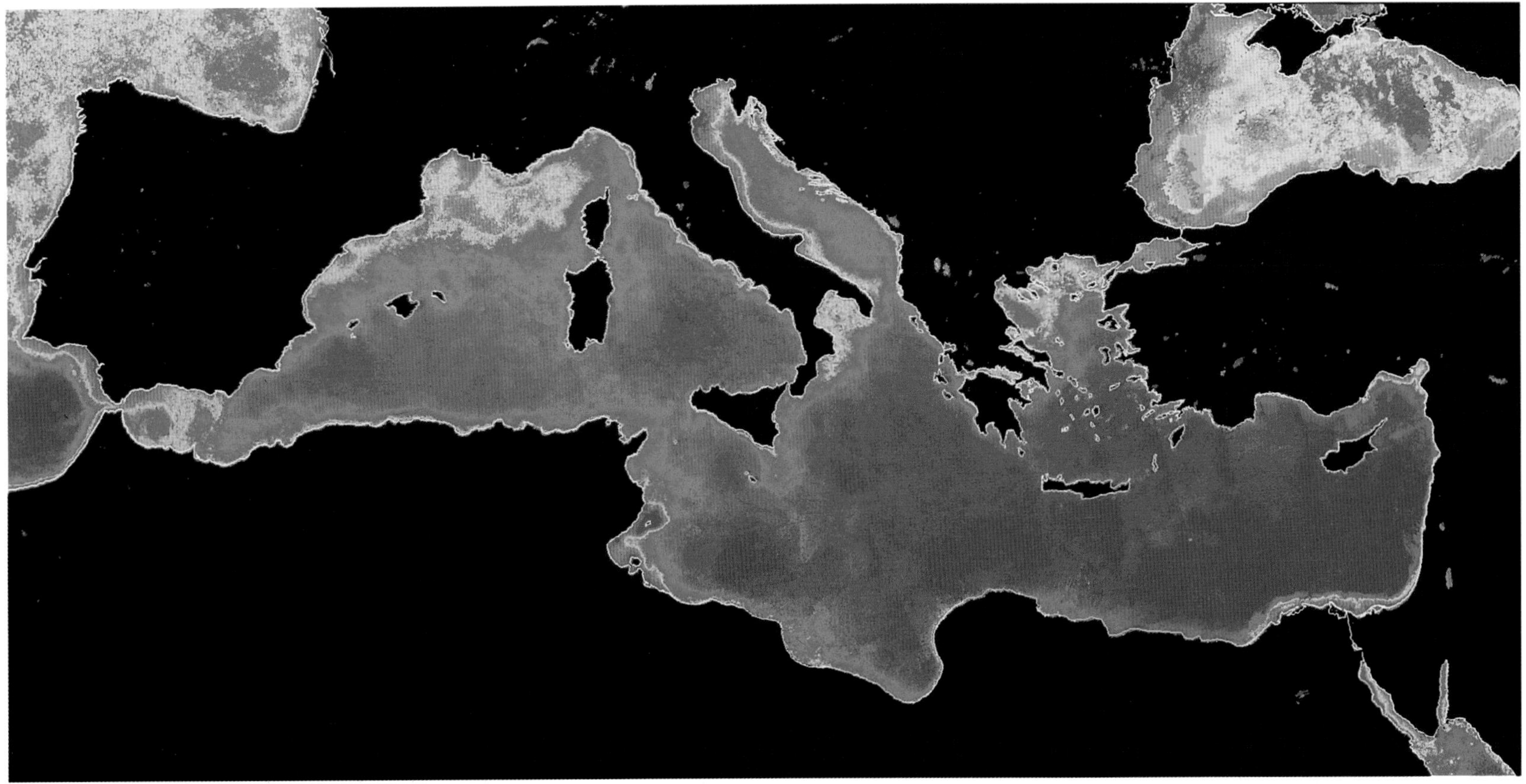

THE MEDITERRANEAN. The 20th century has inaugurated a new age of scientific charting, first with aerial surveys, then with satellite imagery. This image shows the distribution of phytoplankton in the water, from red (most dense) through orange, yellow and green to blue (least dense). The Mediterranean is relatively barren compared with the Atlantic and the Black Sea. NASA/SPL.

speeds involved are so great, and because aircraft cannot heave-to as a ship can, an almost instant position fix was essential. The first answer was to develop analogue calculators which quickly converted celestial observations into positions, but ultimately electronic signalling was needed. Hyperbolic navigation was the earliest system, in which two or more transmitters produce related signals whose point of intersection gives the position of the ship. Sea-charts were published overprinted with a lattice of hyperbolic lines for use in the system, known as Loran, an acronym for long-range navigation. This method was to be refined and prove durable for many decades. Soon after the war came another breakthrough in inertial navigation. In this system a reference weight is suspended within a housing, and the slightest motion between the two is translated electrically into the vessel's movement in three dimensions. It is essentially a highly sensitive method of dead rackoning, especially valuable to submarines, and with its aid the American submarine *Nautilus* traversed the Arctic Ocean beneath the ice-cap in 1958. The culmination of electrical and electronic navigation is the modern satellite positioning system, whose signals can give the receiver's position to within a few metres anywhere on the earth's surface. Sea-charts are now being issued in digital image form displayed on-screen, and these can now be linked with a satellite geo-referencing system, providing instant and accurate positioning.

Where does all this leave the traditional chart? The modern navigator spends little time watching the stars or making calculations from nautical almanacs; instead he manages electronic systems. To that extent he has become distanced from the elements, the sea and the sky, which were fundamental to the mariner of the past, and reconnaissance has given way to data manipulation. But the chart, although strictly designed as a navigational instrument, does have a wider validity as a picture of the ship's environment: it provides an essential conceptual model of the world or part of it, and mariners, like the rest of humanity, will continue to need such a model. The charts of the world's historic navies were also symbols of man's mastery of his world. This mastery had a political dimension, for each nation which aspired to dominate the seas sought to become the leading chart-maker of the age, and it was through these rivalries and ambitions that the oceans of the world were charted between 1500 and 1800. The technological revolution had made the enormous chart base truly international: any mariner of any nation has access to global positioning systems of unparalleled power. Yet it should never be forgotten that behind them lie five centuries of exploration, science, courage and many deaths.

Bibliography

Admiralty Hydrographic Department: *A Summary of Selected Manuscript Documents of Historic Importance Preserved in the Archives of the Department*, 1950.

J. N. L. Baker: *History of Geographical Exploration and Discovery*, new ed., 1963.

J. B. Harley & D. Woodward: *History of Cartography*, vol. 1, 1987; vol. 2, part 1, 1993.

D. Howse & M. Sanderson: *The Sea Chart*, 1973.

J. Jobé: *The Great Age of Sail*, 1977.

M. Mollat du Jourdin et. al.: *Sea-Charts of the Early Explorers*, 1984.

E. Newby: *World Atlas of Exploration*, 1975.

J. Pryor: *Geography, Technology and War: the Maritime History of the Mediterranean*, 1988.

G. S. Ritchie: *The Admiralty Chart*, new ed., 1995.

E. G. R. Taylor: *The Haven-Finding Art*, 1956.

J. Taylor: *Marine Painting*, 1995.

O. Warner: *Great Sea Battles*, 1963.

J. E. Williams: *Sails to Satellites: the Origin and Development of Navigational Science*, 1992.

Index